بِسْمِ اللَّهِ الرَّحْمٰنِ الرَّحِيمِ

Bismi Allahi Ar-Rahmani Ar-Rahimee

In the name of Allah, the Most Merciful, the Most Merciful

Surah Yasseen, Al-Waqiah, Ar-Rahman and Al-Mulk

Powerful Surahs in the Holy Quran for Wealth, Healing and Relaxing

Surah Al Fatiha (the Opener) الفاتحة

Bismi Allāhi Ar-Rahmāni Ar-Rahīmi
(1) «In the name of God, the Gracious, the Merciful.»

١ - بِسْمِ اللَّهِ الرَّحْمَٰنِ الرَّحِيمِ

Al-Hamdu Lillāhi Rabbi Al-`Ālamīna
(2) « Praise be to God, Lord of the Worlds.»

٢ - الْحَمْدُ لِلَّهِ رَبِّ الْعَالَمِينَ

Ar-Rahmāni Ar-Rahīmi
(3) «The Most Gracious, the Most Merciful.»

٣ - الرَّحْمَٰنِ الرَّحِيمِ

Māliki Yawmi Ad-Dīni
(4) Master of the Day of Judgment.»

٤ - مَالِكِ يَوْمِ الدِّينِ

'Īyāka Na`budu Wa 'Īyāka Nasta`īnu
(5) «It is You we worship, and upon You we call for help.»

٥ - إِيَّاكَ نَعْبُدُ وَإِيَّاكَ نَسْتَعِينُ

Ihdinā Aş-Şirāţa Al-Mustaqīma
(6) «Guide us to the straight path.»

٦ - اهْدِنَا الصِّرَاطَ الْمُسْتَقِيمَ

Şirāţa Al-Ladhīna 'An`amta `Alayhim Ghayri Al-Maghđūbi `Alayhim Wa Lā Ađ-Đāllīna
(7) «The path of those You have blessed, not of those against whom there is anger, nor of those who are misguided.»

٧ صِرَاطَ الَّذِينَ أَنْعَمْتَ عَلَيْهِمْ غَيْرِ الْمَغْضُوبِ عَلَيْهِمْ وَلَا الضَّالِّينَ

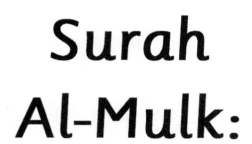

Surah
Al-Mulk:

Arabic & Phonetic

Bismi Allāhi Ar-Raĥmāni Ar-Raĥīmi

بِسْمِ اللهِ الرَّحْمٰنِ الرَّحِيمِ

(1) Tabāraka Al-Ladhī Biyadihi Al-Mulku Wa Huwa `Alá Kulli Shay'in Qadīrun

١- تَبَارَكَ الَّذِي بِيَدِهِ الْمُلْكُ وَهُوَ عَلَىٰ كُلِّ شَيْءٍ قَدِيرٌ

(2) Al-Ladhī Khalaqa Al-Mawta Wa Al-Ĥayāata Liyabluwakum 'Ayyukum 'Aĥsanu `Amalāan Wa Huwa Al-`Azīzu Al-Ghafūru

٢- الَّذِي خَلَقَ الْمَوْتَ وَالْحَيَاةَ لِيَبْلُوَكُمْ أَيُّكُمْ أَحْسَنُ عَمَلاً ۚ وَهُوَ الْعَزِيزُ الْغَفُورُ

(3) Al-Ladhī Khalaqa Sab`a Samāwātin Ţibāqāan Mā Tará Fī Khalqi Ar-Raĥmāni Min Tafāwutin Fārji`i Al-Başara Hal Tará Min Fuţūrin

٣- الَّذِي خَلَقَ سَبْعَ سَمَاوَاتٍ طِبَاقًا ۖ مَا تَرَىٰ فِي خَلْقِ الرَّحْمٰنِ مِنْ تَفَاوُتٍ ۖ فَارْجِعِ الْبَصَرَ هَلْ تَرَىٰ مِنْ فُطُورٍ

(4) Thumma Arji`i Al-Başara Karratayni Yanqalib 'Ilayka Al-Başaru Khāsi'āan Wa Huwa Ĥasīrun

٤- ثُمَّ ارْجِعِ الْبَصَرَ كَرَّتَيْنِ يَنْقَلِبْ إِلَيْكَ الْبَصَرُ خَاسِئًا وَهُوَ حَسِيرٌ

(5) Wa Laqad Zayyannā As-Samā'a Ad-Dunyā Bimaşābīĥa Wa Ja`alnāhā Rujūmāan Lilshayāţīni Wa 'A`tadnā Lahum `Adhāba As-Sa`īri

٥- وَلَقَدْ زَيَّنَّا السَّمَاءَ الدُّنْيَا بِمَصَابِيحَ وَجَعَلْنَاهَا رُجُومًا لِلشَّيَاطِينِ ۖ وَأَعْتَدْنَا لَهُمْ عَذَابَ السَّعِيرِ

(6) Wa Lilladhīna Kafarū Birabbihim `Adhābu Jahannama Wa Bi'sa Al-Maşīru	٦ـ وَلِلَّذِينَ كَفَرُوا بِرَبِّهِمْ عَذَابُ جَهَنَّمَ ۖ وَبِئْسَ الْمَصِيرُ
(7) 'Idhā 'Ulqū Fīhā Sami`ū Lahā Shahīqāan Wa Hiya Tafūru	٧ـ إِذَا أُلْقُوا فِيهَا سَمِعُوا لَهَا شَهِيقًا وَهِيَ تَفُورُ
(8) Takādu Tamayyazu Mina Al-Ghayži Kullamā 'Ulqiya Fīhā Fawjun Sa'alahum Khazanatuhā 'Alam Ya'tikum Nadhīrun	٨ـ تَكَادُ تَمَيَّزُ مِنَ الْغَيْظِ ۖ كُلَّمَا أُلْقِيَ فِيهَا فَوْجٌ سَأَلَهُمْ خَزَنَتُهَا أَلَمْ يَأْتِكُمْ نَذِيرٌ
(9) Qālū Balá Qad Jā'anā Nadhīrun Fakadhabnā Wa Qulnā Mā Nazzala Allāhu Min Shay'in 'In 'Antum 'Illā Fī Đalālin Kabīrin	٩ـ قَالُوا بَلَىٰ قَدْ جَاءَنَا نَذِيرٌ فَكَذَّبْنَا وَقُلْنَا مَا نَزَّلَ اللَّهُ مِنْ شَيْءٍ إِنْ أَنْتُمْ إِلَّا فِي ضَلَالٍ كَبِيرٍ
(10) Wa Qālū Law Kunnā Nasma`u 'Aw Na`qilu Mā Kunnā Fī 'Aşĥābi As-Sa`īri	١٠ـ وَقَالُوا لَوْ كُنَّا نَسْمَعُ أَوْ نَعْقِلُ مَا كُنَّا فِي أَصْحَابِ السَّعِيرِ
(11) Fā`tarafū Bidhanbihim Fasuĥqāan Li'şĥābi As-Sa`īri	١١ـ فَاعْتَرَفُوا بِذَنْبِهِمْ فَسُحْقًا لِأَصْحَابِ السَّعِيرِ
(12) 'Inna Al-Ladhīna Yakhshawna Rabbahum Bil-Ghaybi Lahum Maghfiratun Wa 'Ajrun Kabīrun	١٢ـ إِنَّ الَّذِينَ يَخْشَوْنَ رَبَّهُمْ بِالْغَيْبِ لَهُمْ مَغْفِرَةٌ وَأَجْرٌ كَبِيرٌ

(13) Wa 'Asirrū Qawlakum 'Aw Ajharū Bihi 'Innahu `Alīmun Bidhāti Aş-Şudūri	١٣- وَأَسِرُّوا قَوْلَكُمْ أَوِ اجْهَرُوا بِهِ ۗ إِنَّهُ عَلِيمٌ بِذَاتِ الصُّدُورِ
(14) 'Alā Ya`lamu Man Khalaqa Wa Huwa Al-Laţīfu Al-Khabīru	١٤- أَلَا يَعْلَمُ مَنْ خَلَقَ وَهُوَ اللَّطِيفُ الْخَبِيرُ
(15) Huwa Al-Ladhī Ja`ala Lakumu Al-'Arđa Dhalūlāan Fāmshū Fī Manākibihā Wa Kulū Min Rizqihi Wa 'Ilayhi An-Nushūru	١٥- هُوَ الَّذِي جَعَلَ لَكُمُ الْأَرْضَ ذَلُولًا فَامْشُوا فِي مَنَاكِبِهَا وَكُلُوا مِنْ رِزْقِهِ ۖ وَإِلَيْهِ النُّشُورُ
(16) 'A'amintum Man Fī As-Samā'i 'An Yakhsifa Bikumu Al-'Arđa Fa'idhā Hiya Tamūru	١٦- أَأَمِنْتُمْ مَنْ فِي السَّمَاءِ أَنْ يَخْسِفَ بِكُمُ الْأَرْضَ فَإِذَا هِيَ تَمُورُ
(17) 'Am 'Amintum Man Fī As-Samā'i 'An Yursila `Alaykum Ĥāşibāan Fasata`lamūna Kayfa Nadhīri	١٧- أَمْ أَمِنْتُمْ مَنْ فِي السَّمَاءِ أَنْ يُرْسِلَ عَلَيْكُمْ حَاصِبًا ۖ فَسَتَعْلَمُونَ كَيْفَ نَذِيرِ
(18) Wa Laqad Kadhaba Aladhīna Min Qablihim Fakayfa Kāna Nakīri	١٨- وَلَقَدْ كَذَّبَ الَّذِينَ مِنْ قَبْلِهِمْ فَكَيْفَ كَانَ نَكِيرِ
(19) 'Awalam Yaraw 'Ilá Aţ-Ţayri Fawqahum Şāffātin Wa Yaqbiđna Mā Yumsikuhunna 'Illā Ar-Raĥmānu 'Innahu Bikulli Shay'in Başīrun	١٩- أَوَلَمْ يَرَوْا إِلَى الطَّيْرِ فَوْقَهُمْ صَافَّاتٍ وَيَقْبِضْنَ ۚ مَا يُمْسِكُهُنَّ إِلَّا الرَّحْمَٰنُ ۚ إِنَّهُ بِكُلِّ شَيْءٍ بَصِيرٌ

(20) 'Amman Hādhā Al-Ladhī Huwa Jundun Lakum Yanşurukum Min Dūni Ar-Raĥmāni 'Ini Al-Kāfirūna 'Illā Fī Ghurūrin	٢٠ أَمَّنْ هٰذَا الَّذِي هُوَ جُندٌ لَكُمْ يَنصُرُكُم مِّن دُونِ الرَّحْمٰنِ ۚ إِنِ الْكَافِرُونَ إِلَّا فِي غُرُورٍ
(21) 'Amman Hādhā Al-Ladhī Yarzuqukum 'In 'Amsaka Rizqahu Bal Lajjū Fī `Utūwin Wa Nufūrin	٢١ أَمَّنْ هٰذَا الَّذِي يَرْزُقُكُمْ إِنْ أَمْسَكَ رِزْقَهُ ۚ بَل لَّجُّوا فِي عُتُوٍّ وَنُفُورٍ
(22) 'Afaman Yamshī Mukibbāan `Alá Wajhihi 'Ahdá 'Amman Yamshī Sawīyāan `Alá Şirāţin Mustaqīm	٢٢ أَفَمَن يَمْشِي مُكِبًّا عَلَىٰ وَجْهِهِ أَهْدَىٰ أَمَّن يَمْشِي سَوِيًّا عَلَىٰ صِرَاطٍ مُّسْتَقِيمٍ
(23) Qul Huwa Al-Ladhī 'Ansha'akum Wa Ja`ala Lakumu As-Sam`a Wa Al-'Abşāra Wa Al-'Af'idata Qalīlāan Mā Tashkurūna	٢٣ قُلْ هُوَ الَّذِي أَنشَأَكُمْ وَجَعَلَ لَكُمُ السَّمْعَ وَالْأَبْصَارَ وَالْأَفْئِدَةَ ۖ قَلِيلًا مَّا تَشْكُرُونَ
(24) Qul Huwa Aladhī Dhara'kum Fī Al-'Arđi Wa 'Ilayhi Tuĥsharūna	٢٤ قُلْ هُوَ الَّذِي ذَرَأَكُمْ فِي الْأَرْضِ وَإِلَيْهِ تُحْشَرُونَ
(25) Wa Yaqūlūna Matá Hādhā Al-Wa`du 'In Kuntum Şādiqīna	٢٥ وَيَقُولُونَ مَتَىٰ هٰذَا الْوَعْدُ إِن كُنتُمْ صَادِقِينَ
(26) Qul 'Innamā Al-`Ilmu `Inda Allāhi Wa 'Innamā 'Anā Nadhīrun Mubīnun	٢٦ قُلْ إِنَّمَا الْعِلْمُ عِندَ اللَّهِ وَإِنَّمَا أَنَا نَذِيرٌ مُّبِينٌ

(27) Falammā Ra'awhu Zulfatan
Sī'at Wujūhu Al-Ladhīna Kafarū
Wa Qīla Hādhā Al-Ladhī Kuntum
Bihi Tadda`ūna

٢٧ فَلَمَّا رَأَوْهُ زُلْفَةً سِيئَتْ وُجُوهُ الَّذِينَ
كَفَرُوا وَقِيلَ هَذَا الَّذِي كُنْتُمْ بِهِ تَدَّعُونَ

(28) Qul 'Ara'aytum 'In
'Ahlakaniya Allāhu Wa Man Ma`ī
'Aw Raḥimanā Faman Yujīru Al-
Kāfirīna Min `Adhābin 'Alīmin

٢٨ قُلْ أَرَأَيْتُمْ إِنْ أَهْلَكَنِيَ اللَّهُ وَمَنْ مَعِيَ أَوْ
رَحِمَنَا فَمَنْ يُجِيرُ الْكَافِرِينَ مِنْ عَذَابٍ أَلِيمٍ

(29) Qul Huwa Ar-Raḥmānu
'Āmannā Bihi Wa `Alayhi
Tawakkalnā Fasata`lamūna Man
Huwa Fī Đalālin Mubīnin

٢٩ قُلْ هُوَ الرَّحْمَنُ آمَنَّا بِهِ وَعَلَيْهِ تَوَكَّلْنَا
فَسَتَعْلَمُونَ مَنْ هُوَ فِي ضَلَالٍ مُبِينٍ

(30) Qul 'Ara'aytum 'In 'Aşbaḥa
Mā'uukum Ghawrāan Faman
Ya'tīkum Bimā'in Ma`īnin

٣٠ قُلْ أَرَأَيْتُمْ إِنْ أَصْبَحَ مَاؤُكُمْ غَوْرًا فَمَنْ
يَأْتِيكُمْ بِمَاءٍ مَعِينٍ

Surah
Al-Mulk:

Arabic & English

In the name of God, the Gracious, the Merciful.

بِسْمِ اللَّهِ الرَّحْمَٰنِ الرَّحِيمِ

1 Blessed is He in whose hand is the sovereignty, and Who has power over everything.

١- تَبَارَكَ الَّذِي بِيَدِهِ الْمُلْكُ وَهُوَ عَلَىٰ كُلِّ شَيْءٍ قَدِيرٌ

2 He who created death and life—to test you—as to which of you is better in conduct. He is the Almighty, the Forgiving.

٢- الَّذِي خَلَقَ الْمَوْتَ وَالْحَيَاةَ لِيَبْلُوَكُمْ أَيُّكُمْ أَحْسَنُ عَمَلًا ۚ وَهُوَ الْعَزِيزُ الْغَفُورُ

3 He who created seven heavens in layers. You see no discrepancy in the creation of the Compassionate. Look again. Can you see any cracks?

٣- الَّذِي خَلَقَ سَبْعَ سَمَاوَاتٍ طِبَاقًا ۖ مَا تَرَىٰ فِي خَلْقِ الرَّحْمَٰنِ مِنْ تَفَاوُتٍ ۖ فَارْجِعِ الْبَصَرَ هَلْ تَرَىٰ مِنْ فُطُورٍ

4 Then look again, and again, and your sight will return to you dazzled and exhausted.

٤- ثُمَّ ارْجِعِ الْبَصَرَ كَرَّتَيْنِ يَنْقَلِبْ إِلَيْكَ الْبَصَرُ خَاسِئًا وَهُوَ حَسِيرٌ

5 We have adorned the lower heaven with lanterns, and made them missiles against the devils; and We have prepared for them the punishment of the Blaze.

٥- وَلَقَدْ زَيَّنَّا السَّمَاءَ الدُّنْيَا بِمَصَابِيحَ وَجَعَلْنَاهَا رُجُومًا لِلشَّيَاطِينِ ۖ وَأَعْتَدْنَا لَهُمْ عَذَابَ السَّعِيرِ

6 For those who reject their Lord, there is the torment of Hell. What an evil destination!	٦- وَلِلَّذِينَ كَفَرُوا بِرَبِّهِمْ عَذَابُ جَهَنَّمَ ۖ وَبِئْسَ الْمَصِيرُ
7 When they are thrown into it, they will hear it roaring, as it seethes.	٧- إِذَا أُلْقُوا فِيهَا سَمِعُوا لَهَا شَهِيقًا وَهِيَ تَفُورُ
8 It almost bursts with fury. Every time a batch is thrown into it, its keepers will ask them, "Has no warner come to you?"	٨- تَكَادُ تَمَيَّزُ مِنَ الْغَيْظِ ۖ كُلَّمَا أُلْقِيَ فِيهَا فَوْجٌ سَأَلَهُمْ خَزَنَتُهَا أَلَمْ يَأْتِكُمْ نَذِيرٌ
9 They will say, "Yes, a warner did come to us, but we disbelieved, and said, 'God did not send down anything; you are very much mistaken.'"	٩- قَالُوا بَلَىٰ قَدْ جَاءَنَا نَذِيرٌ فَكَذَّبْنَا وَقُلْنَا مَا نَزَّلَ اللَّهُ مِنْ شَيْءٍ إِنْ أَنْتُمْ إِلَّا فِي ضَلَالٍ كَبِيرٍ
10 And they will say, "Had we listened or reasoned, we would not have been among the inmates of the Blaze."	١٠- وَقَالُوا لَوْ كُنَّا نَسْمَعُ أَوْ نَعْقِلُ مَا كُنَّا فِي أَصْحَابِ السَّعِيرِ
11 So they will acknowledge their sins. So away with the inmates of the Blaze.	١١- فَاعْتَرَفُوا بِذَنْبِهِمْ فَسُحْقًا لِأَصْحَابِ السَّعِيرِ
12 As for those who fear their Lord in secret—for them is forgiveness and a great reward.	١٢- إِنَّ الَّذِينَ يَخْشَوْنَ رَبَّهُمْ بِالْغَيْبِ لَهُمْ مَغْفِرَةٌ وَأَجْرٌ كَبِيرٌ

13 Whether you keep your words secret, or declare them—He is Aware of the inner thoughts.	١٣- وَأَسِرُّوا قَوْلَكُمْ أَوِ اجْهَرُوا بِهِ ۖ إِنَّهُ عَلِيمٌ بِذَاتِ الصُّدُورِ
14 Would He not know, He Who created? He is the Refined, the Expert.	١٤- أَلَا يَعْلَمُ مَنْ خَلَقَ وَهُوَ اللَّطِيفُ الْخَبِيرُ
15 It is He who made the earth manageable for you, so travel its regions, and eat of His provisions. To Him is the Resurgence.	١٥- هُوَ الَّذِي جَعَلَ لَكُمُ الْأَرْضَ ذَلُولًا فَامْشُوا فِي مَنَاكِبِهَا وَكُلُوا مِنْ رِزْقِهِ ۖ وَإِلَيْهِ النُّشُورُ
16 Are you confident that the One in heaven will not cause the earth to collapse beneath you as it spins?	١٦- أَأَمِنْتُمْ مَنْ فِي السَّمَاءِ أَنْ يَخْسِفَ بِكُمُ الْأَرْضَ فَإِذَا هِيَ تَمُورُ
17 Or are you confident that the One in Heaven will not unleash against you a violent storm? Then you will know what My warning is like.	١٧- أَمْ أَمِنْتُمْ مَنْ فِي السَّمَاءِ أَنْ يُرْسِلَ عَلَيْكُمْ حَاصِبًا ۖ فَسَتَعْلَمُونَ كَيْفَ نَذِيرِ
18 Those before them also denied the truth; and how was My disapproval?	١٨- وَلَقَدْ كَذَّبَ الَّذِينَ مِنْ قَبْلِهِمْ فَكَيْفَ كَانَ نَكِيرِ
19 Have they not seen the birds above them, spreading their wings, and folding them? None holds them except the Compassionate. He is Perceiver of everything.	١٩- أَوَلَمْ يَرَوْا إِلَى الطَّيْرِ فَوْقَهُمْ صَافَّاتٍ وَيَقْبِضْنَ ۚ مَا يُمْسِكُهُنَّ إِلَّا الرَّحْمَٰنُ ۚ إِنَّهُ بِكُلِّ شَيْءٍ بَصِيرٌ

20 Or who is this who is a force for you to protect you against the Compassionate? The disbelievers are in nothing but delusion.

٢٠ أَمَّنْ هَٰذَا الَّذِي هُوَ جُنْدٌ لَكُمْ يَنْصُرُكُمْ مِنْ دُونِ الرَّحْمَٰنِ ۚ إِنِ الْكَافِرُونَ إِلَّا فِي غُرُورٍ

21 Or who is this that will provide for you, if He withholds His provision? Yet they persist in defiance and aversion.

٢١ أَمَّنْ هَٰذَا الَّذِي يَرْزُقُكُمْ إِنْ أَمْسَكَ رِزْقَهُ ۚ بَلْ لَجُّوا فِي عُتُوٍّ وَنُفُورٍ

22 Is he who walks bent on his own design better guided, or he who walks upright on a straight path?

٢٢ أَفَمَنْ يَمْشِي مُكِبًّا عَلَىٰ وَجْهِهِ أَهْدَىٰ أَمَّنْ يَمْشِي سَوِيًّا عَلَىٰ صِرَاطٍ مُسْتَقِيمٍ

23 Say, "It is He who produced you; and made for you the hearing, and the vision, and the organs. But rarely do you give thanks."

٢٣ قُلْ هُوَ الَّذِي أَنْشَأَكُمْ وَجَعَلَ لَكُمُ السَّمْعَ وَالْأَبْصَارَ وَالْأَفْئِدَةَ ۖ قَلِيلًا مَا تَشْكُرُونَ

24 Say, "It is He who scattered you on earth, and to Him you will be rounded up."

٢٤ قُلْ هُوَ الَّذِي ذَرَأَكُمْ فِي الْأَرْضِ وَإِلَيْهِ تُحْشَرُونَ

25 And they say, "When will this promise be fulfilled, if you are truthful?"

٢٥ وَيَقُولُونَ مَتَىٰ هَٰذَا الْوَعْدُ إِنْ كُنْتُمْ صَادِقِينَ

26 Say, "Knowledge is with God, and I am only a clear warner."

٢٦ قُلْ إِنَّمَا الْعِلْمُ عِنْدَ اللَّهِ وَإِنَّمَا أَنَا نَذِيرٌ مُبِينٌ

27 But when they see it approaching, the faces of those who disbelieved will turn gloomy, and it will be said, "This is what you used to call for."

٢٧ فَلَمَّا رَأَوْهُ زُلْفَةً سِيئَتْ وُجُوهُ الَّذِينَ كَفَرُوا وَقِيلَ هَٰذَا الَّذِي كُنْتُمْ بِهِ تَدَّعُونَ

28 Say, "Have you considered? Should God make me perish, and those with me; or else He bestows His mercy on us; who will protect the disbelievers from an agonizing torment?"

٢٨ قُلْ أَرَأَيْتُمْ إِنْ أَهْلَكَنِيَ اللَّهُ وَمَنْ مَعِيَ أَوْ رَحِمَنَا فَمَنْ يُجِيرُ الْكَافِرِينَ مِنْ عَذَابٍ أَلِيمٍ

29 Say, "He is the Compassionate. We have faith in Him, and in Him we trust. Soon you will know who is in evident error."

٢٩ قُلْ هُوَ الرَّحْمَٰنُ آمَنَّا بِهِ وَعَلَيْهِ تَوَكَّلْنَا فَسَتَعْلَمُونَ مَنْ هُوَ فِي ضَلَالٍ مُبِينٍ

30 Say, "Have you considered? If your water drains away, who will bring you pure running water?"

٣٠ قُلْ أَرَأَيْتُمْ إِنْ أَصْبَحَ مَاؤُكُمْ غَوْرًا فَمَنْ يَأْتِيكُمْ بِمَاءٍ مَعِينٍ

Surah Ar-Rahman:

Arabic & Phonetic

Bismi Allāhi Ar-Raĥmāni Ar-Raĥīmi	بِسْمِ اللهِ الرَّحْمٰنِ الرَّحِيمِ
(1) Ar-Raĥmānu	١ الرَّحْمٰنُ
(2) `Allama Al-Qur'āna	٢ عَلَّمَ الْقُرْآنَ
(3) Khalaqa Al-'Insāna	٣ خَلَقَ الْإِنْسَانَ
(4) `Allamahu Al-Bayāna	٤ عَلَّمَهُ الْبَيَانَ
(5) Ash-Shamsu Wa Al-Qamaru Biĥusbānin	٥ الشَّمْسُ وَالْقَمَرُ بِحُسْبَانٍ
(6) Wa An-Najmu Wa Ash-Shajaru Yasjudāni	٦ وَالنَّجْمُ وَالشَّجَرُ يَسْجُدَانِ
(7) Wa As-Samā'a Rafa`ahā Wa Waďa`a Al-Mīzāna	٧ وَالسَّمَاءَ رَفَعَهَا وَوَضَعَ الْمِيزَانَ
(8) 'Allā Taţghaw Fī Al-Mīzāni	٨ أَلَّا تَطْغَوْا فِي الْمِيزَانِ
(9) Wa 'Aqīmū Al-Wazna Bil-Qisţi Wa Lā Tukhsirū Al-Mīzāna	٩ وَأَقِيمُوا الْوَزْنَ بِالْقِسْطِ وَلَا تُخْسِرُوا الْمِيزَانَ

(10) Wa Al-'Arđa Wađa`ahā Lil'anāmi	١٠ وَالْأَرْضَ وَضَعَهَا لِلْأَنَامِ
(11) Fīhā Fākihatun Wa An-Nakhlu Dhātu Al-'Akmāmi	١١ فِيهَا فَاكِهَةٌ وَالنَّخْلُ ذَاتُ الْأَكْمَامِ
(12) Wa Al-Ĥabbu Dhū Al-`Aşfi Wa Ar-Rayĥānu	١٢ وَالْحَبُّ ذُو الْعَصْفِ وَالرَّيْحَانُ
(13) Fabi'ayyi 'Ālā'i Rabbikumā Tukadhibāni	١٣ فَبِأَيِّ آلَاءِ رَبِّكُمَا تُكَذِّبَانِ
(14) Khalaqa Al-'Insāna Min Şalşālin Kālfakhkhāri	١٤ خَلَقَ الْإِنْسَانَ مِنْ صَلْصَالٍ كَالْفَخَّارِ
(15) Wa Khalaqa Al-Jānna Min Mārijin Min Nārin	١٥ وَخَلَقَ الْجَانَّ مِنْ مَارِجٍ مِنْ نَارٍ
(16) Fabi'ayyi 'Ālā'i Rabbikumā Tukadhibāni	١٦ فَبِأَيِّ آلَاءِ رَبِّكُمَا تُكَذِّبَانِ
(17) Rabbu Al-Mashriqayni Wa Rabbu Al-Maghribayni	١٧ رَبُّ الْمَشْرِقَيْنِ وَرَبُّ الْمَغْرِبَيْنِ
(18) Fabi'ayyi 'Ālā'i Rabbikumā Tukadhibāni	١٨ فَبِأَيِّ آلَاءِ رَبِّكُمَا تُكَذِّبَانِ

(19) Maraja Al-Baĥrayni Yaltaqiyāni	١٩ مَرَجَ الْبَحْرَيْنِ يَلْتَقِيَانِ
(20) Baynahumā Barzakhun Lā Yabghiyān	٢٠ بَيْنَهُمَا بَرْزَخٌ لَا يَبْغِيَانِ
(21) Fabi'ayyi 'Ālā'i Rabbikumā Tukadhibāni	٢١ فَبِأَيِّ آلَاءِ رَبِّكُمَا تُكَذِّبَانِ
(22) Yakhruju Minhumā Al-Lu'ulu'uu Wa Al-Marjānu	٢٢ يَخْرُجُ مِنْهُمَا اللُّؤْلُؤُ وَالْمَرْجَانُ
(23) Fabi'ayyi 'Ālā'i Rabbikumā Tukadhibāni	٢٣ فَبِأَيِّ آلَاءِ رَبِّكُمَا تُكَذِّبَانِ
(24) Wa Lahu Al-Jawāri Al-Munsha'ātu Fī Al-Baĥri Kāl'a`lāmi	٢٤ وَلَهُ الْجَوَارِ الْمُنْشَآتُ فِي الْبَحْرِ كَالْأَعْلَامِ
(25) Fabi'ayyi 'Ālā'i Rabbikumā Tukadhibāni	٢٥ فَبِأَيِّ آلَاءِ رَبِّكُمَا تُكَذِّبَانِ
(26) Kullu Man `Alayhā Fānin	٢٦ كُلُّ مَنْ عَلَيْهَا فَانٍ
(27) Wa Yabqá Wajhu Rabbika Dhū Al-Jalāli Wa Al-'Ikrāmi	٢٧ وَيَبْقَىٰ وَجْهُ رَبِّكَ ذُو الْجَلَالِ وَالْإِكْرَامِ

(28) Fabi'ayyi 'Ālā'i Rabbikumā Tukadhibāni	٢٨ فَبِأَيِّ آلَاءِ رَبِّكُمَا تُكَذِّبَانِ
(29) Yas'aluhu Man Fī As-Samāwāti Wa Al-'Arđi Kulla Yawmin Huwa Fī Sha'nin	٢٩ يَسْأَلُهُ مَن فِي السَّمَاوَاتِ وَالْأَرْضِ ۚ كُلَّ يَوْمٍ هُوَ فِي شَأْنٍ
(30) Fabi'ayyi 'Ālā'i Rabbikumā Tukadhibāni	٣٠ فَبِأَيِّ آلَاءِ رَبِّكُمَا تُكَذِّبَانِ
(31) Sanafrughu Lakum 'Ayyuhā Ath-Thaqalāni	٣١ سَنَفْرُغُ لَكُمْ أَيُّهَ الثَّقَلَانِ
(32) Fabi'ayyi 'Ālā'i Rabbikumā Tukadhibāni	٣٢ فَبِأَيِّ آلَاءِ رَبِّكُمَا تُكَذِّبَانِ
(33) Yā Ma`shara Al-Jinni Wa Al-'Insi 'Ini Astaţa`tum 'An Tanfudhū Min 'Aqţāri As-Samāwāti Wa Al-'Arđi Fānfudhū Lā Tanfudhūna 'Illā Bisulţānin	٣٣ يَا مَعْشَرَ الْجِنِّ وَالْإِنسِ إِنِ اسْتَطَعْتُمْ أَن تَنفُذُوا مِنْ أَقْطَارِ السَّمَاوَاتِ وَالْأَرْضِ فَانفُذُوا ۚ لَا تَنفُذُونَ إِلَّا بِسُلْطَانٍ
(34) Fabi'ayyi 'Ālā'i Rabbikumā Tukadhibāni	٣٤ فَبِأَيِّ آلَاءِ رَبِّكُمَا تُكَذِّبَانِ
(35) Yursalu `Alaykumā Shuwāžun Min Nārin Wa Nuĥāsun Falā Tantaşirāni	٣٥ يُرْسَلُ عَلَيْكُمَا شُوَاظٌ مِّن نَّارٍ وَنُحَاسٌ فَلَا تَنتَصِرَانِ

(36) Fabi'ayyi 'Ālā'i Rabbikumā Tukadhibāni	٣٦ فَبِأَيِّ آلَاءِ رَبِّكُمَا تُكَذِّبَانِ
(37) Fa'idhā Anshaqqati As-Samā'u Fakānat Wardatan Kālddihāni	٣٧ فَإِذَا انْشَقَّتِ السَّمَاءُ فَكَانَتْ وَرْدَةً كَالدِّهَانِ
(38) Fabi'ayyi 'Ālā'i Rabbikumā Tukadhibāni	٣٨ فَبِأَيِّ آلَاءِ رَبِّكُمَا تُكَذِّبَانِ
(39) Fayawma'idhin Lā Yus'alu `An Dhanbihi 'Insun Wa Lā Jānnun	٣٩ فَيَوْمَئِذٍ لَا يُسْأَلُ عَنْ ذَنْبِهِ إِنْسٌ وَلَا جَانٌّ
(40) Fabi'ayyi 'Ālā'i Rabbikumā Tukadhibāni	٤٠ فَبِأَيِّ آلَاءِ رَبِّكُمَا تُكَذِّبَانِ
(41) Yu`rafu Al-Mujrimūna Bisīmāhum Fayu'ukhadhu Bin-Nawāşī Wa Al-'Aqdāmi	٤١ يُعْرَفُ الْمُجْرِمُونَ بِسِيمَاهُمْ فَيُؤْخَذُ بِالنَّوَاصِي وَالْأَقْدَامِ
(42) Fabi'ayyi 'Ālā'i Rabbikumā Tukadhibāni	٤٢ فَبِأَيِّ آلَاءِ رَبِّكُمَا تُكَذِّبَانِ
(43) Hadhihi Jahannamu Allatī Yukadhibu Bihā Al-Mujrimūna	٤٣ هَٰذِهِ جَهَنَّمُ الَّتِي يُكَذِّبُ بِهَا الْمُجْرِمُونَ

(44) Yaţūfūna Baynahā Wa Bayna Ĥamīmin 'Ānin	٤٤ يَطُوفُونَ بَيْنَهَا وَبَيْنَ حَمِيمٍ آنٍ
(45) Fabi'ayyi 'Ālā'i Rabbikumā Tukadhibāni	٤٥ فَبِأَيِّ آلَاءِ رَبِّكُمَا تُكَذِّبَانِ
(46) Wa Liman Khāfa Maqāma Rabbihi Jannatāni	٤٦ وَلِمَنْ خَافَ مَقَامَ رَبِّهِ جَنَّتَانِ
(47) Fabi'ayyi 'Ālā'i Rabbikumā Tukadhibāni	٤٧ فَبِأَيِّ آلَاءِ رَبِّكُمَا تُكَذِّبَانِ
(48) Dhawātā 'Afnānin	٤٨ ذَوَاتَا أَفْنَانٍ
(49) Fabi'ayyi 'Ālā'i Rabbikumā Tukadhibāni	٤٩ فَبِأَيِّ آلَاءِ رَبِّكُمَا تُكَذِّبَانِ
(50) Fīhimā `Aynāni Tajriyāni	٥٠ فِيهِمَا عَيْنَانِ تَجْرِيَانِ
(51) Fabi'ayyi 'Ālā'i Rabbikumā Tukadhibāni	٥١ فَبِأَيِّ آلَاءِ رَبِّكُمَا تُكَذِّبَانِ
(52) Fīhimā Min Kulli Fākihatin Zawjāni	٥٢ فِيهِمَا مِنْ كُلِّ فَاكِهَةٍ زَوْجَانِ

(53) Fabi'ayyi 'Ālā'i Rabbikumā Tukadhibāni	٥٣ فَبِأَيِّ آلَاءِ رَبِّكُمَا تُكَذِّبَانِ
(54) Muttaki'īna `Alá Furushin Baṭā'inuhā Min 'Istabraqin Wa Janá Al-Jannatayni Dānin	٥٤ مُتَّكِئِينَ عَلَىٰ فُرُشٍ بَطَائِنُهَا مِنْ إِسْتَبْرَقٍ ۚ وَجَنَى الْجَنَّتَيْنِ دَانٍ
(55) Fabi'ayyi 'Ālā'i Rabbikumā Tukadhibāni	٥٥ فَبِأَيِّ آلَاءِ رَبِّكُمَا تُكَذِّبَانِ
(56) Fīhinna Qāṣirātu Aṭ-Ṭarfi Lam Yaṭmithhunna 'Insun Qablahum Wa Lā Jānnun	٥٦ فِيهِنَّ قَاصِرَاتُ الطَّرْفِ لَمْ يَطْمِثْهُنَّ إِنْسٌ قَبْلَهُمْ وَلَا جَانٌّ
(57) Fabi'ayyi 'Ālā'i Rabbikumā Tukadhibāni	٥٧ فَبِأَيِّ آلَاءِ رَبِّكُمَا تُكَذِّبَانِ
(58) Ka'annahunna Al-Yāqūtu Wa Al-Marjānu	٥٨ كَأَنَّهُنَّ الْيَاقُوتُ وَالْمَرْجَانُ
(59) Fabi'ayyi 'Ālā'i Rabbikumā Tukadhibāni	٥٩ فَبِأَيِّ آلَاءِ رَبِّكُمَا تُكَذِّبَانِ
(60) Hal Jazā'u Al-'Iĥsāni 'Illā Al-'Iĥsānu	٦٠ هَلْ جَزَاءُ الْإِحْسَانِ إِلَّا الْإِحْسَانُ

(61) Fabi'ayyi 'Ālā'i Rabbikumā Tukadhibāni	٦١ فَبِأَيِّ آلَاءِ رَبِّكُمَا تُكَذِّبَانِ
(62) Wa Min Dūnihimā Jannatāni	٦٢ وَمِنْ دُونِهِمَا جَنَّتَانِ
(63) Fabi'ayyi 'Ālā'i Rabbikumā Tukadhibāni	٦٣ فَبِأَيِّ آلَاءِ رَبِّكُمَا تُكَذِّبَانِ
(64) Mud/hāmmatāni	٦٤ مُدْهَامَّتَانِ
(65) Fabi'ayyi 'Ālā'i Rabbikumā Tukadhibāni	٦٥ فَبِأَيِّ آلَاءِ رَبِّكُمَا تُكَذِّبَانِ
(66) Fīhimā `Aynāni Naḍākhatāni	٦٦ فِيهِمَا عَيْنَانِ نَضَّاخَتَانِ
(67) Fabi'ayyi 'Ālā'i Rabbikumā Tukadhibāni	٦٧ فَبِأَيِّ آلَاءِ رَبِّكُمَا تُكَذِّبَانِ
(68) Fīhimā Fākihatun Wa Nakhlun Wa Rummānun	٦٨ فِيهِمَا فَاكِهَةٌ وَنَخْلٌ وَرُمَّانٌ
(69) Fabi'ayyi 'Ālā'i Rabbikumā Tukadhibāni	٦٩ فَبِأَيِّ آلَاءِ رَبِّكُمَا تُكَذِّبَانِ
(70) Fīhinna Khayrātun Ĥisānun	٧٠ فِيهِنَّ خَيْرَاتٌ حِسَانٌ

(71) Fabi'ayyi 'Ālā'i Rabbikumā Tukadhibāni	٧١ فَبِأَيِّ آلَاءِ رَبِّكُمَا تُكَذِّبَانِ
(72) Ĥūrun Maqşūrātun Fī Al-Khiyāmi	٧٢ حُورٌ مَقْصُورَاتٌ فِي الْخِيَامِ
(73) Fabi'ayyi 'Ālā'i Rabbikumā Tukadhibāni	٧٣ فَبِأَيِّ آلَاءِ رَبِّكُمَا تُكَذِّبَانِ
(74) Lam Yaţmithhunna 'Insun Qablahum Wa Lā Jānnun	٧٤ لَمْ يَطْمِثْهُنَّ إِنْسٌ قَبْلَهُمْ وَلَا جَانٌّ
(75) Fabi'ayyi 'Ālā'i Rabbikumā Tukadhibāni	٧٥ فَبِأَيِّ آلَاءِ رَبِّكُمَا تُكَذِّبَانِ
(76) Muttaki'īna `Alá Rafrafin Khuđrin Wa `Abqarīyin Ĥisānin	٧٦ مُتَّكِئِينَ عَلَىٰ رَفْرَفٍ خُضْرٍ وَعَبْقَرِيٍّ حِسَانٍ
(77) Fabi'ayyi 'Ālā'i Rabbikumā Tukadhibāni	٧٧ فَبِأَيِّ آلَاءِ رَبِّكُمَا تُكَذِّبَانِ
(78) Tabāraka Asmu Rabbika Dhī Al-Jalāli Wa Al-'Ikrāmi	٧٨ تَبَارَكَ اسْمُ رَبِّكَ ذِي الْجَلَالِ وَالْإِكْرَامِ

Surah Ar-Rahman:

Arabic & English

In the name of God, the Gracious, the Merciful.	بِسْمِ اللَّهِ الرَّحْمَٰنِ الرَّحِيمِ
1 The Compassionate.	١ الرَّحْمَٰنُ
2 Has taught the Quran.	٢ عَلَّمَ الْقُرْآنَ
3 He created man.	٣ خَلَقَ الْإِنْسَانَ
4 And taught him clear expression.	٤ عَلَّمَهُ الْبَيَانَ
5 The sun and the moon move according to plan.	٥ الشَّمْسُ وَالْقَمَرُ بِحُسْبَانٍ
6 And the stars and the trees prostrate themselves.	٦ وَالنَّجْمُ وَالشَّجَرُ يَسْجُدَانِ
7 And the sky, He raised; and He set up the balance.	٧ وَالسَّمَاءَ رَفَعَهَا وَوَضَعَ الْمِيزَانَ
8 So do not transgress in the balance.	٨ أَلَّا تَطْغَوْا فِي الْمِيزَانِ
9 But maintain the weights with justice, and do not violate the balance.	٩ وَأَقِيمُوا الْوَزْنَ بِالْقِسْطِ وَلَا تُخْسِرُوا الْمِيزَانَ

10 And the earth; He set up for the creatures.	١٠ وَالْأَرْضَ وَضَعَهَا لِلْأَنَامِ
11 In it are fruits, and palms in clusters.	١١ فِيهَا فَاكِهَةٌ وَالنَّخْلُ ذَاتُ الْأَكْمَامِ
12 And grains in the blades, and fragrant plants.	١٢ وَالْحَبُّ ذُو الْعَصْفِ وَالرَّيْحَانُ
13 So which of your Lord's marvels will you deny?	١٣ فَبِأَيِّ آلَاءِ رَبِّكُمَا تُكَذِّبَانِ
14 He created man from hard clay, like bricks.	١٤ خَلَقَ الْإِنْسَانَ مِنْ صَلْصَالٍ كَالْفَخَّارِ
15 And created the jinn from a fusion of fire.	١٥ وَخَلَقَ الْجَانَّ مِنْ مَارِجٍ مِنْ نَارٍ
16 So which of your Lord's marvels will you deny?	١٦ فَبِأَيِّ آلَاءِ رَبِّكُمَا تُكَذِّبَانِ
17 Lord of the two Easts and Lord of the two Wests.	١٧ رَبُّ الْمَشْرِقَيْنِ وَرَبُّ الْمَغْرِبَيْنِ
18 So which of your Lord's marvels will you deny?	١٨ فَبِأَيِّ آلَاءِ رَبِّكُمَا تُكَذِّبَانِ

19 He merged the two seas, converging together.	١٩ مَرَجَ الْبَحْرَيْنِ يَلْتَقِيَانِ
20 Between them is a barrier, which they do not overrun.	٢٠ بَيْنَهُمَا بَرْزَخٌ لَا يَبْغِيَانِ
21 So which of your Lord's marvels will you deny?	٢١ فَبِأَيِّ آلَاءِ رَبِّكُمَا تُكَذِّبَانِ
22 From them emerge pearls and coral.	٢٢ يَخْرُجُ مِنْهُمَا اللُّؤْلُؤُ وَالْمَرْجَانُ
23 So which of your Lord's marvels will you deny?	٢٣ فَبِأَيِّ آلَاءِ رَبِّكُمَا تُكَذِّبَانِ
24 His are the ships, raised above the sea like landmarks.	٢٤ وَلَهُ الْجَوَارِ الْمُنْشَآتُ فِي الْبَحْرِ كَالْأَعْلَامِ
25 So which of your Lord's marvels will you deny?	٢٥ فَبِأَيِّ آلَاءِ رَبِّكُمَا تُكَذِّبَانِ
26 Everyone upon it is perishing.	٢٦ كُلُّ مَنْ عَلَيْهَا فَانٍ
27 But will remain the Presence of your Lord, Full of Majesty and Splendor.	٢٧ وَيَبْقَى وَجْهُ رَبِّكَ ذُو الْجَلَالِ وَالْإِكْرَامِ

28 So which of your Lord's marvels will you deny?	٢٨ فَبِأَيِّ آلَاءِ رَبِّكُمَا تُكَذِّبَانِ
29 Everyone in the heavens and the earth asks Him. Every day He is managing.	٢٩ يَسْأَلُهُ مَنْ فِي السَّمَاوَاتِ وَالْأَرْضِ ۚ كُلَّ يَوْمٍ هُوَ فِي شَأْنٍ
30 So which of your Lord's marvels will you deny?	٣٠ فَبِأَيِّ آلَاءِ رَبِّكُمَا تُكَذِّبَانِ
31 We will attend to you, O prominent two.	٣١ سَنَفْرُغُ لَكُمْ أَيُّهَ الثَّقَلَانِ
32 So which of your Lord's marvels will you deny?	٣٢ فَبِأَيِّ آلَاءِ رَبِّكُمَا تُكَذِّبَانِ
33 O society of jinn and humans! If you can pass through the bounds of the heavens and the earth, go ahead and pass. But you will not pass except with authorization.	٣٣ يَا مَعْشَرَ الْجِنِّ وَالْإِنْسِ إِنِ اسْتَطَعْتُمْ أَنْ تَنْفُذُوا مِنْ أَقْطَارِ السَّمَاوَاتِ وَالْأَرْضِ فَانْفُذُوا ۚ لَا تَنْفُذُونَ إِلَّا بِسُلْطَانٍ
34 So which of your Lord's marvels will you deny?	٣٤ فَبِأَيِّ آلَاءِ رَبِّكُمَا تُكَذِّبَانِ
35 You will be bombarded with flares of fire and brass, and you will not succeed.	٣٥ يُرْسَلُ عَلَيْكُمَا شُوَاظٌ مِنْ نَارٍ وَنُحَاسٌ فَلَا تَنْتَصِرَانِ

36 So which of your Lord's marvels will you deny?	٣٦ فَبِأَيِّ آلَاءِ رَبِّكُمَا تُكَذِّبَانِ
37 When the sky splits apart, and becomes rose, like paint.	٣٧ فَإِذَا انْشَقَّتِ السَّمَاءُ فَكَانَتْ وَرْدَةً كَالدِّهَانِ
38 So which of your Lord's marvels will you deny?	٣٨ فَبِأَيِّ آلَاءِ رَبِّكُمَا تُكَذِّبَانِ
39 On that Day, no human and no jinn will be asked about his sins.	٣٩ فَيَوْمَئِذٍ لَا يُسْأَلُ عَنْ ذَنْبِهِ إِنْسٌ وَلَا جَانٌّ
40 So which of your Lord's marvels will you deny?	٤٠ فَبِأَيِّ آلَاءِ رَبِّكُمَا تُكَذِّبَانِ
41 The guilty will be recognized by their marks; they will be taken by the forelocks and the feet.	٤١ يُعْرَفُ الْمُجْرِمُونَ بِسِيمَاهُمْ فَيُؤْخَذُ بِالنَّوَاصِي وَالْأَقْدَامِ
42 So which of your Lord's marvels will you deny?	٤٢ فَبِأَيِّ آلَاءِ رَبِّكُمَا تُكَذِّبَانِ
43 This is Hell that the guilty denied.	٤٣ هَٰذِهِ جَهَنَّمُ الَّتِي يُكَذِّبُ بِهَا الْمُجْرِمُونَ

44 They circulate between it and between a seething bath.	٤٤ يَطُوفُونَ بَيْنَهَا وَبَيْنَ حَمِيمٍ آنٍ
45 So which of your Lord's marvels will you deny?	٤٥ فَبِأَيِّ آلَاءِ رَبِّكُمَا تُكَذِّبَانِ
46 But for him who feared the standing of his Lord are two gardens.	٤٦ وَلِمَنْ خَافَ مَقَامَ رَبِّهِ جَنَّتَانِ
47 So which of your Lord's marvels will you deny?	٤٧ فَبِأَيِّ آلَاءِ رَبِّكُمَا تُكَذِّبَانِ
48 Full of varieties.	٤٨ ذَوَاتَا أَفْنَانٍ
49 So which of your Lord's marvels will you deny?	٤٩ فَبِأَيِّ آلَاءِ رَبِّكُمَا تُكَذِّبَانِ
50 In them are two flowing springs.	٥٠ فِيهِمَا عَيْنَانِ تَجْرِيَانِ
51 So which of your Lord's marvels will you deny?	٥١ فَبِأَيِّ آلَاءِ رَبِّكُمَا تُكَذِّبَانِ
52 In them are fruits of every kind, in pairs.	٥٢ فِيهِمَا مِنْ كُلِّ فَاكِهَةٍ زَوْجَانِ

53 So which of your Lord's marvels will you deny?	٥٣ فَبِأَيِّ آلَاءِ رَبِّكُمَا تُكَذِّبَانِ
54 Reclining on furnishings lined with brocade, and the fruits of the two gardens are near at hand.	٥٤ مُتَّكِئِينَ عَلَى فُرُشٍ بَطَائِنُهَا مِنْ إِسْتَبْرَقٍ ۚ وَجَنَى الْجَنَّتَيْنِ دَانٍ
55 So which of your Lord's marvels will you deny?	٥٥ فَبِأَيِّ آلَاءِ رَبِّكُمَا تُكَذِّبَانِ
56 In them are maidens restraining their glances, untouched before by any man or jinn.	٥٦ فِيهِنَّ قَاصِرَاتُ الطَّرْفِ لَمْ يَطْمِثْهُنَّ إِنْسٌ قَبْلَهُمْ وَلَا جَانٌّ
57 So which of your Lord's marvels will you deny?	٥٧ فَبِأَيِّ آلَاءِ رَبِّكُمَا تُكَذِّبَانِ
58 As though they were rubies and corals.	٥٨ كَأَنَّهُنَّ الْيَاقُوتُ وَالْمَرْجَانُ
59 So which of your Lord's marvels will you deny?	٥٩ فَبِأَيِّ آلَاءِ رَبِّكُمَا تُكَذِّبَانِ
60 Is the reward of goodness anything but goodness?	٦٠ هَلْ جَزَاءُ الْإِحْسَانِ إِلَّا الْإِحْسَانُ

61 So which of your Lord's marvels will you deny?	٦١ فَبِأَيِّ آلَاءِ رَبِّكُمَا تُكَذِّبَانِ
62 And beneath them are two gardens.	٦٢ وَمِنْ دُونِهِمَا جَنَّتَانِ
63 So which of your Lord's marvels will you deny?	٦٣ فَبِأَيِّ آلَاءِ رَبِّكُمَا تُكَذِّبَانِ
64 Deep green.	٦٤ مُدْهَامَّتَانِ
65 So which of your Lord's marvels will you deny?	٦٥ فَبِأَيِّ آلَاءِ رَبِّكُمَا تُكَذِّبَانِ
66 In them are two gushing springs.	٦٦ فِيهِمَا عَيْنَانِ نَضَّاخَتَانِ
67 So which of your Lord's marvels will you deny?	٦٧ فَبِأَيِّ آلَاءِ رَبِّكُمَا تُكَذِّبَانِ
68 In them are fruits, and date-palms, and pomegranates.	٦٨ فِيهِمَا فَاكِهَةٌ وَنَخْلٌ وَرُمَّانٌ
69 So which of your Lord's marvels will you deny?	٦٩ فَبِأَيِّ آلَاءِ رَبِّكُمَا تُكَذِّبَانِ
70 In them are good and beautiful ones.	٧٠ فِيهِنَّ خَيْرَاتٌ حِسَانٌ

71 So which of your Lord's marvels will you deny?	٧١ فَبِأَيِّ آلَاءِ رَبِّكُمَا تُكَذِّبَانِ
72 Companions, secluded in the tents.	٧٢ حُورٌ مَقْصُورَاتٌ فِي الْخِيَامِ
73 So which of your Lord's marvels will you deny?	٧٣ فَبِأَيِّ آلَاءِ رَبِّكُمَا تُكَذِّبَانِ
74 Whom no human has touched before, nor jinn.	٧٤ لَمْ يَطْمِثْهُنَّ إِنْسٌ قَبْلَهُمْ وَلَا جَانٌّ
75 So which of your Lord's marvels will you deny?	٧٥ فَبِأَيِّ آلَاءِ رَبِّكُمَا تُكَذِّبَانِ
76 Reclining on green cushions, and exquisite carpets.	٧٦ مُتَّكِئِينَ عَلَى رَفْرَفٍ خُضْرٍ وَعَبْقَرِيٍّ حِسَانٍ
77 So which of your Lord's marvels will you deny?	٧٧ فَبِأَيِّ آلَاءِ رَبِّكُمَا تُكَذِّبَانِ
78 Blessed be the name of your Lord, Full of Majesty and Splendor.	٧٨ تَبَارَكَ اسْمُ رَبِّكَ ذِي الْجَلَالِ وَالْإِكْرَامِ

Surah Yaseen:

Arabic & Phonetic

Bismi Allāhi Ar-Raĥmāni Ar-Raĥīmi	بِسْمِ اللَّهِ الرَّحْمَٰنِ الرَّحِيمِ
(1) Yā -Sīn	١- يس
(2) Wa Al-Qur'āni Al-Ĥakīmi	٢- وَالْقُرْآنِ الْحَكِيمِ
(3) 'Innaka Lamina Al-Mursalīna	٣- إِنَّكَ لَمِنَ الْمُرْسَلِينَ
(4) `Alá Şirāţin Mustaqīmin	٤- عَلَىٰ صِرَاطٍ مُسْتَقِيمٍ
(5) Tanzīla Al-`Azīzi Ar-Raĥīmi	٥- تَنْزِيلَ الْعَزِيزِ الرَّحِيمِ
(6) Litundhira Qawmāan Mā 'Undhira 'Ābā'uuhum Fahum Ghāfilūna	٦- لِتُنْذِرَ قَوْمًا مَا أُنْذِرَ آبَاؤُهُمْ فَهُمْ غَافِلُونَ
(7) Laqad Ĥaqqa Al-Qawlu `Alá 'Aktharihim Fahum Lā Yu'uminūna	٧- لَقَدْ حَقَّ الْقَوْلُ عَلَىٰ أَكْثَرِهِمْ فَهُمْ لَا يُؤْمِنُونَ
(8) 'Innā Ja`alnā Fī 'A`nāqihim 'Aghlālāan Fahiya 'Ilá Al-'Adhqāni Fahum Muqmaĥūna	٨- إِنَّا جَعَلْنَا فِي أَعْنَاقِهِمْ أَغْلَالًا فَهِيَ إِلَى الْأَذْقَانِ فَهُمْ مُقْمَحُونَ
(9) Wa Ja`alnā Min Bayni 'Aydīhim Saddāan Wa Min Khalfihim Saddāan	٩- وَجَعَلْنَا مِنْ بَيْنِ أَيْدِيهِمْ سَدًّا وَمِنْ خَلْفِهِمْ سَدًّا فَأَغْشَيْنَاهُمْ فَهُمْ لَا يُبْصِرُونَ

Fa'aghshaynāhum Fahum Lā
Yubşirūna

(10) Wa Sawā'un `Alayhim
'A'andhartahum 'Am Lam
Tundhirhum Lā Yu'uminūna

١٠- وَسَوَاءٌ عَلَيْهِمْ أَأَنْذَرْتَهُمْ أَمْ لَمْ تُنْذِرْهُمْ لَا يُؤْمِنُونَ

(11) 'Innamā Tundhiru Mani
Attaba`a Adh-Dhikra Wa Khashiya
Ar-Raĥmana Bil-Ghaybi
Fabashirhu Bimaghfiratin Wa
'Ajrin Karīmin

١١- إِنَّمَا تُنْذِرُ مَنِ اتَّبَعَ الذِّكْرَ وَخَشِيَ الرَّحْمَنَ بِالْغَيْبِ ۖ فَبَشِّرْهُ بِمَغْفِرَةٍ وَأَجْرٍ كَرِيمٍ

(12) 'Innā Naĥnu Nuĥyi Al-Mawtá
Wa Naktubu Mā Qaddamū Wa
'Āthārahum Wa Kulla Shay'in
'Ĥşaynāhu Fī 'Imāmin Mubīnin

١٢- إِنَّا نَحْنُ نُحْيِي الْمَوْتَى وَنَكْتُبُ مَا قَدَّمُوا وَآثَارَهُمْ ۚ وَكُلَّ شَيْءٍ أَحْصَيْنَاهُ فِي إِمَامٍ مُبِينٍ

(13) Wa Ađrib Lahum Mathalāan
'Aşĥāba Al-Qaryati 'Idh Jā'ahā Al-
Mursalūna

١٣- وَاضْرِبْ لَهُمْ مَثَلًا أَصْحَابَ الْقَرْيَةِ إِذْ جَاءَهَا الْمُرْسَلُونَ

(14) 'Idh 'Arsalnā 'Ilayhimu
Athnayni Fakadhabūhumā
Fa`azzaznā Bithālithin Faqālū 'Innā
'Ilaykum Mursalūna

١٤- إِذْ أَرْسَلْنَا إِلَيْهِمُ اثْنَيْنِ فَكَذَّبُوهُمَا فَعَزَّزْنَا بِثَالِثٍ فَقَالُوا إِنَّا إِلَيْكُمْ مُرْسَلُونَ

(15) Qālū Mā 'Antum 'Illā Basharun Mithlunā Wa Mā 'Anzala Ar-Raĥmānu Min Shay'in 'In 'Antum 'Illā Takdhibūna	١٥ـ قَالُوا مَا أَنْتُمْ إِلَّا بَشَرٌ مِثْلُنَا وَمَا أَنْزَلَ الرَّحْمَٰنُ مِنْ شَيْءٍ إِنْ أَنْتُمْ إِلَّا تَكْذِبُونَ
(16) Qālū Rabbunā Ya`lamu 'Innā 'Ilaykum Lamursalūna	١٦ـ قَالُوا رَبُّنَا يَعْلَمُ إِنَّا إِلَيْكُمْ لَمُرْسَلُونَ
(17) Wa Mā `Alaynā 'Illā Al-Balāghu Al-Mubīnu	١٧ـ وَمَا عَلَيْنَا إِلَّا الْبَلَاغُ الْمُبِينُ
(18) Qālū 'Innā Taţayyarnā Bikum La'in Lam Tantahū Lanarjuma-nnakum Wa Layamassannakum Minnā `Adhābun 'Alīmun	١٨ـ قَالُوا إِنَّا تَطَيَّرْنَا بِكُمْ لَئِنْ لَمْ تَنْتَهُوا لَنَرْجُمَنَّكُمْ وَلَيَمَسَّنَّكُمْ مِنَّا عَذَابٌ أَلِيمٌ
(19) Qālū Ţā'irukum Ma`akum 'A'in Dhukkirtum Bal 'Antum Qawmun Musrifūna	١٩ـ قَالُوا طَائِرُكُمْ مَعَكُمْ أَئِنْ ذُكِّرْتُمْ بَلْ أَنْتُمْ قَوْمٌ مُسْرِفُونَ
(20) Wa Jā'a Min 'Aqşá Al-Madīnati Rajulun Yas`á Qāla Yā Qawmi Attabi`ū Al-Mursalīna	٢٠ـ وَجَاءَ مِنْ أَقْصَى الْمَدِينَةِ رَجُلٌ يَسْعَىٰ قَالَ يَا قَوْمِ اتَّبِعُوا الْمُرْسَلِينَ
(21) Attabi`ū Man Lā Yas'alukum 'Ajrāan Wa Hum Muhtadūna	٢١ـ اتَّبِعُوا مَنْ لَا يَسْأَلُكُمْ أَجْرًا وَهُمْ مُهْتَدُونَ

(22) Wa Mā Liya Lā 'A`budu Al-Ladhī Faţaranī Wa 'Ilayhi Turja`ūna	٢٢ـ وَمَا لِيَ لَا أَعْبُدُ الَّذِي فَطَرَنِي وَإِلَيْهِ تُرْجَعُونَ
(23) 'A'attakhidhu Min Dūnihi 'Ālihatan 'In Yuridni Ar-Raĥmānu Biđurrin Lā Tughni `Annī Shafā`atuhum Shay'āan Wa Lā Yunqidhūni	٢٣ـ أَأَتَّخِذُ مِنْ دُونِهِ آلِهَةً إِنْ يُرِدْنِ الرَّحْمَنُ بِضُرٍّ لَا تُغْنِ عَنِّي شَفَاعَتُهُمْ شَيْئًا وَلَا يُنْقِذُونِ
(24) 'Innī 'Idhāan Lafī Đalālin Mubīnin	٢٤ـ إِنِّي إِذًا لَفِي ضَلَالٍ مُبِينٍ
(25) 'Innī 'Āmantu Birabbikum Fāsma`ūni	٢٥ـ إِنِّي آمَنْتُ بِرَبِّكُمْ فَاسْمَعُونِ
(26) Qīla Adkhuli Al-Jannata Qāla Yā Layta Qawmī Ya`lamūna	٢٦ـ قِيلَ ادْخُلِ الْجَنَّةَ قَالَ يَا لَيْتَ قَوْمِي يَعْلَمُونَ
(27) Bimā Ghafara Lī Rabbī Wa Ja`alanī Mina Al-Mukramīna	٢٧ـ بِمَا غَفَرَ لِي رَبِّي وَجَعَلَنِي مِنَ الْمُكْرَمِينَ
(28) Wa Mā 'Anzalnā `Alá Qawmihi Min Ba`dihi Min Jundin Mina As-Samā'i Wa Mā Kunnā Munzilīna	٢٨ـ وَمَا أَنْزَلْنَا عَلَى قَوْمِهِ مِنْ بَعْدِهِ مِنْ جُنْدٍ مِنَ السَّمَاءِ وَمَا كُنَّا مُنْزِلِينَ

(29) 'In Kānat 'Illā Şayĥatan Wāĥidatan Fa'idhā Hum Khāmidūna	٢٩ - إِنْ كَانَتْ إِلَّا صَيْحَةً وَاحِدَةً فَإِذَا هُمْ خَامِدُونَ
(30) Yā Ĥasratan `Alá Al-`Ibādi Mā Ya'tīhim Min Rasūlin 'Illā Kānū Bihi Yastahzi'ūn	٣٠ - يَا حَسْرَةً عَلَى الْعِبَادِ ۚ مَا يَأْتِيهِمْ مِنْ رَسُولٍ إِلَّا كَانُوا بِهِ يَسْتَهْزِئُونَ
(31) 'Alam Yaraw Kam 'Ahlaknā Qablahum Mina Al-Qurūni 'Annahum 'Ilayhim Lā Yarji`ūna	٣١ - أَلَمْ يَرَوْا كَمْ أَهْلَكْنَا قَبْلَهُمْ مِنَ الْقُرُونِ أَنَّهُمْ إِلَيْهِمْ لَا يَرْجِعُونَ
(32) Wa 'In Kullun Lammā Jamī`un Ladaynā Muĥđarūna	٣٢ - وَإِنْ كُلٌّ لَمَّا جَمِيعٌ لَدَيْنَا مُحْضَرُونَ
(33) Wa 'Āyatun Lahumu Al-'Arđu Al-Maytatu 'Aĥyaynāhā Wa 'Akhrajnā Minhā Ĥabbāan Faminhu Ya'kulūna	٣٣ - وَآيَةٌ لَهُمُ الْأَرْضُ الْمَيْتَةُ أَحْيَيْنَاهَا وَأَخْرَجْنَا مِنْهَا حَبًّا فَمِنْهُ يَأْكُلُونَ
(34) Wa Ja`alnā Fīhā Jannātin Min Nakhīlin Wa 'A`nābin Wa Fajjarnā Fīhā Mina Al-`Uyūni	٣٤ - وَجَعَلْنَا فِيهَا جَنَّاتٍ مِنْ نَخِيلٍ وَأَعْنَابٍ وَفَجَّرْنَا فِيهَا مِنَ الْعُيُونِ
(35) Liya'kulū Min Thamarihi Wa Mā `Amilat/hu 'Aydīhim 'Afalā Yashkurūna	٣٥ - لِيَأْكُلُوا مِنْ ثَمَرِهِ وَمَا عَمِلَتْهُ أَيْدِيهِمْ ۖ أَفَلَا يَشْكُرُونَ

(36) Subĥāna Al-Ladhī Khalaqa Al-'Azwāja Kullahā Mimmā Tunbitu Al-'Arđu Wa Min 'Anfusihim Wa Mimmā Lā Ya`lamūna

٣٦ـ سُبْحَانَ الَّذِي خَلَقَ الْأَزْوَاجَ كُلَّهَا مِمَّا تُنْبِتُ الْأَرْضُ وَمِنْ أَنْفُسِهِمْ وَمِمَّا لَا يَعْلَمُونَ

(37) Wa 'Āyatun Lahumu Al-Laylu Naslakhu Minhu An-Nahāra Fa'idhā Hum Mužlimūna

٣٧ـ وَآيَةٌ لَهُمُ اللَّيْلُ نَسْلَخُ مِنْهُ النَّهَارَ فَإِذَا هُمْ مُظْلِمُونَ

(38) Wa Ash-Shamsu Tajrī Limustaqarrin Lahā Dhālika Taqdīru Al-`Azīzi Al-`Alīmi

٣٨ـ وَالشَّمْسُ تَجْرِي لِمُسْتَقَرٍّ لَهَا ۚ ذَٰلِكَ تَقْدِيرُ الْعَزِيزِ الْعَلِيمِ

(39) Wa Al-Qamara Qaddarnāhu Manāzila Ĥattá `Āda Kāl`urjūni Al-Qadīmi

٣٩ـ وَالْقَمَرَ قَدَّرْنَاهُ مَنَازِلَ حَتَّىٰ عَادَ كَالْعُرْجُونِ الْقَدِيمِ

(40) Lā Ash-Shamsu Yanbaghī Lahā 'An Tudrika Al-Qamara Wa Lā Al-Laylu Sābiqu An-Nahāri Wa Kullun Fī Falakin Yasbaĥūna

٤٠ـ لَا الشَّمْسُ يَنْبَغِي لَهَا أَنْ تُدْرِكَ الْقَمَرَ وَلَا اللَّيْلُ سَابِقُ النَّهَارِ ۚ وَكُلٌّ فِي فَلَكٍ يَسْبَحُونَ

(41) Wa 'Āyatun Lahum 'Annā Ĥamalnā Dhurrīyatahum Fī Al-Fulki Al-Mashĥūni

٤١ـ وَآيَةٌ لَهُمْ أَنَّا حَمَلْنَا ذُرِّيَّتَهُمْ فِي الْفُلْكِ الْمَشْحُونِ

(42) Wa Khalaqnā Lahum Min Mithlihi Mā Yarkabūna

٤٢ـ وَخَلَقْنَا لَهُمْ مِنْ مِثْلِهِ مَا يَرْكَبُونَ

(43) Wa 'In Nasha' Nughriqhum Falā Şarīkha Lahum Wa Lā Hum Yunqadhūna	٤٣- وَإِنْ نَشَأْ نُغْرِقْهُمْ فَلَا صَرِيخَ لَهُمْ وَلَا هُمْ يُنْقَذُونَ
(44) 'Illā Raĥmatan Minnā Wa Matā`āan 'Ilá Ĥīnin	٤٤- إِلَّا رَحْمَةً مِنَّا وَمَتَاعًا إِلَى حِينٍ
(45) Wa 'Idhā Qīla Lahumu Atta-qū Mā Bayna 'Aydīkum Wa Mā Khalfakum La`allakum Turĥamūna	٤٥- وَإِذَا قِيلَ لَهُمُ اتَّقُوا مَا بَيْنَ أَيْدِيكُمْ وَمَا خَلْفَكُمْ لَعَلَّكُمْ تُرْحَمُونَ
(46) Wa Mā Ta'tīhim Min 'Āyatin Min 'Āyāti Rabbihim 'Illā Kānū `Anhā Mu`riđīna	٤٦- وَمَا تَأْتِيهِمْ مِنْ آيَةٍ مِنْ آيَاتِ رَبِّهِمْ إِلَّا كَانُوا عَنْهَا مُعْرِضِينَ
(47) Wa 'Idhā Qīla Lahum 'Anfiqū Mimmā Razaqakumu Allāhu Qāla Al-Ladhīna Kafarū Lilladhīna 'Āmanū 'Anuţ`imu Man Law Yashā'u Allāhu 'Aţ`amahu 'In 'Antum 'Illā Fī Đalālin Mubīnin	٤٧- وَإِذَا قِيلَ لَهُمْ أَنْفِقُوا مِمَّا رَزَقَكُمُ اللَّهُ قَالَ الَّذِينَ كَفَرُوا لِلَّذِينَ آمَنُوا أَنُطْعِمُ مَنْ لَوْ يَشَاءُ اللَّهُ أَطْعَمَهُ إِنْ أَنْتُمْ إِلَّا فِي ضَلَالٍ مُبِينٍ
(48) Wa Yaqūlūna Matá Hādhā Al-Wa`du 'In Kuntum Şādiqīna	٤٨- وَيَقُولُونَ مَتَى هَذَا الْوَعْدُ إِنْ كُنْتُمْ صَادِقِينَ
(49) Mā Yanzurūna 'Illā Şayĥatan Wāĥidatan Ta'khudhuhum Wa Hum Yakhişşimūna	٤٩- مَا يَنْظُرُونَ إِلَّا صَيْحَةً وَاحِدَةً تَأْخُذُهُمْ وَهُمْ يَخِصِّمُونَ

(50) Falā Yastaṭī`ūna Tawṣiyatan Wa Lā 'Ilá 'Ahlihim Yarji`ūna	٥٠ـ فَلَا يَسْتَطِيعُونَ تَوْصِيَةً وَلَا إِلَى أَهْلِهِمْ يَرْجِعُونَ
(51) Wa Nufikha Fī Aṣ-Ṣūri Fa'idhā Hum Mina Al-'Ajdāthi 'Ilá Rabbihim Yansilūna	٥١ـ وَنُفِخَ فِي الصُّورِ فَإِذَا هُم مِنَ الْأَجْدَاثِ إِلَى رَبِّهِمْ يَنسِلُونَ
(52) Qālū Yā Waylanā Man Ba`athanā Min Marqadinā Hādhā Mā Wa`ada Ar-Raḥmānu Wa Ṣadaqa Al-Mursalūna	٥٢ـ قَالُوا يَا وَيْلَنَا مَن بَعَثَنَا مِن مَرْقَدِنَا هَٰذَا مَا وَعَدَ الرَّحْمَٰنُ وَصَدَقَ الْمُرْسَلُونَ
(53) 'In Kānat 'Illā Ṣayḥatan Wāḥidatan Fa'idhā Hum Jamī`un Ladaynā Muḥḍarūna	٥٣ـ إِن كَانَتْ إِلَّا صَيْحَةً وَاحِدَةً فَإِذَا هُمْ جَمِيعٌ لَدَيْنَا مُحْضَرُونَ
(54) Fālyawma Lā Tuẓlamu Nafsun Shay'āan Wa Lā Tujzawna 'Illā Mā Kuntum Ta`malūna	٥٤ـ فَالْيَوْمَ لَا تُظْلَمُ نَفْسٌ شَيْئًا وَلَا تُجْزَوْنَ إِلَّا مَا كُنتُمْ تَعْمَلُونَ
(55) 'Inna 'Aṣḥāba Al-Jannati Al-Yawma Fī Shughulin Fākihūna	٥٥ـ إِنَّ أَصْحَابَ الْجَنَّةِ الْيَوْمَ فِي شُغُلٍ فَاكِهُونَ
(56) Hum Wa 'Azwājuhum Fī Ẓilālin `Alá Al-'Arā'iki Muttaki'ūna	٥٦ـ هُمْ وَأَزْوَاجُهُمْ فِي ظِلَالٍ عَلَى الْأَرَائِكِ مُتَّكِئُونَ

(57) Lahum Fīhā Fākihatun Wa Lahum Mā Yadda`ūna	٥٧- لَهُمْ فِيهَا فَاكِهَةٌ وَلَهُمْ مَا يَدَّعُونَ
(58) Salāmun Qawlāan Min Rabbin Rahīmin	٥٨- سَلَامٌ قَوْلًا مِنْ رَبٍّ رَحِيمٍ
(59) Wa Amtāzū Al-Yawma 'Ayyuhā Al-Mujrimūna	٥٩- وَامْتَازُوا الْيَوْمَ أَيُّهَا الْمُجْرِمُونَ
(60) 'Alam 'A`had 'Ilaykum Yā Banī 'Ādama 'An Lā Ta`budū Ash-Shaytāna 'Innahu Lakum `Adūwun Mubīnun	٦٠- أَلَمْ أَعْهَدْ إِلَيْكُمْ يَا بَنِي آدَمَ أَنْ لَا تَعْبُدُوا الشَّيْطَانَ ۖ إِنَّهُ لَكُمْ عَدُوٌّ مُبِينٌ
(61) Wa 'Ani A`budūnī Hādhā Şirātun Mustaqīmun	٦١- وَأَنِ اعْبُدُونِي ۚ هَٰذَا صِرَاطٌ مُسْتَقِيمٌ
(62) Wa Laqad 'Adalla Minkum Jibillāan Kathīrāan 'Afalam Takūnū Ta`qilūna	٦٢- وَلَقَدْ أَضَلَّ مِنْكُمْ جِبِلًّا كَثِيرًا ۖ أَفَلَمْ تَكُونُوا تَعْقِلُونَ
(63) Hadhihi Jahannamu Allatī Kuntum Tū`adūna	٦٣- هَٰذِهِ جَهَنَّمُ الَّتِي كُنْتُمْ تُوعَدُونَ
(64) Aşlawhā Al-Yawma Bimā Kuntum Takfurūna	٦٤- اصْلَوْهَا الْيَوْمَ بِمَا كُنْتُمْ تَكْفُرُونَ

(65) Al-Yawma Nakhtimu `Alá 'Afwāhihim Wa Tukallimunā 'Aydīhim Wa Tash/hadu 'Arjuluhum Bimā Kānū Yaksibūna	٦٥۔ الْيَوْمَ نَخْتِمُ عَلَىٰ أَفْوَاهِهِمْ وَتُكَلِّمُنَا أَيْدِيهِمْ وَتَشْهَدُ أَرْجُلُهُم بِمَا كَانُوا يَكْسِبُونَ
(66) Wa Law Nashā'u Laţamasnā `Alá 'A`yunihim Fāstabaqū Aş-Şirāţa Fa'anná Yubşirūna	٦٦۔ وَلَوْ نَشَاءُ لَطَمَسْنَا عَلَىٰ أَعْيُنِهِمْ فَاسْتَبَقُوا الصِّرَاطَ فَأَنَّىٰ يُبْصِرُونَ
(67) Wa Law Nashā'u Lamasakhnāhum `Alá Makānatihim Famā Astaţā`ū Muđīyāan Wa Lā Yarji`ūna	٦٧۔ وَلَوْ نَشَاءُ لَمَسَخْنَاهُمْ عَلَىٰ مَكَانَتِهِمْ فَمَا اسْتَطَاعُوا مُضِيًّا وَلَا يَرْجِعُونَ
(68) Wa Man Nu`ammirhu Nunakkis/hu Fī Al-Khalqi 'Afalā Ya`qilūna	٦٨۔ وَمَن نُّعَمِّرْهُ نُنَكِّسْهُ فِي الْخَلْقِ ۚ أَفَلَا يَعْقِلُونَ
(69) Wa Mā `Allamnāhu Ash-Shi`ra Wa Mā Yanbaghī Lahu 'In Huwa 'Illā Dhikrun Wa Qur'ānun Mubīnun	٦٩۔ وَمَا عَلَّمْنَاهُ الشِّعْرَ وَمَا يَنبَغِي لَهُ ۚ إِنْ هُوَ إِلَّا ذِكْرٌ وَقُرْآنٌ مُّبِينٌ
(70) Liyundhira Man Kāna Ĥayyāan Wa Yaĥiqqa Al-Qawlu `Alá Al-Kāfirīna	٧٠۔ لِيُنذِرَ مَن كَانَ حَيًّا وَيَحِقَّ الْقَوْلُ عَلَى الْكَافِرِينَ

(71) 'Awalam Yaraw 'Annā Khalaqnā Lahum Mimmā `Amilat 'Aydīnā 'An`āmāan Fahum Lahā Mālikūna	٧١- أَوَلَمْ يَرَوْا أَنَّا خَلَقْنَا لَهُمْ مِمَّا عَمِلَتْ أَيْدِينَا أَنْعَامًا فَهُمْ لَهَا مَالِكُونَ
(72) Wa Dhallalnāhā Lahum Faminhā Rakūbuhum Wa Minhā Ya'kulūna	٧٢- وَذَلَّلْنَاهَا لَهُمْ فَمِنْهَا رَكُوبُهُمْ وَمِنْهَا يَأْكُلُونَ
(73) Wa Lahum Fīhā Manāfi`u Wa Mashāribu 'Afalā Yashkurūna	٧٣- وَلَهُمْ فِيهَا مَنَافِعُ وَمَشَارِبُ ۖ أَفَلَا يَشْكُرُونَ
(74) Wa Attakhadhū Min Dūni Allāhi 'Ālihatan La`allahum Yunşarūna	٧٤- وَاتَّخَذُوا مِنْ دُونِ اللَّهِ آلِهَةً لَعَلَّهُمْ يُنْصَرُونَ
(75) Lā Yastaţī`ūna Naşrahum Wa Hum Lahum Jundun Muĥđarūna	٧٥- لَا يَسْتَطِيعُونَ نَصْرَهُمْ وَهُمْ لَهُمْ جُنْدٌ مُحْضَرُونَ
(76) Falā Yaĥzunka Qawluhum 'Innā Na`lamu Mā Yusirrūna Wa Mā Yu`linūna	٧٦- فَلَا يَحْزُنْكَ قَوْلُهُمْ ۘ إِنَّا نَعْلَمُ مَا يُسِرُّونَ وَمَا يُعْلِنُونَ
(77) 'Awalam Yara Al-'Insānu 'Annā Khalaqnāhu Min Nuţfatin Fa'idhā Huwa Khaşīmun Mubīnun	٧٧- أَوَلَمْ يَرَ الْإِنْسَانُ أَنَّا خَلَقْنَاهُ مِنْ نُطْفَةٍ فَإِذَا هُوَ خَصِيمٌ مُبِينٌ

(78) Wa Đaraba Lanā Mathalāan Wa Nasiya Khalqahu Qāla Man Yuĥyī Al-`Ižāma Wa Hiya Ramīmun	٧٨ـ وَضَرَبَ لَنَا مَثَلًا وَنَسِيَ خَلْقَهُ ۖ قَالَ مَنْ يُحْيِي الْعِظَامَ وَهِيَ رَمِيمٌ
(79) Qul Yuĥyīhā Al-Ladhī 'Ansha'ahā 'Awwala Marratin Wa Huwa Bikulli Khalqin `Alīmun	٧٩ـ قُلْ يُحْيِيهَا الَّذِي أَنشَأَهَا أَوَّلَ مَرَّةٍ ۖ وَهُوَ بِكُلِّ خَلْقٍ عَلِيمٌ
(80) Al-Ladhī Ja`ala Lakum Mina Ash-Shajari Al-'Akhđari Nārāan Fa'idhā 'Antum Minhu Tūqidūna	٨٠ـ الَّذِي جَعَلَ لَكُم مِّنَ الشَّجَرِ الْأَخْضَرِ نَارًا فَإِذَا أَنتُم مِّنْهُ تُوقِدُونَ
(81) 'Awalaysa Al-Ladhī Khalaqa As-Samāwāti Wa Al-'Arđa Biqādirin `Alá 'An Yakhluqa Mithlahum Balá Wa Huwa Al-Khallāqu Al-`Alīmu	٨١ـ أَوَلَيْسَ الَّذِي خَلَقَ السَّمَاوَاتِ وَالْأَرْضَ بِقَادِرٍ عَلَىٰ أَن يَخْلُقَ مِثْلَهُم ۚ بَلَىٰ وَهُوَ الْخَلَّاقُ الْعَلِيمُ
(82) 'Innamā 'Amruhu 'Idhā 'Arāda Shay'āan 'An Yaqūla Lahu Kun Fayakūnu	٨٢ـ إِنَّمَا أَمْرُهُ إِذَا أَرَادَ شَيْئًا أَن يَقُولَ لَهُ كُن فَيَكُونُ
(83) Fasubĥāna Al-Ladhī Biyadihi Malakūtu Kulli Shay'in Wa 'Ilayhi Turja`ūna	٨٣ـ فَسُبْحَانَ الَّذِي بِيَدِهِ مَلَكُوتُ كُلِّ شَيْءٍ وَإِلَيْهِ تُرْجَعُونَ

Surah Yaseen:

Arabic & English

Bismi Allāhi Ar-Raḥmāni Ar-Raḥīmi

بِسْمِ اللَّهِ الرَّحْمَٰنِ الرَّحِيمِ

1 Ya, Seen.

١- يس

2 By the Wise Quran.

٢- وَالْقُرْآنِ الْحَكِيمِ

3 You are one of the messengers.

٣- إِنَّكَ لَمِنَ الْمُرْسَلِينَ

4 On a straight path.

٤- عَلَىٰ صِرَاطٍ مُسْتَقِيمٍ

5 The revelation of the Almighty, the Merciful.

٥- تَنْزِيلَ الْعَزِيزِ الرَّحِيمِ

6 To warn a people whose ancestors were not warned, and so they are unaware.

٦- لِتُنْذِرَ قَوْمًا مَا أُنْذِرَ آبَاؤُهُمْ فَهُمْ غَافِلُونَ

7 The Word was realized against most of them, for they do not believe.

٧- لَقَدْ حَقَّ الْقَوْلُ عَلَىٰ أَكْثَرِهِمْ فَهُمْ لَا يُؤْمِنُونَ

8 We placed shackles around their necks, up to their chins, so they are stiff-necked.

٨- إِنَّا جَعَلْنَا فِي أَعْنَاقِهِمْ أَغْلَالًا فَهِيَ إِلَى الْأَذْقَانِ فَهُمْ مُقْمَحُونَ

9 And We placed a barrier in front of them, and a barrier behind them, and We have enshrouded them, so they

٩- وَجَعَلْنَا مِنْ بَيْنِ أَيْدِيهِمْ سَدًّا وَمِنْ خَلْفِهِمْ سَدًّا فَأَغْشَيْنَاهُمْ فَهُمْ لَا يُبْصِرُونَ

cannot see.

10 It is the same for them, whether you warn them, or do not warn them—they will not believe.

١٠۔ وَسَوَاءٌ عَلَيْهِمْ أَأَنْذَرْتَهُمْ أَمْ لَمْ تُنْذِرْهُمْ لَا يُؤْمِنُونَ

11 You warn only him who follows the Message, and fears the Most Gracious inwardly. So give him good news of forgiveness, and a generous reward.

١١۔ إِنَّمَا تُنْذِرُ مَنِ اتَّبَعَ الذِّكْرَ وَخَشِيَ الرَّحْمٰنَ بِالْغَيْبِ فَبَشِّرْهُ بِمَغْفِرَةٍ وَأَجْرٍ كَرِيمٍ

12 It is We who revive the dead; and We write down what they have forwarded, and their traces. We have tallied all things in a Clear Record.

١٢۔ إِنَّا نَحْنُ نُحْيِي الْمَوْتَىٰ وَنَكْتُبُ مَا قَدَّمُوا وَآثَارَهُمْ وَكُلَّ شَيْءٍ أَحْصَيْنَاهُ فِي إِمَامٍ مُبِينٍ

13 And cite for them the parable of the landlords of the town—when the messengers came to it.

١٣۔ وَاضْرِبْ لَهُمْ مَثَلًا أَصْحَابَ الْقَرْيَةِ إِذْ جَاءَهَا الْمُرْسَلُونَ

14 We sent them two messengers, but they denied them both, so We reinforced them with a third. They said, "We are messengers to you."

١٤۔ إِذْ أَرْسَلْنَا إِلَيْهِمُ اثْنَيْنِ فَكَذَّبُوهُمَا فَعَزَّزْنَا بِثَالِثٍ فَقَالُوا إِنَّا إِلَيْكُمْ مُرْسَلُونَ

15 They said, "You are nothing but humans like us, and the Gracious did not send down anything; you are only lying."	١٥ـ قَالُوا مَا أَنْتُمْ إِلَّا بَشَرٌ مِثْلُنَا وَمَا أَنْزَلَ الرَّحْمَٰنُ مِنْ شَيْءٍ إِنْ أَنْتُمْ إِلَّا تَكْذِبُونَ
16 They said, "Our Lord knows that we are messengers to you.	١٦ـ قَالُوا رَبُّنَا يَعْلَمُ إِنَّا إِلَيْكُمْ لَمُرْسَلُونَ
17 And our only duty is clear communication."	١٧ـ وَمَا عَلَيْنَا إِلَّا الْبَلَاغُ الْمُبِينُ
18 They said, "We see an evil omen in you; if you do not give up, we will stone you, and a painful punishment from us will befall you."	١٨ـ قَالُوا إِنَّا تَطَيَّرْنَا بِكُمْ لَئِنْ لَمْ تَنْتَهُوا لَنَرْجُمَنَّكُمْ وَلَيَمَسَّنَّكُمْ مِنَّا عَذَابٌ أَلِيمٌ
19 They said, "Your evil omen is upon you. Is it because you were reminded? But you are an extravagant people."	١٩ـ قَالُوا طَائِرُكُمْ مَعَكُمْ أَئِنْ ذُكِّرْتُمْ بَلْ أَنْتُمْ قَوْمٌ مُسْرِفُونَ
20 Then a man came running from the remotest part of the city. He said, "O my people, follow the messengers.	٢٠ـ وَجَاءَ مِنْ أَقْصَى الْمَدِينَةِ رَجُلٌ يَسْعَىٰ قَالَ يَا قَوْمِ اتَّبِعُوا الْمُرْسَلِينَ
21 Follow those who ask you of no wage, and are themselves guided.	٢١ـ اتَّبِعُوا مَنْ لَا يَسْأَلُكُمْ أَجْرًا وَهُمْ مُهْتَدُونَ

22 "And why should I not worship Him Who created me, and to Whom you will be returned?	٢٢- وَمَا لِيَ لَا أَعْبُدُ الَّذِي فَطَرَنِي وَإِلَيْهِ تُرْجَعُونَ
23 Shall I take other gods instead of Him? If the Merciful desires harm for me, their intercession will not avail me at all, nor will they save me.	٢٣- أَأَتَّخِذُ مِنْ دُونِهِ آلِهَةً إِنْ يُرِدْنِ الرَّحْمَنُ بِضُرٍّ لَا تُغْنِ عَنِّي شَفَاعَتُهُمْ شَيْئًا وَلَا يُنْقِذُونِ
24 In that case, I would be completely lost.	٢٤- إِنِّي إِذًا لَفِي ضَلَالٍ مُبِينٍ
25 I have believed in your Lord, so listen to me."	٢٥- إِنِّي آمَنْتُ بِرَبِّكُمْ فَاسْمَعُونِ
26 It was said, "Enter Paradise." He said, "If only my people knew.	٢٦- قِيلَ ادْخُلِ الْجَنَّةَ ۖ قَالَ يَا لَيْتَ قَوْمِي يَعْلَمُونَ
27 How my Lord has forgiven me, and made me one of the honored."	٢٧- بِمَا غَفَرَ لِي رَبِّي وَجَعَلَنِي مِنَ الْمُكْرَمِينَ
28 After him, We sent down no hosts from heaven to his people; nor would We ever send any down.	٢٨- وَمَا أَنْزَلْنَا عَلَى قَوْمِهِ مِنْ بَعْدِهِ مِنْ جُنْدٍ مِنَ السَّمَاءِ وَمَا كُنَّا مُنْزِلِينَ

29 It was just one Cry, and they were stilled.	٢٩ـ إِنْ كَانَتْ إِلَّا صَيْحَةً وَاحِدَةً فَإِذَا هُمْ خَامِدُونَ
30 Alas for the servants. No messenger ever came to them, but they ridiculed him.	٣٠ـ يَا حَسْرَةً عَلَى الْعِبَادِ ۚ مَا يَأْتِيهِمْ مِنْ رَسُولٍ إِلَّا كَانُوا بِهِ يَسْتَهْزِئُونَ
31 Have they not considered how many generations We destroyed before them; and that unto them they will not return?	٣١ـ أَلَمْ يَرَوْا كَمْ أَهْلَكْنَا قَبْلَهُمْ مِنَ الْقُرُونِ أَنَّهُمْ إِلَيْهِمْ لَا يَرْجِعُونَ
32 All of them, every single one of them, will be arraigned before Us.	٣٢ـ وَإِنْ كُلٌّ لَمَّا جَمِيعٌ لَدَيْنَا مُحْضَرُونَ
33 And there is a sign for them in the dead land: We give it life, and produce from it grains from which they eat.	٣٣ـ وَآيَةٌ لَهُمُ الْأَرْضُ الْمَيْتَةُ أَحْيَيْنَاهَا وَأَخْرَجْنَا مِنْهَا حَبًّا فَمِنْهُ يَأْكُلُونَ
34 And We place in it gardens of palm-trees and vines, and cause springs to gush out of it.	٣٤ـ وَجَعَلْنَا فِيهَا جَنَّاتٍ مِنْ نَخِيلٍ وَأَعْنَابٍ وَفَجَّرْنَا فِيهَا مِنَ الْعُيُونِ
35 That they may eat from its fruits, although their hands did not make it. Will they not be appreciative?	٣٥ـ لِيَأْكُلُوا مِنْ ثَمَرِهِ وَمَا عَمِلَتْهُ أَيْدِيهِمْ ۖ أَفَلَا يَشْكُرُونَ

36 Glory be to Him who created all the pairs; of what the earth produces, and of their own selves, and of what they do not know.	٣٦- سُبْحَانَ الَّذِي خَلَقَ الْأَزْوَاجَ كُلَّهَا مِمَّا تُنْبِتُ الْأَرْضُ وَمِنْ أَنْفُسِهِمْ وَمِمَّا لَا يَعْلَمُونَ
37 Another sign for them is the night: We strip the day out of it—and they are in darkness.	٣٧- وَآيَةٌ لَهُمُ اللَّيْلُ نَسْلَخُ مِنْهُ النَّهَارَ فَإِذَا هُمْ مُظْلِمُونَ
38 And the sun runs towards its destination. Such is the design of the Almighty, the All-Knowing.	٣٨- وَالشَّمْسُ تَجْرِي لِمُسْتَقَرٍّ لَهَا ۚ ذَٰلِكَ تَقْدِيرُ الْعَزِيزِ الْعَلِيمِ
39 And the moon: We have disposed it in phases, until it returns like the old twig.	٣٩- وَالْقَمَرَ قَدَّرْنَاهُ مَنَازِلَ حَتَّىٰ عَادَ كَالْعُرْجُونِ الْقَدِيمِ
40 The sun is not to overtake the moon, nor is the night to outpace the day. Each floats in an orbit.	٤٠- لَا الشَّمْسُ يَنْبَغِي لَهَا أَنْ تُدْرِكَ الْقَمَرَ وَلَا اللَّيْلُ سَابِقُ النَّهَارِ ۚ وَكُلٌّ فِي فَلَكٍ يَسْبَحُونَ
41 Another sign for them is that We carried their offspring in the laden Ark.	٤١- وَآيَةٌ لَهُمْ أَنَّا حَمَلْنَا ذُرِّيَّتَهُمْ فِي الْفُلْكِ الْمَشْحُونِ
42 And We created for them the like of it, in which they ride.	٤٢- وَخَلَقْنَا لَهُمْ مِنْ مِثْلِهِ مَا يَرْكَبُونَ

43 If We will, We can drown them—with no screaming to be heard from them, nor will they be saved.

٤٣ ـ وَإِنْ نَشَأْ نُغْرِقْهُمْ فَلَا صَرِيخَ لَهُمْ وَلَا هُمْ يُنْقَذُونَ

44 Except by a mercy from Us, and enjoyment for a while.

٤٤ ـ إِلَّا رَحْمَةً مِنَّا وَمَتَاعًا إِلَى حِينٍ

45 Yet when it is said to them, "Beware of what lies before you, and what lies behind you, that you may receive mercy."

٤٥ ـ وَإِذَا قِيلَ لَهُمُ اتَّقُوا مَا بَيْنَ أَيْدِيكُمْ وَمَا خَلْفَكُمْ لَعَلَّكُمْ تُرْحَمُونَ

46 Yet never came to them a sign of their Lord's signs, but they turned away from it.

٤٦ ـ وَمَا تَأْتِيهِمْ مِنْ آيَةٍ مِنْ آيَاتِ رَبِّهِمْ إِلَّا كَانُوا عَنْهَا مُعْرِضِينَ

47 And when it is said to them, "Spend of what God has provided for you," those who disbelieve say to those who believe, "Shall we feed someone whom God could feed, if He so willed? You must be deeply misguided."

٤٧ ـ وَإِذَا قِيلَ لَهُمْ أَنْفِقُوا مِمَّا رَزَقَكُمُ اللَّهُ قَالَ الَّذِينَ كَفَرُوا لِلَّذِينَ آمَنُوا أَنُطْعِمُ مَنْ لَوْ يَشَاءُ اللَّهُ أَطْعَمَهُ إِنْ أَنْتُمْ إِلَّا فِي ضَلَالٍ مُبِينٍ

48 And they say, "When will this promise be, if you are truthful?"

٤٨ ـ وَيَقُولُونَ مَتَى هَذَا الْوَعْدُ إِنْ كُنْتُمْ صَادِقِينَ

49 All they can expect is a single blast, which will seize them while they feud.

٤٩ ـ مَا يَنْظُرُونَ إِلَّا صَيْحَةً وَاحِدَةً تَأْخُذُهُمْ وَهُمْ يَخِصِّمُونَ

50 They will not be able to make a will, nor will they return to their families.	٥٠ ـ فَلَا يَسْتَطِيعُونَ تَوْصِيَةً وَلَا إِلَىٰ أَهْلِهِمْ يَرْجِعُونَ
51 The Trumpet will be blown, then behold, they will rush from the tombs to their Lord.	٥١ ـ وَنُفِخَ فِي الصُّورِ فَإِذَا هُم مِنَ الْأَجْدَاثِ إِلَىٰ رَبِّهِمْ يَنْسِلُونَ
52 They will say, "Woe to us! Who resurrected us from our resting-place?" This is what the Most Gracious had promised, and the messengers have spoken the truth."	٥٢ ـ قَالُوا يَا وَيْلَنَا مَن بَعَثَنَا مِن مَرْقَدِنَا ۜ هَٰذَا مَا وَعَدَ الرَّحْمَٰنُ وَصَدَقَ الْمُرْسَلُونَ
53 It will be but a single scream; and behold, they will all be brought before Us.	٥٣ ـ إِنْ كَانَتْ إِلَّا صَيْحَةً وَاحِدَةً فَإِذَا هُمْ جَمِيعٌ لَدَيْنَا مُحْضَرُونَ
54 On that Day, no soul will be wronged in the least, and you will be recompensed only for what you used to do.	٥٤ ـ فَالْيَوْمَ لَا تُظْلَمُ نَفْسٌ شَيْئًا وَلَا تُجْزَوْنَ إِلَّا مَا كُنتُمْ تَعْمَلُونَ
55 The inhabitants of Paradise, on that Day, will be happily busy.	٥٥ ـ إِنَّ أَصْحَابَ الْجَنَّةِ الْيَوْمَ فِي شُغُلٍ فَاكِهُونَ
56 They and their spouses, in shades, reclining on couches.	٥٦ ـ هُمْ وَأَزْوَاجُهُمْ فِي ظِلَالٍ عَلَى الْأَرَائِكِ مُتَّكِئُونَ

57 They will have therein fruits. They will have whatever they call for.	٥٧ـ لَهُمْ فِيهَا فَاكِهَةٌ وَلَهُمْ مَا يَدَّعُونَ
58 Peace—a saying from a Most Merciful Lord.	٥٨ـ سَلَامٌ قَوْلًا مِنْ رَبٍّ رَحِيمٍ
59 But step aside today, you criminals.	٥٩ـ وَامْتَازُوا الْيَوْمَ أَيُّهَا الْمُجْرِمُونَ
60 Did I not covenant with you, O Children of Adam, that you shall not serve the devil? That he is your sworn enemy?	٦٠ـ أَلَمْ أَعْهَدْ إِلَيْكُمْ يَا بَنِي آدَمَ أَنْ لَا تَعْبُدُوا الشَّيْطَانَ ۖ إِنَّهُ لَكُمْ عَدُوٌّ مُبِينٌ
61 And that you shall serve Me? This is a straight path.	٦١ـ وَأَنِ اعْبُدُونِي ۚ هَٰذَا صِرَاطٌ مُسْتَقِيمٌ
62 He has misled a great multitude of you. Did you not understand?	٦٢ـ وَلَقَدْ أَضَلَّ مِنْكُمْ جِبِلًّا كَثِيرًا ۖ أَفَلَمْ تَكُونُوا تَعْقِلُونَ
63 This is Hellfire, which you were promised.	٦٣ـ هَٰذِهِ جَهَنَّمُ الَّتِي كُنْتُمْ تُوعَدُونَ
64 Roast in it today, because you persistently disbelieved.	٦٤ـ اصْلَوْهَا الْيَوْمَ بِمَا كُنْتُمْ تَكْفُرُونَ

65 On this Day, We will seal their mouths, and their hands will speak to Us, and their feet will testify to everything they had done.	٦٥- الْيَوْمَ نَخْتِمُ عَلَىٰ أَفْوَاهِهِمْ وَتُكَلِّمُنَا أَيْدِيهِمْ وَتَشْهَدُ أَرْجُلُهُمْ بِمَا كَانُوا يَكْسِبُونَ
66 If We will, We can blind their eyes as they rush towards the path—but how will they see?	٦٦- وَلَوْ نَشَاءُ لَطَمَسْنَا عَلَىٰ أَعْيُنِهِمْ فَاسْتَبَقُوا الصِّرَاطَ فَأَنَّىٰ يُبْصِرُونَ
67 And if We will, We can cripple them in their place; so they can neither move forward, nor go back.	٦٧- وَلَوْ نَشَاءُ لَمَسَخْنَاهُمْ عَلَىٰ مَكَانَتِهِمْ فَمَا اسْتَطَاعُوا مُضِيًّا وَلَا يَرْجِعُونَ
68 Whomever We grant old age, We reverse his development. Do they not understand?	٦٨- وَمَنْ نُعَمِّرْهُ نُنَكِّسْهُ فِي الْخَلْقِ ۚ أَفَلَا يَعْقِلُونَ
69 We did not teach him poetry, nor is it proper for him. It is only a reminder, and a Clear Quran.	٦٩- وَمَا عَلَّمْنَاهُ الشِّعْرَ وَمَا يَنْبَغِي لَهُ ۚ إِنْ هُوَ إِلَّا ذِكْرٌ وَقُرْآنٌ مُبِينٌ
70 That he may warn whoever is alive, and prove the Word against the faithless.	٧٠- لِيُنْذِرَ مَنْ كَانَ حَيًّا وَيَحِقَّ الْقَوْلُ عَلَى الْكَافِرِينَ

71 Have they not seen that We created for them, of Our Handiwork, livestock that they own?

٧١ـ أَوَلَمْ يَرَوْا أَنَّا خَلَقْنَا لَهُمْ مِمَّا عَمِلَتْ أَيْدِينَا أَنْعَامًا فَهُمْ لَهَا مَالِكُونَ

72 And We subdued them for them. Some they ride, and some they eat.

٧٢ـ وَذَلَّلْنَاهَا لَهُمْ فَمِنْهَا رَكُوبُهُمْ وَمِنْهَا يَأْكُلُونَ

73 And they have in them other benefits, and drinks. Will they not give thanks?

٧٣ـ وَلَهُمْ فِيهَا مَنَافِعُ وَمَشَارِبُ ۖ أَفَلَا يَشْكُرُونَ

74 Yet they have taken to themselves gods other than God, that perhaps they may be helped.

٧٤ـ وَاتَّخَذُوا مِنْ دُونِ اللَّهِ آلِهَةً لَعَلَّهُمْ يُنْصَرُونَ

75 They cannot help them, although they are arrayed as troops for them.

٧٥ـ لَا يَسْتَطِيعُونَ نَصْرَهُمْ وَهُمْ لَهُمْ جُنْدٌ مُحْضَرُونَ

76 So let their words not sadden you. We know what they conceal, and what they reveal.

٧٦ـ فَلَا يَحْزُنْكَ قَوْلُهُمْ ۘ إِنَّا نَعْلَمُ مَا يُسِرُّونَ وَمَا يُعْلِنُونَ

77 Does the human being not consider that We created him from a seed? Yet he becomes a fierce adversary.

٧٧ـ أَوَلَمْ يَرَ الْإِنْسَانُ أَنَّا خَلَقْنَاهُ مِنْ نُطْفَةٍ فَإِذَا هُوَ خَصِيمٌ مُبِينٌ

78 And he produces arguments against Us, and he forgets his own creation. He says, "Who will revive the bones when they have decayed?"	٧٨- وَضَرَبَ لَنَا مَثَلًا وَنَسِيَ خَلْقَهُ ۖ قَالَ مَنْ يُحْيِي الْعِظَامَ وَهِيَ رَمِيمٌ
79 Say, "He who initiated them in the first instance will revive them. He has knowledge of every creation."	٧٩- قُلْ يُحْيِيهَا الَّذِي أَنْشَأَهَا أَوَّلَ مَرَّةٍ ۖ وَهُوَ بِكُلِّ خَلْقٍ عَلِيمٌ
80 He who produced fuel for you from the green trees, with which you kindle a fire.	٨٠- الَّذِي جَعَلَ لَكُمْ مِنَ الشَّجَرِ الْأَخْضَرِ نَارًا فَإِذَا أَنْتُمْ مِنْهُ تُوقِدُونَ
81 Is not He who created the heavens and the earth able to create the like of them? Certainly. He is the Supreme All-Knowing Creator.	٨١- أَوَلَيْسَ الَّذِي خَلَقَ السَّمَاوَاتِ وَالْأَرْضَ بِقَادِرٍ عَلَىٰ أَنْ يَخْلُقَ مِثْلَهُمْ ۚ بَلَىٰ وَهُوَ الْخَلَّاقُ الْعَلِيمُ
82 His command, when He wills a thing, is to say to it, "Be," and it comes to be.	٨٢- إِنَّمَا أَمْرُهُ إِذَا أَرَادَ شَيْئًا أَنْ يَقُولَ لَهُ كُنْ فَيَكُونُ
83 So glory be to Him in whose hand is the dominion of everything, and to Him you will be returned.	٨٣- فَسُبْحَانَ الَّذِي بِيَدِهِ مَلَكُوتُ كُلِّ شَيْءٍ وَإِلَيْهِ تُرْجَعُونَ

Surah Al-Waqiah:

Arabic & Phonetic

Bismi Allāhi Ar-Raĥmāni Ar-Raĥīmi	بِسْمِ اللَّهِ الرَّحْمَٰنِ الرَّحِيمِ
(1) 'Idhā Waqa`ati Al-Wāqi`ahu	١ إِذَا وَقَعَتِ الْوَاقِعَةُ
(2) Laysa Liwaq`atihā Kādhibahun	٢ لَيْسَ لِوَقْعَتِهَا كَاذِبَةٌ
(3) Khāfiđatun Rāfi`ahun	٣ خَافِضَةٌ رَافِعَةٌ
(4) 'Idhā Rujjati Al-'Arđu Rajjāan	٤ إِذَا رُجَّتِ الْأَرْضُ رَجًّا
(5) Wa Bussati Al-Jibālu Bassāan	٥ وَبُسَّتِ الْجِبَالُ بَسًّا
(6) Fakānat Habā'an Munba-thrāan	٦ فَكَانَتْ هَبَاءً مُنْبَثًّا
(7) Wa Kuntum 'Azwājāan Thalāthahan	٧ وَكُنْتُمْ أَزْوَاجًا ثَلَاثَةً
(8) Fa'aşĥābu Al-Maymanati Mā 'Aşĥābu Al-Maymanahi	٨ فَأَصْحَابُ الْمَيْمَنَةِ مَا أَصْحَابُ الْمَيْمَنَةِ
(9) Wa 'Aşĥābu Al-Mash'amati Mā 'Aşĥābu Al-Mash'amahi	٩ وَأَصْحَابُ الْمَشْأَمَةِ مَا أَصْحَابُ الْمَشْأَمَةِ

(10) Wa As-Sābiqūna As-Sābiqūna	١٠ وَالسَّابِقُونَ السَّابِقُونَ
(11) 'Ūlā'ika Al-Muqarrabūna	١١ أُولَٰئِكَ الْمُقَرَّبُونَ
(12) Fī Jannāti An-Na`īmi	١٢ فِي جَنَّاتِ النَّعِيمِ
(13) Thullatun Mina Al-'Awwalīna	١٣ ثُلَّةٌ مِنَ الْأَوَّلِينَ
(14) Wa Qalīlun Mina Al-'Ākhirīna	١٤ وَقَلِيلٌ مِنَ الْآخِرِينَ
(15) `Alá Sururin Mawđūnahin	١٥ عَلَىٰ سُرُرٍ مَوْضُونَةٍ
(16) Muttaki'īna `Alayhā Mutaqābilīna	١٦ مُتَّكِئِينَ عَلَيْهَا مُتَقَابِلِينَ
(17) Yaṭūfu `Alayhim Wildānun Mukhalladūna	١٧ يَطُوفُ عَلَيْهِمْ وِلْدَانٌ مُخَلَّدُونَ
(18) Bi'akwābin Wa 'Abārīqa Wa Ka'sin Min Ma`īnin	١٨ بِأَكْوَابٍ وَأَبَارِيقَ وَكَأْسٍ مِنْ مَعِينٍ
(19) Lā Yuşadda`ūna `Anhā Wa Lā Yunzifūna	١٩ لَا يُصَدَّعُونَ عَنْهَا وَلَا يُنْزِفُونَ

(20) Wa Fākihatin Mimmā Yatakhayyarūna	٢٠ وَفَاكِهَةٍ مِمَّا يَتَخَيَّرُونَ
(21) Wa Laĥmi Ţayrin Mimmā Yashtahūna	٢١ وَلَحْمِ طَيْرٍ مِمَّا يَشْتَهُونَ
(22) Wa Ĥūrun `Īnun	٢٢ وَحُورٌ عِينٌ
(23) Ka'amthāli Al-Lu'ulu'ui Al-Maknūni	٢٣ كَأَمْثَالِ اللُّؤْلُؤِ الْمَكْنُونِ
(24) Jazā'an Bimā Kānū Ya`malūna	٢٤ جَزَاءً بِمَا كَانُوا يَعْمَلُونَ
(25) Lā Yasma`ūna Fīhā Laghwan Wa Lā Ta'thīmāan	٢٥ لَا يَسْمَعُونَ فِيهَا لَغْوًا وَلَا تَأْثِيمًا
(26) 'Illā Qīlāan Salāmāan Salāmāan	٢٦ إِلَّا قِيلًا سَلَامًا سَلَامًا
(27) Wa 'Aşĥābu Al-Yamīni Mā 'Aşĥābu Al-Yamīni	٢٧ وَأَصْحَابُ الْيَمِينِ مَا أَصْحَابُ الْيَمِينِ
(28) Fī Sidrin Makhđūdin	٢٨ فِي سِدْرٍ مَخْضُودٍ
(29) Wa Ţalĥin Manđūdin	٢٩ وَطَلْحٍ مَنْضُودٍ

(30) Wa Žillin Mamdūdin	٣٠ وَظِلٍّ مَمْدُودٍ
(31) Wa Mā'in Maskūbin	٣١ وَمَاءٍ مَسْكُوبٍ
(32) Wa Fākihatin Kathīrahin	٣٢ وَفَاكِهَةٍ كَثِيرَةٍ
(33) Lā Maqṭū`atin Wa Lā Mamnū`ahin	٣٣ لَا مَقْطُوعَةٍ وَلَا مَمْنُوعَةٍ
(34) Wa Furushin Marfū`ahin	٣٤ وَفُرُشٍ مَرْفُوعَةٍ
(35) 'Innā 'Ansha'nāhunna 'Inshā'an	٣٥ إِنَّا أَنْشَأْنَاهُنَّ إِنْشَاءً
(36) Faja`alnāhunna 'Abkārāan	٣٦ فَجَعَلْنَاهُنَّ أَبْكَارًا
(37) `Urubāan 'Atrābāan	٣٧ عُرُبًا أَتْرَابًا
(38) Li'aṣĥābi Al-Yamīni	٣٨ لِأَصْحَابِ الْيَمِينِ
(39) Thullatun Mina Al-'Awwalīna	٣٩ ثُلَّةٌ مِنَ الْأَوَّلِينَ
(40) Wa Thullatun Mina Al-'Ākhirīna	٤٠ وَثُلَّةٌ مِنَ الْآخِرِينَ

(41) Wa 'Aşĥābu Ash-Shimāli Mā 'Aşĥābu Ash-Shimāli	٤١ وَأَصْحَابُ الشِّمَالِ مَا أَصْحَابُ الشِّمَالِ
(42) Fī Samūmin Wa Ĥamīmin	٤٢ فِي سَمُومٍ وَحَمِيمٍ
(43) Wa Žillin Min Yaĥmūmin	٤٣ وَظِلٍّ مِنْ يَحْمُومٍ
(44) Lā Bāridin Wa Lā Karīmin	٤٤ لَا بَارِدٍ وَلَا كَرِيمٍ
(45) 'Innahum Kānū Qabla Dhālika Mutrafīna	٤٥ إِنَّهُمْ كَانُوا قَبْلَ ذَلِكَ مُتْرَفِينَ
(46) Wa Kānū Yuşirrūna `Alá Al-Ĥinthi Al-`Ažīmi	٤٦ وَكَانُوا يُصِرُّونَ عَلَى الْحِنْثِ الْعَظِيمِ
(47) Wa Kānū Yaqūlūna 'A'idhā Mitnā Wa Kunnā Turābāan Wa `Ižāmāan 'A'innā Lamab`ūthūna	٤٧ وَكَانُوا يَقُولُونَ أَئِذَا مِتْنَا وَكُنَّا تُرَابًا وَعِظَامًا أَئِنَّا لَمَبْعُوثُونَ
(48) 'Awa 'Ābā'uunā Al-Awwalūna	٤٨ أَوَآبَاؤُنَا الْأَوَّلُونَ
(49) Qul 'Inna Al-'Awwalīna Wa Al-'Ākhirīna	٤٩ قُلْ إِنَّ الْأَوَّلِينَ وَالْآخِرِينَ
(50) Lamajmū`ūna 'Ilá Mīqāti Yawmin Ma`lūmin	٥٠ لَمَجْمُوعُونَ إِلَى مِيقَاتِ يَوْمٍ مَعْلُومٍ

(51) Thumma 'Innakum 'Ayyuhā Ađ-Đāllūna Al-Mukadhibūna	٥١ ثُمَّ إِنَّكُمْ أَيُّهَا الضَّالُّونَ الْمُكَذِّبُونَ
(52) La'ākilūna Min Shajarin Min Zaqqūmin	٥٢ لَآكِلُونَ مِنْ شَجَرٍ مِنْ زَقُّومٍ
(53) Famāli'ūna Minhā Al-Buṭūna	٥٣ فَمَالِئُونَ مِنْهَا الْبُطُونَ
(54) Fashāribūna `Alayhi Mina Al-Ĥamīmi	٥٤ فَشَارِبُونَ عَلَيْهِ مِنَ الْحَمِيمِ
(55) Fashāribūna Shurba Al-Hīmi	٥٥ فَشَارِبُونَ شُرْبَ الْهِيمِ
(56) Hādhā Nuzuluhum Yawma Ad-Dīni	٥٦ هَٰذَا نُزُلُهُمْ يَوْمَ الدِّينِ
(57) Naĥnu Khalaqnākum Falawlā Tuşaddiqūna	٥٧ نَحْنُ خَلَقْنَاكُمْ فَلَوْلَا تُصَدِّقُونَ
(58) 'Afara'aytum Mā Tumnūna	٥٨ أَفَرَأَيْتُمْ مَا تُمْنُونَ
(59) 'A'antum Takhluqūnahu 'Am Naĥnu Al-Khāliqūna	٥٩ أَأَنْتُمْ تَخْلُقُونَهُ أَمْ نَحْنُ الْخَالِقُونَ

(60) Naĥnu Qaddarnā Baynakumu Al-Mawta Wa Mā Naĥnu Bimasbūqīna	٦٠ نَحْنُ قَدَّرْنَا بَيْنَكُمُ الْمَوْتَ وَمَا نَحْنُ بِمَسْبُوقِينَ
(61) `Alá 'An Nubaddila 'Amthālakum Wa Nunshi'akum Fī Mā Lā Ta`lamūna	٦١ عَلَىٰ أَنْ نُبَدِّلَ أَمْثَالَكُمْ وَنُنْشِئَكُمْ فِي مَا لَا تَعْلَمُونَ
(62) Wa Laqad `Alimtumu An-Nash'ata Al-'Ūlá Falawlā Tadhkkarūna	٦٢ وَلَقَدْ عَلِمْتُمُ النَّشْأَةَ الْأُولَىٰ فَلَوْلَا تَذَكَّرُونَ
(63) 'Afara'aytum Mā Taĥruthūna	٦٣ أَفَرَأَيْتُمْ مَا تَحْرُثُونَ
(64) 'A'antum Tazra`ūnahu 'Am Naĥnu Az-Zāri`ūna	٦٤ أَأَنْتُمْ تَزْرَعُونَهُ أَمْ نَحْنُ الزَّارِعُونَ
(65) Law Nashā'u Laja`alnāhu Ĥuţāmāan Fažalaltum Tafakkahūna	٦٥ لَوْ نَشَاءُ لَجَعَلْنَاهُ حُطَامًا فَظَلْتُمْ تَفَكَّهُونَ
(66) 'Innā Lamughramūna	٦٦ إِنَّا لَمُغْرَمُونَ
(67) Bal Naĥnu Maĥrūmūna	٦٧ بَلْ نَحْنُ مَحْرُومُونَ

(68) 'Afara'aytumu Al-Mā'a Al-Ladhī Tashrabūna	٦٨ أَفَرَأَيْتُمُ الْمَاءَ الَّذِي تَشْرَبُونَ
(69) 'A'antum 'Anzaltumūhu Mina Al-Muzni 'Am Nahnu Al-Munzilūna	٦٩ أَأَنْتُمْ أَنْزَلْتُمُوهُ مِنَ الْمُزْنِ أَمْ نَحْنُ الْمُنْزِلُونَ
(70) Law Nashā'u Ja`alnāhu 'Ujājāan Falawlā Tashkurūna	٧٠ لَوْ نَشَاءُ جَعَلْنَاهُ أُجَاجًا فَلَوْلَا تَشْكُرُونَ
(71) 'Afara'aytumu An-Nāra Allatī Tūrūna	٧١ أَفَرَأَيْتُمُ النَّارَ الَّتِي تُورُونَ
(72) 'A'antum 'Ansha'tum Shajaratahā 'Am Nahnu Al-Munshi'ūna	٧٢ أَأَنْتُمْ أَنْشَأْتُمْ شَجَرَتَهَا أَمْ نَحْنُ الْمُنْشِئُونَ
(73) Nahnu Ja`alnāhā Tadhkiratan Wa Matā`āan Lilmuqwīna	٧٣ نَحْنُ جَعَلْنَاهَا تَذْكِرَةً وَمَتَاعًا لِلْمُقْوِينَ
(74) Fasabbih Biāsmi Rabbika Al-`Ažīmi	٧٤ فَسَبِّحْ بِاسْمِ رَبِّكَ الْعَظِيمِ
(75) Falā 'Uqsimu Bimawāqi`i An-Nujūmi	٧٥ فَلَا أُقْسِمُ بِمَوَاقِعِ النُّجُومِ

(76) Wa 'Innahu Laqasamun Law Ta`lamūna `Ažīmun	٧٦ وَإِنَّهُ لَقَسَمٌ لَوْ تَعْلَمُونَ عَظِيمٌ
(77) 'Innahu Laqur'ānun Karīmun	٧٧ إِنَّهُ لَقُرْآنٌ كَرِيمٌ
(78) Fī Kitābin Maknūnin	٧٨ فِي كِتَابٍ مَكْنُونٍ
(79) Lā Yamassuhu 'Illā Al-Muṭahharūna	٧٩ لَا يَمَسُّهُ إِلَّا الْمُطَهَّرُونَ
(80) Tanzīlun Min Rabbi Al-`Ālamīna	٨٠ تَنْزِيلٌ مِنْ رَبِّ الْعَالَمِينَ
(81) 'Afabihadhā Al-Ĥadīthi 'Antum Mud/hinūna	٨١ أَفَبِهَذَا الْحَدِيثِ أَنْتُمْ مُدْهِنُونَ
(82) Wa Taj`alūna Rizqakum 'Annakum Tukadhibūna	٨٢ وَتَجْعَلُونَ رِزْقَكُمْ أَنَّكُمْ تُكَذِّبُونَ
(83) Falawlā 'Idhā Balaghati Al-Ĥulqūma	٨٣ فَلَوْلَا إِذَا بَلَغَتِ الْحُلْقُومَ
(84) Wa 'Antum Ĥīna'idhin Tanžurūna	٨٤ وَأَنْتُمْ حِينَئِذٍ تَنْظُرُونَ

(85) Wa Naĥnu 'Aqrabu 'Ilayhi Minkum Wa Lakin Lā Tubşirūna	٨٤ وَأَنْتُمْ حِينَئِذٍ تَنْظُرُونَ
(86) Falawlā 'In Kuntum Ghayra Madīnīna	٨٥ وَنَحْنُ أَقْرَبُ إِلَيْهِ مِنْكُمْ وَلَكِنْ لَا تُبْصِرُونَ
(87) Tarji`ūnahā 'In Kuntum Şādiqīna	٨٧ تَرْجِعُونَهَا إِنْ كُنْتُمْ صَادِقِينَ
(88) Fa'ammā 'In Kāna Mina Al-Muqarrabīna	٨٨ فَأَمَّا إِنْ كَانَ مِنَ الْمُقَرَّبِينَ
(89) Farawĥun Wa Rayĥānun Wa Jannatu Na`īmin	٨٩ فَرَوْحٌ وَرَيْحَانٌ وَجَنَّتُ نَعِيمٍ
(90) Wa 'Ammā 'In Kāna Min 'Aşĥābi Al-Yamīni	٩٠ وَأَمَّا إِنْ كَانَ مِنْ أَصْحَابِ الْيَمِينِ
(91) Fasalāmun Laka Min 'Aşĥābi Al-Yamīni	٩١ فَسَلَامٌ لَكَ مِنْ أَصْحَابِ الْيَمِينِ
(92) Wa 'Ammā 'In Kāna Mina Al-Mukadhibīna Ađ-Đāllīna	٩٢ وَأَمَّا إِنْ كَانَ مِنَ الْمُكَذِّبِينَ الضَّالِّينَ
(93) Fanuzulun Min Ĥamīmin	٩٣ فَنُزُلٌ مِنْ حَمِيمٍ

(94) Wa Taşliyatu Jaĥīmin	٩٤ وَتَصْلِيَةُ جَحِيمٍ
(95) 'Inna Hādhā Lahuwa Ĥaqqu Al-Yaqīni	٩٥ إِنَّ هَٰذَا لَهُوَ حَقُّ الْيَقِينِ
(96) Fasabbiĥ Biāsmi Rabbika Al-`Ažīmi	٩٦ فَسَبِّحْ بِاسْمِ رَبِّكَ الْعَظِيمِ

Surah

Al-Waqiah:

Arabic & English

In the name of God, the Gracious, the Merciful.	بِسْمِ اللَّهِ الرَّحْمَنِ الرَّحِيمِ
1 When the inevitable occurs.	١ إِذَا وَقَعَتِ الْوَاقِعَةُ
2 Of its occurrence, there is no denial.	٢ لَيْسَ لِوَقْعَتِهَا كَاذِبَةٌ
3 Bringing low, raising high.	٣ خَافِضَةٌ رَافِعَةٌ
4 When the earth is shaken with a shock.	٤ إِذَا رُجَّتِ الْأَرْضُ رَجًّا
5 And the mountains are crushed and crumbled.	٥ وَبُسَّتِ الْجِبَالُ بَسًّا
6 And they become scattered dust.	٦ فَكَانَتْ هَبَاءً مُنْبَثًّا
7 And you become three classes.	٧ وَكُنْتُمْ أَزْوَاجًا ثَلَاثَةً
8 Those on the Right—what of those on the Right?	٨ فَأَصْحَابُ الْمَيْمَنَةِ مَا أَصْحَابُ الْمَيْمَنَةِ
9 And those on the Left—what of those on the Left?	٩ وَأَصْحَابُ الْمَشْأَمَةِ مَا أَصْحَابُ الْمَشْأَمَةِ

10 And the forerunners, the forerunners.	١٠ وَالسَّابِقُونَ السَّابِقُونَ
11 Those are the nearest.	١١ أُولَٰئِكَ الْمُقَرَّبُونَ
12 In the Gardens of Bliss.	١٢ فِي جَنَّاتِ النَّعِيمِ
13 A throng from the ancients.	١٣ ثُلَّةٌ مِنَ الْأَوَّلِينَ
14 And a small band from the latecomers.	١٤ وَقَلِيلٌ مِنَ الْآخِرِينَ
15 On luxurious furnishings.	١٥ عَلَىٰ سُرُرٍ مَوْضُونَةٍ
16 Reclining on them, facing one another.	١٦ مُتَّكِئِينَ عَلَيْهَا مُتَقَابِلِينَ
17 Serving them will be immortalized youth.	١٧ يَطُوفُ عَلَيْهِمْ وِلْدَانٌ مُخَلَّدُونَ
18 With cups, pitchers, and sparkling drinks.	١٨ بِأَكْوَابٍ وَأَبَارِيقَ وَكَأْسٍ مِنْ مَعِينٍ
19 Causing them neither headache, nor intoxication.	١٩ لَا يُصَدَّعُونَ عَنْهَا وَلَا يُنْزِفُونَ

20 And fruits of their choice.	٢٠ وَفَاكِهَةٍ مِّمَّا يَتَخَيَّرُونَ
21 And meat of birds that they may desire.	٢١ وَلَحْمِ طَيْرٍ مِّمَّا يَشْتَهُونَ
22 And lovely companions.	٢٢ وَحُورٌ عِينٌ
23 The likenesses of treasured pearls.	٢٣ كَأَمْثَالِ اللُّؤْلُؤِ الْمَكْنُونِ
24 As a reward for what they used to do.	٢٤ جَزَاءً بِمَا كَانُوا يَعْمَلُونَ
25 Therein they will hear no nonsense, and no accusations.	٢٥ لَا يَسْمَعُونَ فِيهَا لَغْوًا وَلَا تَأْثِيمًا
26 But only the greeting: "Peace, peace."	٢٦ إِلَّا قِيلًا سَلَامًا سَلَامًا
27 And those on the Right—what of those on the Right?	٢٧ وَأَصْحَابُ الْيَمِينِ مَا أَصْحَابُ الْيَمِينِ
28 In lush orchards.	٢٨ فِي سِدْرٍ مَّخْضُودٍ
29 And sweet-smelling plants.	٢٩ وَطَلْحٍ مَّنْضُودٍ

30 And extended shade.	٣٠ وَظِلٍّ مَمْدُودٍ
31 And outpouring water.	٣١ وَمَاءٍ مَسْكُوبٍ
32 And abundant fruit.	٣٢ وَفَاكِهَةٍ كَثِيرَةٍ
33 Neither withheld, nor forbidden.	٣٣ لَا مَقْطُوعَةٍ وَلَا مَمْنُوعَةٍ
34 And uplifted mattresses.	٣٤ وَفُرُشٍ مَرْفُوعَةٍ
35 We have created them of special creation.	٣٥ إِنَّا أَنْشَأْنَاهُنَّ إِنْشَاءً
36 And made them virgins.	٣٦ فَجَعَلْنَاهُنَّ أَبْكَارًا
37 Tender and un-aging.	٣٧ عُرُبًا أَتْرَابًا
38 For those on the Right.	٣٨ لِأَصْحَابِ الْيَمِينِ
39 A throng from the ancients.	٣٩ ثُلَّةٌ مِنَ الْأَوَّلِينَ
40 And a throng from the latecomers.	٤٠ وَثُلَّةٌ مِنَ الْآخِرِينَ

41 And those on the Left what of those on the Left?	٤١ وَأَصْحَابُ الشِّمَالِ مَا أَصْحَابُ الشِّمَالِ
42 Amid searing wind and boiling water.	٤٢ فِي سَمُومٍ وَحَمِيمٍ
43 And a shadow of thick smoke.	٤٣ وَظِلٍّ مِنْ يَحْمُومٍ
44 Neither cool, nor refreshing.	٤٤ لَا بَارِدٍ وَلَا كَرِيمٍ
45 They had lived before that in luxury.	٤٥ إِنَّهُمْ كَانُوا قَبْلَ ذَٰلِكَ مُتْرَفِينَ
46 And they used to persist in immense wrongdoing.	٤٦ وَكَانُوا يُصِرُّونَ عَلَى الْحِنْثِ الْعَظِيمِ
47 And they used to say, "When we are dead and turned into dust and bones, are we to be resurrected?	٤٧ وَكَانُوا يَقُولُونَ أَئِذَا مِتْنَا وَكُنَّا تُرَابًا وَعِظَامًا أَإِنَّا لَمَبْعُوثُونَ
48 And our ancient ancestors too?"	٤٨ أَوَآبَاؤُنَا الْأَوَّلُونَ
49 Say, "The first and the last.	٤٩ قُلْ إِنَّ الْأَوَّلِينَ وَالْآخِرِينَ
50 Will be gathered for the appointment of a familiar Day."	٥٠ لَمَجْمُوعُونَ إِلَىٰ مِيقَاتِ يَوْمٍ مَعْلُومٍ

51 Then you, you misguided, who deny the truth.	٥١ ثُمَّ إِنَّكُمْ أَيُّهَا الضَّالُّونَ الْمُكَذِّبُونَ
52 Will be eating from the Tree of Bitterness.	٥٢ لَآكِلُونَ مِنْ شَجَرٍ مِنْ زَقُّومٍ
53 Will be filling your bellies with it.	٥٣ فَمَالِئُونَ مِنْهَا الْبُطُونَ
54 Will be drinking on top of it boiling water.	٥٤ فَشَارِبُونَ عَلَيْهِ مِنَ الْحَمِيمِ
55 Drinking like thirsty camels drink.	٥٥ فَشَارِبُونَ شُرْبَ الْهِيمِ
56 That is their hospitality on the Day of Retribution.	٥٦ هَٰذَا نُزُلُهُمْ يَوْمَ الدِّينِ
57 We created you—if only you would believe!	٥٧ نَحْنُ خَلَقْنَاكُمْ فَلَوْلَا تُصَدِّقُونَ
58 Have you seen what you ejaculate?	٥٨ أَفَرَأَيْتُمْ مَا تُمْنُونَ
59 Is it you who create it, or are We the Creator?	٥٩ أَأَنْتُمْ تَخْلُقُونَهُ أَمْ نَحْنُ الْخَالِقُونَ

60 We have decreed death among you, and We will not be outstripped.	٦٠ نَحْنُ قَدَّرْنَا بَيْنَكُمُ الْمَوْتَ وَمَا نَحْنُ بِمَسْبُوقِينَ
61 In replacing you with your likes, and transforming you into what you do not know.	٦١ عَلَىٰ أَنْ نُبَدِّلَ أَمْثَالَكُمْ وَنُنْشِئَكُمْ فِي مَا لَا تَعْلَمُونَ
62 You have known the first formation; if only you would remember.	٦٢ وَلَقَدْ عَلِمْتُمُ النَّشْأَةَ الْأُولَىٰ فَلَوْلَا تَذَكَّرُونَ
63 Have you seen what you cultivate?	٦٣ أَفَرَأَيْتُمْ مَا تَحْرُثُونَ
64 Is it you who make it grow, or are We the Grower?	٦٤ أَأَنْتُمْ تَزْرَعُونَهُ أَمْ نَحْنُ الزَّارِعُونَ
65 If We will, We can turn it into rubble; then you will lament.	٦٥ لَوْ نَشَاءُ لَجَعَلْنَاهُ حُطَامًا فَظَلْتُمْ تَفَكَّهُونَ
66 "We are penalized.	٦٦ إِنَّا لَمُغْرَمُونَ
67 No, we are being deprived."	٦٧ بَلْ نَحْنُ مَحْرُومُونَ

68 Have you seen the water you drink?	٦٨ أَفَرَأَيْتُمُ الْمَاءَ الَّذِي تَشْرَبُونَ
69 Is it you who sent it down from the clouds, or are We the Sender?	٦٩ أَأَنْتُمْ أَنْزَلْتُمُوهُ مِنَ الْمُزْنِ أَمْ نَحْنُ الْمُنْزِلُونَ
70 If We will, We can make it salty. Will you not be thankful?	٧٠ لَوْ نَشَاءُ جَعَلْنَاهُ أُجَاجًا فَلَوْلَا تَشْكُرُونَ
71 Have you seen the fire you kindle?	٧١ أَفَرَأَيْتُمُ النَّارَ الَّتِي تُورُونَ
72 Is it you who produce its tree, or are We the Producer?	٧٢ أَأَنْتُمْ أَنْشَأْتُمْ شَجَرَتَهَا أَمْ نَحْنُ الْمُنْشِئُونَ
73 We have made it a reminder, and a comfort for the users.	٧٣ نَحْنُ جَعَلْنَاهَا تَذْكِرَةً وَمَتَاعًا لِلْمُقْوِينَ
74 So glorify the Name of your Great Lord.	٧٤ فَسَبِّحْ بِاسْمِ رَبِّكَ الْعَظِيمِ
75 I swear by the locations of the stars.	٧٥ فَلَا أُقْسِمُ بِمَوَاقِعِ النُّجُومِ

76 It is an oath, if you only knew, that is tremendous.	٧٦ وَإِنَّهُ لَقَسَمٌ لَوْ تَعْلَمُونَ عَظِيمٌ
77 It is a noble Quran.	٧٧ إِنَّهُ لَقُرْآنٌ كَرِيمٌ
78 In a well-protected Book.	٧٨ فِي كِتَابٍ مَكْنُونٍ
79 None can grasp it except the purified.	٧٩ لَا يَمَسُّهُ إِلَّا الْمُطَهَّرُونَ
80 A revelation from the Lord of the Worlds.	٨٠ تَنْزِيلٌ مِنْ رَبِّ الْعَالَمِينَ
81 Is it this discourse that you take so lightly?	٨١ أَفَبِهَٰذَا الْحَدِيثِ أَنْتُمْ مُدْهِنُونَ
82 And you make it your livelihood to deny it?	٨٢ وَتَجْعَلُونَ رِزْقَكُمْ أَنَّكُمْ تُكَذِّبُونَ
83 So when it has reached the throat.	٨٣ فَلَوْلَا إِذَا بَلَغَتِ الْحُلْقُومَ
84 As you are looking on.	٨٤ وَأَنْتُمْ حِينَئِذٍ تَنْظُرُونَ

85 We are nearer to it than you are, but you do not see.	٨٤ وَأَنْتُمْ حِينَئِذٍ تَنْظُرُونَ
86 If you are not held to account.	٨٥ وَنَحْنُ أَقْرَبُ إِلَيْهِ مِنْكُمْ وَلَكِنْ لَا تُبْصِرُونَ
87 Then bring it back, if you are truthful.	٨٧ تَرْجِعُونَهَا إِنْ كُنْتُمْ صَادِقِينَ
88 But if he is one of those brought near.	٨٨ فَأَمَّا إِنْ كَانَ مِنَ الْمُقَرَّبِينَ
89 Then happiness, and flowers, and Garden of Delights.	٨٩ فَرَوْحٌ وَرَيْحَانٌ وَجَنَّتُ نَعِيمٍ
90 And if he is one of those on the Right.	٩٠ وَأَمَّا إِنْ كَانَ مِنْ أَصْحَابِ الْيَمِينِ
91 Then, "Peace upon you," from those on the Right.	٩١ فَسَلَامٌ لَكَ مِنْ أَصْحَابِ الْيَمِينِ
92 But if he is one of the deniers, the mistaken.	٩٢ وَأَمَّا إِنْ كَانَ مِنَ الْمُكَذِّبِينَ الضَّالِّينَ
93 Then a welcome of Inferno.	٩٣ فَنُزُلٌ مِنْ حَمِيمٍ

94 And burning in Hell.	٩٤ وَتَصْلِيَةُ جَحِيمٍ
95 This is the certain truth.	٩٥ إِنَّ هَٰذَا لَهُوَ حَقُّ الْيَقِينِ
96 So glorify the Name of your Lord, the Magnificent	٩٦ فَسَبِّحْ بِاسْمِ رَبِّكَ الْعَظِيمِ

For more books and exercise books, activities or coloring books in Arabic or Islamic, please visit our author page:
"Aicha Mhamed"
You have also found a book that talks about Islam history, Ramadan and others.

Printed in Great Britain
by Amazon

Fermanagh's
Railways

Second Edition

Charles P Friel   Norman Johnston

Enniskillen station in May 1956, viewed from the Omagh end of platform 1. On the right, U class 4-4-0 No 202 *Louth* has just arrived in with the 10.45am from Dundalk. Its coaches will become the 2.05pm to Omagh. On the left a very clean PP class 4-4-0 No 74 has the Bundoran portion of this train, which will be added to it after No 202 goes on shed. No 74 was destined to be the last of this popular class to survive, facing the cutter's torch as late as 1964.

RH Barr

Second Edition
First impression

© Charles Friel and Norman Johnston and
Colourpoint Books, 1998 and 2008

Designed by Colourpoint Books, Newtownards
Printed by W&G Baird Ltd

ISBN 978 1 906578 16 9

Colourpoint Books
Colourpoint House
Jubilee Business Park
21 Jubilee Road
NEWTOWNARDS
County Down
Northern Ireland
BT23 4YH
Tel: 028 9182 6339
Fax: 028 9182 1900
E-mail: info@colourpoint.co.uk
Web site: www.colourpoint.co.uk

Charles Friel was born in
Enniskillen and has been a life
long railway enthusiast, active
preservationist, photographer
and collector of Irish railway
photographs and negatives. He
is author of *Merlin* and *Slieve
Gullion* and numerous railway
articles. His illustrated talks
on railways in the Ardhowen
Theatre at Enniskillen have
inspired this book. He is a
retired Civil Servant.

Norman Johnston has family
roots in Fermanagh and is the
grandson of a GNR Station
Master who served at Newbliss
and Maguiresbridge around the
time of the Great War. He has
written several books including
*Locomotives of the GNRI,
The Great Northern Railway
(Ireland) in colour, Austerity
Ulster 1947-52* and *Ulster
in the 1950s*. He is a retired
school teacher.

A note for the lay person

Readers of this book will see frequent references to
'Up' and 'Down' in relation to trains and platforms. In
railway terminology the 'Up' direction is towards the line's
headquarters. Thus on the GNR(I) 'Up' was towards Dublin
(in Fermanagh, the Clones direction) and 'Down' towards
Bundoran. On the SLNCR 'Up' was towards Enniskillen and
'Down' towards Sligo.

In signalling, a 'distant' signal was a yellow caution signal
on the approaches to a station, a 'home' signal was a red
stop signal controlling entry to it and a 'starter' signal was an
identical red signal controlling departure from a station.

Front and rear cover picture

The approaches to Enniskillen from Clones and Sligo, with a PPs class
4-4-0 and Qs class 4-4-0 No 122 on shed.

ColourRail

CONTENTS

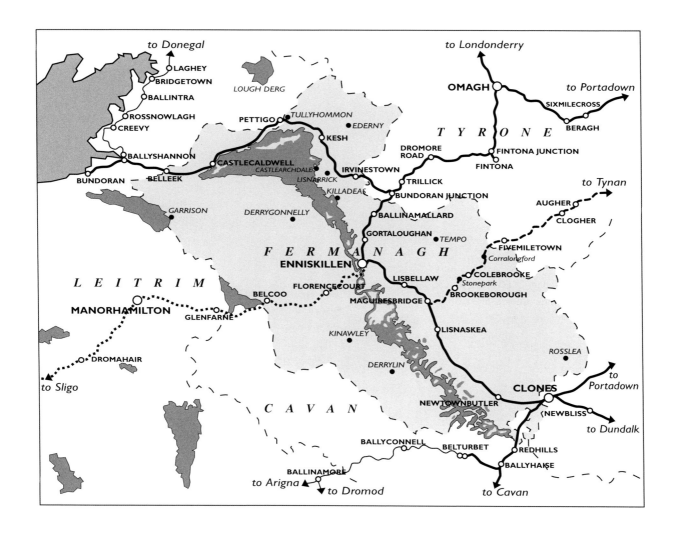

THE RAILWAYS OF COUNTY FERMANAGH

————————— Great Northern Railway (Ireland)

·················· Sligo, Leitrim and Northern Counties Railway

– – – – – – Clogher Valley Railway

——————— other railways

INTRODUCTION

Norman remembers

Fermanagh is rooted deep in my heart. I am linked to it by kinship, by memories and by the charm of its scenery and associations. The bones of my ancestors lie in its soil, and I frequently visit haunts that are as familiar to me today as they were over fifty years ago when I was a child. I knew its railways well in my earliest years and travelled them frequently. Their closure in 1957 brought to me the first sense of bereavement I ever experienced. It was the loss of an old friend. Even today, as I travel the roads of Fermanagh, I can still see the trains – as vivid in my mind's eye as if it were only yesterday. Lisnagole accommodation crossing, on the lane down to my late uncle's farm of the same name, brings me back to days in the mid 1950s when, with my mother, I stood on the lane watching the Enniskillen-bound train passing, hauled by a clean and neat PP 4-4-0. Then, as the exhaust drifted away from the cutting 200 yards away, one of the Armstrong children, who lived in the gatehouse, ran out to open the gates for us. Or again, prior to its recent demolition, I would stand on the derelict platform of Maguiresbridge station, where my grandfather William Johnston was briefly station master in 1918-20 before his untimely death, and look at the cottage, then occupied by Mr Traynor the last station master, where my father lived for those two years as a boy. I remember it as it used to be, and try to imagine it in 1920, with the Clogher Valley Railway connecting with the GNR trains and hustle and bustle going on in the transship shed, as goods were transferred between narrow gauge and standard gauge.

Railways, more than any other form of transport, seem to have a powerful effect on the emotions of many people. Fermanagh is no different in this respect. To this day, when the subject of the railways comes up in conversation, a room can grow uncannily quiet and eyes become a little misty. Then the sense of loss experienced all those years ago surfaces and someone says, "It's an awful shame they closed the railways. The train was a great way of getting about." Then they reminisce about going to school by train, about going to Bundoran on an excursion, and of seeing the 'Bundoran Express' with its clean, polished blue engine passing through Enniskillen at a breathtaking 5-10

mph, the proud name of Fermanagh's only named train hung on the smokebox – and it didn't even stop in Fermanagh! Other things can stimulate the memory. One is the sight and sound of a preserved steam engine – like 85 *Merlin* or 171 *Slieve Gullion* on the 'Portrush Flyer', both blue GNR locomotives – the rich aroma of soot and burnt oil, the hiss of the valves and roar of the blower, the warmth of the firebox, the clank of the coupling rods – can all bring us back to childhood years in the 1940s or 1950s when these smells and everyday sounds were in Fermanagh.

Writing this book in cooperation with my co-author Charles Friel was a labour of love for us both. As teenagers we met in Portadown over forty years ago and discovered not only a common love of trains, but a shared experience of Fermanagh and its railways. These two things led to a lifelong friendship, which resulted in this tribute to our favourite railways. As well as describing the history of the lines and illustrating them with our favourite pictures, we both felt an urge to put down on paper our own very personal feelings and memories of a great railway system. Not that these memories are particularly significant in themselves but we hope that, in sharing them, we will stir equally powerful memories within our readers.

I often meet railway enthusiasts who regret that they have no personal experience of Fermanagh's railways, and it makes me feel privileged and honoured that circumstances and ancestry put me in the position where I had. In some ways

PP No 42 approaching Lisnagole accommodation crossing with the 4.30pm mail train from Enniskillen. In the distance is the cutting, in which my mother, as a girl, was nearly killed by an unexpected train, while taking a short cut to school.

it is not surprising that Belfast people had little experience of railways in Fermanagh. An amazing number of people in Northern Ireland have never even been in Fermanagh. Fermanagh is not really on the way to anywhere if you live in the east of Ulster. You have to be going there to go to it, so to speak. Enniskillen is about two hours from Belfast by road. There is a somewhat fictitious story told about a conversation at a reception in Hillsborough Castle shortly after Sir Patrick Mayhew became N I Secretary. It goes something like this:

Mrs Mayhew:	And where are you from?
Fermanagh man:	I'm from Fermanagh.
Mrs Mayhew:	Fermanagh. Mmm ... Is that in the North or the South?
Fermanagh man:	No, it isn't. It's in the west.
Mrs Mayhew:	Well, I can't say I've heard of it. Is it near anywhere?
Fermanagh man:	No, it's not. We kinda keep ourselves to ourselves!

However, if you do go there, Fermanagh is a wonderful place. Known as 'Ulster's Lakeland', it is by far the most picturesque of the six Ulster counties that became part of Northern Ireland in 1921. It has close links with those other three Ulster counties – Monaghan, Cavan, and Donegal – which ended up in the Irish Free State at that time. With them it shared the self-reliance and independence of spirit that resulted from their remoteness from both Dublin and Belfast, and the cooperation that is characteristic of the 'border counties'. Fermanagh's railways crossed into all three of them as well as into its northern neighbour Tyrone, where I spent 25 happy years.

Fermanagh is dominated by its lakes and islands, which are a playground for both fishermen and weekend sailors. Upper and Lower Lough Erne, and the River Erne which links them, effectively divide the county in two. Those who live to the south and west of the county are often known as the folk 'beyond the lough' and have their own distinct dialect, different from but as unmistakably 'Fermanagh' as the accent in east Fermanagh. Wherever they live, Fermanagh folk are renowned for their friendliness and hospitality. It is virtually a cardinal sin to let someone who calls at your house, leave without the obligatory 'cup of tea' (pronounced 'tay' in Fermanagh, in the French fashion). A 'cup of tea' means buns, scones, and buttered cake or fruit bread (brack) – in other words, the complete works

– and refusal to accept is a matter of some offence!

Kinship is very important to Fermanagh folk. Relations are counted to second or third cousins, sometimes to once or twice removed as well. If you have any connection with the county, they will know your grandfather or your aunt or someone who 'belongs' to you. In the other five Northern Ireland counties Fermanagh folk living in exile have an especially warm spot for other Fermanagh folk. They seek each other out, have 'cups of tay' and talk knowledgeably about places like Derrygonnelly, Kinawley, Lisnarick and 'The Round O'. Since only about 60,000 people live in Fermanagh, everyone seems to know at least a quarter of the population. In this regard I am on firm ground. My father was a Johnston from Maguiresbridge and my mother a Moore from Lisnaskea. They spent the first half of their lives in Fermanagh, and came back there to live in their old age and eventually to be buried. Although they spent their married lives in Portadown, they brought me back to Fermanagh to be christened in the little country church in Maguiresbridge where they had been married eighteen months earlier. In 1994, within five months of each other, that same little church was the setting for their respective funeral services. To my mother, Fermanagh was always 'home', and although I have never actually lived there myself, I share that sense of belonging.

My first contact with the railways of Fermanagh was in April 1949 when my mother brought me from Portadown, via Clones, to Lisnaskea to be shown off to the relatives and to be christened in the 'right' county. Being only ten weeks old I didn't get the number of the engine! My father followed a few days later, travelling on the 5.35pm to Derry as far as Omagh, from where he reached Lisnaskea via Enniskillen. This illustrated one superb feature of the Fermanagh lines – there were two alternative routes to Enniskillen, via Clones and via Omagh. This allowed a flexibility in travel arrangements and a wide choice of trains. Travelling from Portadown, you could go via Clones at 12 noon or 3.40pm, and via Omagh at 5.45pm.

I soon became a seasoned traveller. In 1949 alone I made the trip to Fermanagh six times, once by Omagh and the rest by Clones. This became the pattern in the years that followed, with additional local trips between Enniskillen and Lisnaskea. I never travelled on the Sligo Leitrim line, mainly because by parents had no relations in the Florencecourt-Belcoo area, but I did once venture onto the Bundoran branch. This was on 6 June 1953 when we took the 12 noon from Portadown to Omagh, changed to the Enniskillen train, changed again at Bundoran Junction and took the branch train as far as Irvinestown from which, after an hour's wait, we got a bus to our final destination, Lisnarick, where my mother's older sister lived. We retraced our steps a week later. A few years later this same aunt and her husband moved to a farm near Kesh, the front garden of which gave an excellent view of trains passing on the Bundoran branch. After the railway closed we used to walk the line at this point and, in 1961, I remember UG class 0-6-0 No 47 (GNR 82) on the lifting train.

As soon as I could talk, my father set about broadening my education. Coming from a railway family, he was a mine of information about trains. I learnt all about signals and the procedures for starting a train. The Fermanagh journeys were used to teach me about steam engines. I would be stood on the platform next the engine and taught the names of all the bits from the chimney down to the coupling rods. I think the first six words I learnt were 'Daddy, Mummy, dome, whistle, home and distant', in roughly that order, the last two referring to signals rather than the house and relatives!

It was in Fermanagh too that I was presented with my first train set. Having messed about with various unsatisfactory O gauge clockwork trains, I had discovered Hornby-Dublo electric trains, being often found glued to the display cabinet in Jeffers shop in Portadown. So a letter was duly sent to Santa coming up to Christmas 1956, and on Christmas morning in Lisnagole farmhouse there it was – A4 4-6-2 *Silver King* and two gleaming red and cream coaches, with an oval of track and, as an extra bonus from my financially hard-pressed father, a siding and three wagons as well! How he ever got this lot smuggled down to Fermanagh on the train without me noticing, still exercises my mind. Mind you, Lisnagole had no electricity, so trying it out had to wait until we got back to Gilford, the village near Portadown where we lived up to 1957.

Many images of rail travel to Fermanagh are still very vivid in my mind. I especially remember Clones, which was a very large station by the standards of the GNR. It was a busy junction where the routes from Dundalk and Portadown converged before continuing over the border into Fermanagh. In addition, there was a branch to Cavan on the Down side. Passengers from Portadown to Fermanagh had to change into the train from Dundalk to Enniskillen. With customs clearance, this usually involved waiting half an hour or more for the connection. Often the Up train from Enniskillen would arrive during this

delay, also making connection with the Portadown train and the branch train from Cavan. Clones had a third road between the Up and Down platforms, and the station pilot often sat in here, ready to make a quick shunt of a parcels van from one train to another.

I remember on one such occasion sitting with my parents in the Enniskillen train at Platform 1 waiting for customs clearance. GNR third class carriages were centre corridor with two bays of eight seats to each compartment, every other bay having a door. Each window, whether with door or not, consisted of two side lights and a drop light window. I had the drop light open in our compartment and was leaning out watching all the bustle at Platforms 2/3 (the island platform). I remember the station pilot arriving right beside us on the middle road with the cab just at our window. It was a big black engine – most likely an LQG or SG3 0-6-0 – and the driver, having a spare moment, put chat on us. I remember him saying, "Would you like to see the fire, son?" and with that he threw open the firebox door, only six feet away. It was most impressive with the blast of heat that hit my face and this huge blazing furnace, much bigger even than my uncle's Wellstood cooker. Then his fireman threw a shovel of coal into the back and he slammed the door shut.

After the wait in Clones, the train then left, but, at Newtownbutler, faced another delay with the British customs. My father as always good at finding the best train to use, and one of his favourites was the new direct Portadown-Enniskillen (via Clones) diesel train introduced in 1953. It can be seen on page 62 arriving at Enniskillen. The GNR had helped pioneer diesel traction in the British Isles and, in 1950, introduced a fleet of ten three-coach AEC diesel trains. These were widely used on a variety of services. The new train left Portadown at 12.10pm, travelling by Clones, and reaching Enniskillen at about 2.00pm, returning at 3.00pm. This avoided having to change trains at Clones. On 29 December 1953, I remember travelling on the return working from Enniskillen as far as Lisnaskea. We were travelling with my father's brother Joseph and his wife and son. The first class compartments in these trains faced front and allowed a panoramic view of the line ahead. The train was far from crowded and, by some arrangement or other, the guard let us travel first class (Joseph worked for British Railways and my father for the UTA, which may have counted for something). Anyway my cousin Colin and I took up position in the very front, directly behind the GNR driver. To improve the view even more, we stood

A busy scene at Clones photographed from the footbridge about 6.30pm on Saturday 16 June 1951. The loco at the bottom of the picture is PP class 4-4-0 No 107, with Fireman G McKeown watching the photographer, and there is a load of briquetted coal in her tender. No 107 is sitting in the middle road between Platforms One and Two and is probably waiting to shunt a van on or off the back of the 4.25pm Dundalk to Enniskillen train. The middle engine is QL class 4-4-0 No 156 with the 6.15pm for Portadown and Belfast. At the top of the picture is an unidentified UG class 0-6-0 with the 1.25pm from Derry to Dundalk.

A Donaldson, courtesy WT Scott

on the first class seats. To this day I can remember the look of disapproval which the driver bestowed upon us when he noticed what we were doing. As we shrank down in our seats Colin said innocently "I wonder what's bothering him?" But we had a fair idea and behaved ourselves the rest of the way! The following day we caught the same diesel at 3.25pm in Lisnaskea and were in Portadown by 5.30pm, a saving of nearly an hour on the usual train. In the summer this train ran much earlier, at 9.00am, and started at Belfast, reaching Clones at 10.57am and Enniskillen at 11.37am, certainly much faster than by road. The return working was at 12.30pm.

In case the reader is remarking on what a head for detail I had at the age of four, I will let you into a secret – my father kept a diary! I now own all these diaries and with hindsight it is remarkably fortunate that my father recorded his travel arrangements so meticulously. He usually noted what trains he travelled on, though never, unfortunately, the engine number.

One very frequently used diesel in our family was the 6.20pm from Enniskillen to Clones. This was a useful service for anyone who had spent the afternoon in Enniskillen and found catching the 5.00pm steam train a trifle tight. This train was either a railbus or a Gardner articulated-railcar like No C3. This vehicle dated from 1935, and was a regular on the Bundoran branch in the winter. The railbus features in the photographic section and was a genuine road bus, with steel flanged wheels at the front and a steel tyre placed over its pneumatic tyre at the back. I have come across many dated photographs of the 6.20pm and often check my father's diary to see if by chance I might have been on it. The closest I have come is a Colin Hogg photograph taken on 22 August 1955, exactly a week after I had travelled on it!

Of all the stations that are etched in my mind's eye, I suppose Lisnaskea is the one that has the most poignant memories. Perhaps this is because so many journeys started and ended there. It was one of the smallest of the Irish North stations and apparently the least photographed. Lisnaskea consisted of a single platform on the Up side, with a passing loop and a level crossing at the Enniskillen end just past the points. Like many other GNR stations in Fermanagh, the name 'LISNASKEA' was cast in large whitewashed concrete letters set into the bank opposite the platform. The only other trackwork was a single siding (with headshunt) into the goods shed on the Up side, trailing from the Newtownbutler end. This meant that wagons for Lisnaskea could most easily be shunted by the Up goods but I never saw this, as it came through at 6.15am in the morning.

I only once ever saw the loop being used, mainly because we usually travelled on the early afternoon or evening trains. However I can pinpoint the date from my father's diary – it was on Monday 5 November 1956, when we rather unusually took the 10.09am to Clones (8.25am ex-Omagh). I remember watching the Down goods being shunted into the loop on this occasion. However this was a daily occurrence, as the 8.55am goods from Clones always crossed the 8.25am Omagh to Dundalk passenger at Lisnaskea, where the goods stopped over for 40 minutes. By leaving the goods in the loop the engine could run round and add wagons from Lisnaskea to the rear of the train, should that be needed.

The very last occasion I ever used Lisnaskea station, or indeed travelled on any Fermanagh train, was on Saturday 24 August 1957, just seven weeks before the line closed. It was a dreadful day, with heavy rain, and a fierce storm, and we were returning on the 5.00pm from Enniskillen, which got into Lisnaskea at 5.26pm, having started at Derry at 1.35pm and would reach Dundalk at 7.45pm. We walked the half mile from my aunt's house to the station with our luggage and took refuge in the waiting room, the window of which gave a view of the level crossing and the approaching train. In normal weather we would have waited on the platform. I remember consciously thinking "I want to remember this moment. This is the last time I will ever travel on this line." So I drank in the experience, and I can still see the train coming in over the level crossing and slowing for the platform, as we stood watching from the window. The engine was small and black with a tall chimney, so I know with hindsight that it was a PP 4-4-0.

I was in Portadown on the night of the actual closure of the Fermanagh lines – 30 September 1957. The line from Portadown to Clones was closing the same night and, as the last

train came in from Clones, detonators placed on the line near Portadown shed exploded in the usual railwaymen's tribute to last trains. We heard them up in the house and our first reaction was that it was an IRA raid on the police station (An IRA campaign had begun earlier in the year, particularly affecting Fermanagh). However a few seconds later my father realised a more likely explanation for the explosions, "Of course, it's the last train on the Armagh line", he said.

At the time, the shock of the closures took a long time to sink in at family level. For a long period there was an optimistic hope that wiser councils would prevail, and the lines would be reopened in due course. Throughout 1958-9 my mother resolutely kept saying, "As long as the tracks are not lifted there's hope." For those two years they lay derelict and weeds began to grow among the rails. On 1 October 1958 the old GNR was split up between the UTA and CIE, but this made little impact in Fermanagh, though in Portadown, from the middle of 1959, the GNR mahogany-coloured coaches began to appear in UTA green. Thankfully, only six of the blue engines were repainted black in 1961-2 and a few survived to 1965 in GNR sky blue.

Now and then, if we happened to be in Enniskillen on market day, we would look in at Enniskillen station and take a walk down its forlorn platforms. At Lisnaskea, my cousin Sandra and I sometimes walked the half mile down to the station and explored its ghostly atmosphere. The UTA had begun using it as a stabling point for its buses. Travelling to Fermanagh, particularly Lisnaskea, now became problematical for the family. Ever faithful to rail travel, we took the train to Omagh, from where, after a wait, there was a green No 24 bus to Enniskillen. I now have a lovely model of one of these buses (34 seat Leyland PS1 No Z800; GZ 4696) with '24' 'Enniskillen via Dromore' on the blind. In those days the Omagh-Enniskillen road was poor and I really did not look forward to these trips. I was always sick on the bus and positively miserable. The 25 miles to Enniskillen were continuous Z-bends and I felt every one! At Enniskillen the journey was still not over as we had to get a local UTA bus via Maguiresbridge or a cream Erne bus on the direct Enniskillen-Lisnaskea road. As we huddled at Enniskillen bus depot on winter days (it was nowhere as hospitable as its modern counterpart) we thought longingly of the direct Portadown to Enniskillen GNR diesel, and silently cursed the Northern Ireland government for its short-sighted transport policy.

Little wonder that we often opted for the lazy option of

Lisnaskea station in 1962. The goods shed in the background later became part of Mealiff's garage.

D Lawrence, Photos from the Fifties

taking a lift in one of my Uncle Robert Donaldson's Erne Engineering Company's Ford cars which, in the days before car-carriers, were actually driven new from the docks in Belfast by young apprentices of the Erne. This procedure involved a car with four drivers going to Belfast and returning in three brand new cars. Uncle Robert could arrange for a driver to detour to our house in Portadown (no motorway in those days!), pick us up and drop us in Lisnaskea. Of course this only worked if there happened to be cars going on the day we needed to travel. Thus it was that in the 1958-62 era we got to sample quite a wide variety of Henry Ford's Dagenham products! It was an interesting sort of lottery, as you never knew quite what to expect. It could be a black side-valve Ford Popular, with the prewar body shell, a Prefect, one of the new 1959 Anglias or, if we were lucky, a Consul or Zephyr. On one occasion in 1958, I well remember the driver arriving in an absolutely brand new light green upright Anglia, a model phased out in 1953. It even had shiny clear plastic taped over the seats. The story was that

it was for an elderly lady in Enniskillen who had one before and who found the new model much too new-fangled. Ford had actually gone to the trouble of building a one-off Anglia to please her!

However, I digress from the subject, though I am making the point that the closure of Fermanagh's railways led to a much poorer availability of transport. Journeys took longer and were much less comfortable.

Easter 1960 was, as usual, spent in Lisnaskea. By this time the line had been closed over two and a half years. I was playing in the garden with my cousin one morning when we heard the distinct whistle of a steam engine. But it was no ghost train. Down at the level crossing gates, which were within sight of the house, was a steam locomotive! We dashed into the house shouting, "There's a train down at the station!" And of course everyone came out to see. It was in fact the lifting train, which has started work on the Clones to Newtownbutler section (see

This was the scene just west of Kesh in early 1961 when Bobby Perry had the melancholy job of driving the lifting train. The engine is UG class 0-6-0 No 82 but now renumbered as UTA No 47. The loco worked on these trains for some time although it was, in theory at least, now shedded at Portadown where it was known as 'the Bundoran engine'. The van to the left of the engine is an ex-NCC goods brake van which is equipped with a petrol-powered winch for the sad job of hauling the redundant rails onto flat wagons. This was the train Norman saw at Dromard several times that Easter.

J Richardson

page 170). The very last occasion that I ever saw a train in Fermanagh was the following Easter, which was spent at Kesh, in my other aunt's house at Dromard, beside the Bundoran Branch. On 6-7 April 1961 the lifting train passed three times. On the Thursday I presumably saw it returning to Omagh in the evening, and on the Friday it passed in the morning heading towards Kesh and again in the evening returning. I remember getting a friendly wave from the fireman. That was the very end of the railway as far as I was concerned. The next time I was back the tracks had all gone. In 1962 my Kesh aunt was obliged by the government to buy (at minimal cost) the portion of the Bundoran branch that passed through her land. Apparently the owner of the farm in 1866 had sold the same land to the Enniskillen, Bundoran and Sligo Railway a century earlier. Many farmers were given the same deal in the early 1960s. On a holiday in the 1990s I met a retired Civil Servant who had been involved in administering these sales, and she

confirmed what I always suspected – that the purpose of these sales was to make sure that the lines could never possibly be reopened.

As a final personal postscript, I often regret that I did not persuade my father to take even one photograph of the railways in his native county. In those days money was tight and he rationed himself to one eight-exposure film a year. I began my own photography in 1962 when it was too late, though my first ever photograph was appropriately at Omagh station, while waiting for a No 24 bus to Enniskillen. One day in 1967, when I was into colour slide photography, my Lisnaskea cousin and I, now adults, walked down to the remains of the old station, derelict but still standing. We wandered along the overgrown platform and through the ticket office and entrance hall. Then we entered the old waiting room and there in front of me was the window through which in August 1957 I had watched the 5.00pm from Enniskillen arriving to take me on my last trip on Fermanagh's railways. It was a very sad moment as I looked through the by now glassless window at the empty trackbed and the road where the gates had been. But I could still see the train and it brought a lump to my throat. Today the edge of Carrowshee housing estate occupies the site of the old station and the children who play there probably don't even know that trains once passed by. The only bit still standing is the goods shed, now part of Mealiff's garage. After leaving the station, my cousin and I walked towards the town and then turned right to reach the bridge that carried a minor road over the railway. The slide I took is reproduced below. It shows the station buildings and the trackbed and by a happy irony may well be the only colour picture ever taken of Lisnaskea station. If any reader has a photograph of Lisnaskea station in black and white or colour, I would dearly love them to get in touch with me.

Lisnaskea station in 1967. It was demolished the following year. The goods shed still stands and the side next the hedge is still unrendered.

Norman Johnston

Charles Remembers

I sometimes wonder if I was born listening to a steam engine at work!

Away back in the late summer of 1946, I was born in the County Hospital in Enniskillen. 'The County' was on a hill between the Tempo Road and the railway. There is a Sandown Home there nowadays. The maternity ward was on the first floor, in the corner overlooking the Sligo Leitrim and Northern Counties Railway's yard. The joint SLNCR and Great Northern passenger station was beyond that and the GNR engine shed off to the right. Indeed, the first photograph taken of me was on the balcony of that ward with my godparents. I was just three days old and about to be whisked off to be christened – they didn't hang about in those days! No matter how I try to print the negative, I can't get any of the railway into it!

My parents lived at Wickham Drive, a terrace of eight three-storey houses which is now the Belmore Court Motel. We lived at No 2, which later became No 7 Tempo Road, when the imposition of postcodes rationalised all sorts of addresses and almost wiped out our townland names. The Tempo Road was at the back of the house and the Dublin Road ran at the bottom of the long gardens at the front of the houses. The house was, in a way, almost surrounded by railways. From the front of the house you could see the Sligo Leitrim and, from the top room at the back of the house, you could see part of the joint passenger station.

When I was about three, I had the impression that there

The east side of Enniskillen as seen from the Cole Monument about 1935. In the left foreground is the Fair Green with part of Gaol Square on the extreme right and the Derrychara Road at the far end of the first terrace of houses. In the centre of the picture, the V of the Tempo Road (to the left of the picture) and the Dublin Road to the right, contains the Masonic Hall. Wickham Drive, where we lived, is just to the left of the Masonic Hall. The terrace of houses to the left is Westville while, away to the right, are the houses of Lower Celtic Park with the Castlecoole Woods behind.

CP Friel collection

was another station in Enniskillen! My mother's youngest brother emigrated to America. He left from our house and I got the idea that he had gone all the way by train. Soon after that I was ill and spent a day or two in my parents' bedroom at the front of the house. From there I could see steam sometimes billowing about the Taylor Woods nylon factory. I put two and two together and came to the conclusion that this modern-looking building was the station for America!

But back to reality and what we really saw from the front of the house. Trains from Sligo came across the Weirs Bridge and the Dublin Road before coming into view. They skirted the edge of the Castlecoole Woods on what appeared to be a high embankment above the houses of Lower Celtic Park, before disappearing from view behind the Model School. I have few memories of seeing railbuses or the railcar on this high bit of track but even a six year old could not help noticing the many long trains of cattle wagons, each complete with a brake van, which, to our untutored eyes, was known as 'a last wagon'. The incoming cattle or goods trains sometimes stopped alongside the Woods and we would watch for a small lineside fire once they had moved off.

The view from the top room at the back of the house was,

if anything, even more interesting. You had to look past the garage of J G Forde, Motor Engineer (later West's) and across the top of Fairbairn's one-storey chicken hatchery. There was a distant, almost side-on, view of the yellow footbridge, some of the main passenger buildings on its left and part of the engine shed area to the right.

I am the eldest of three children and, in the days before I started school, my mother (probably to get peace to attend to Mary and John) would send me up to the top room "to watch the puff puffs". I needed a tin box to stand on but the ploy worked every time. One very early memory is of watching an engine blowing off vigorously and being fascinated to see what would happen to the tall column of steam when it met the footbridge.

My first railway journey was just after Christmas 1946 when my parents brought me to my mother's family home near Mullaghmore in north Sligo. This was my introduction to train travel and where better than on the Bundoran branch? We came back to Enniskillen in early January, just before the big snow of 1947 closed everything down.

From my mother's diaries, I see that we were on the train to Bundoran again on 30 July, coming home on 19 August.

Then, just a couple of days before my first birthday, we travelled with my father's mother, brother and sister to their house in Rosnakill in north Donegal. Our route was, of course, via Omagh and on to Strabane, where we changed into a narrow gauge train for Letterkenny. The journey was completed in a Lough Swilly bus on the Fanad route. We retraced our steps just under three weeks later. Not surprisingly, I have no recollection of these pioneering trips, though my brother and I later distinguished Donegal railcars from Great Northern ones by our ability to see out the front of the former. I remember thinking, in later years, that the Donegal cars were safer, since they had the entrance door at the top of the steps rather than at the bottom (as in Railcar C1). The doorwell in C1 struck me as a dangerous place to drop a toy.

My strongest railway memories from before I started school centre on the frequent afternoon walks out the Tempo Road with Mary, John and my mother. En route we passed the Breandrum Cemetery on one side and 'the County' with its tennis courts, on the other. My mother would sometimes recall playing tennis here in her nursing days and the long searches for lost balls amongst the graves. Slightly further on, the Sligo Leitrim's engine sheds came into view, where the railway was on an embankment about twelve feet high. Lockingtons had a coal yard here and received coal from wagons at the top of the embankment. These wagons were unloaded by simply shovelling the coal over the side where it cascaded down the embankment; indeed the whole embankment seemed to be made of coal. I remember being fascinated at how each shovelful of coal kept its shape as it arched through the air, before it landed with a light, flittering sound and scattered about the middle of the hill.

Then our walk brought us under the Sligo Leitrim's metal bridge where little seemed to happen. Beyond this bridge, though, the Tempo Road ran parallel to the GNR's Clones line for about half a mile, before the road dog-legged over the railway on another bridge at the outer end of the Killynure siding. This was a metal bridge, built to accommodate double track and the siding made use of this by finishing a few yards on the Clones side of the bridge with a square buffer, built of sleepers and earth, I think. The bridge, with its handrails and high-domed rivets, was painted a blue-grey colour which had fascinating silvery sparkling specks embedded in its mirror-smooth finish. I was told once that this was a painting system that involved electrically-charged metallic paint being

The author with his sister Mary on the Tempo Road one Sunday afternoon in 1951. In the top left corner is the accommodation crossing which gave access to the tennis court and marked the start of the Killynure siding.

CP Friel collection

sprayed onto metal with an opposite charge. This was well beyond me at the time – and still is, a bit! Some of the bigger boys from Wickham Drive used this bridge to try and either spit into or drop stones down the engines' chimneys. I was always too young for this hooliganism (thank goodness) and knew only the simpler delight of hoping to see a train.

One glorious memory is of seeing Driver Jimmy Kelly storming alongside the Tempo Road as he left with a passenger train for Clones. He was on our side of the cab and waving what looked like a white hankie to us as he passed. I can remember that there was much whistling and the engine had a tall chimney, so it might have been a P or a PP class locomotive. Mr Kelly lived in Lower Celtic Park with his wife Kate and daughter Angela. Mrs Kelly came from near Tullaghan in north Leitrim and had, by a remarkable coincidence, been at National School with my mother.

The Killynure siding diverged from the Clones line just past the access road to another tennis court. The siding often had about ten or twenty goods wagons. Some were wagons of coal for Lockingtons. The others were probably waiting for attention at the town's relatively small goods yard. The siding was about three quarters of a mile from our house and probably at a point where four-year-old legs were likely to be giving up. I do not know whether or not this was the reason for my 'job' here; I had to call out the wagon numbers

U class 4-4-0 No 202 *Louth* passes the Killynure siding with a train from Clones. The ground frame controlling access to the siding is in the foreground. To the right the Tempo Road follows the line, before crossing it at the far end of the siding.

RM Arnold

and read any words or letters on the wagons. One afternoon there was big excitement – there was an engine in the siding! I remember us watching it make several attempts to lift a rake of wagons in the siding. Each time the engine started away there were angry shouts and cross words as the men realised that they didn't have all of the rake with them. There was much crashing of buffers and ringing of couplings before all were safely gathered in. My mother explained that 'the bad boys' had undone the couplings!

There was an interesting sequel to this story over 45 years later. I was giving an illustrated talk in Enniskillen's splendid Ardhowen Theatre, to commemorate the 40th anniversary of the closure of the railways. I recounted the above incident and thought little of it. Afterwards, though, one of the audience, a man of about my own years and who had then lived in Westville, told me how young fellas from around there used to play in the Sligo Leitrim yard on a Sunday when no-one was about. One of the things they used to do was undo as many wagon couplings as they could. This man went on to tell me that his mother had once given him a terrible telling off for being with 'the bad boys' who did this. And, 45 years later, when I recounted my story, he could hear his mother telling him how disappointed she was with him. And there he was, sitting in the audience at the Ardhowen, going red in the face and the sweat breaking on him as he felt guilty all over again!

Family Sunday afternoon walks were often out the Castlecoole Road which crossed over the SLNCR line. But the Sligo trains hardly ever ran on Sundays and, anyway, the attention of the young Friels was directed towards a flock of red and black hens in a small yard that backed onto the line. Our walk then lay through the grounds of Castlecoole, a large 18th century mansion and the home of Lord Belmore. Here the concrete bases of army huts were still visible and there was a concrete roadway, a legacy of wartime military use. I remember a Red Cross fête in the grounds of Castlecoole, probably about 1953. One stallholder had a baseboard with an oval of Hornby 0 gauge track and a black clockwork tank engine. Around the outer edge of the track, short lengths had labels for many of the stations between Enniskillen and Bundoran and there were also blank spaces between each label. The idea was that you put a penny at the 'station' where you thought the engine would stop and, if you were right, you won another penny! It is now all too obvious that partial winding by the operator could have resulted in very few wins, but those were simpler times.

But back to those Sunday walks. Before reaching Castlecoole House itself, we took a different road out of the estate and this brought us onto the Dublin Road near the Weirs Bridge. The line crossed the Dublin Road on a metal bridge with a stone pier in the middle of the road. There was something of a bad bend on the approach from the Enniskillen direction and we were always cautioned about crossing the road hereabouts. Sometime about 1955, a motorcyclist was killed when he failed to take the corner properly and hit the stone pier.

It was said that the Weirs Bridge was unsafe and a cautionary tale was often told of a woman who took a short cut across the bridge and fell through rotten boards. This tale was more relevant to older children who were known to be tempted to walk the track on a trainless Sunday afternoon. Sadly, I have no memories of seeing anything cross the bridge though I did cross it a few times, of which more later. The area below the bridge was a magnet for people out for a Sunday stroll. We usually played or just sat around under the trees while others swam and dived in the river. You had to be a big boy to do that and there was something approaching a scandal when one swimmer cut his foot on broken glass and got a terrible infection.

The other big scandal from those days was when the new fire station at the junction of the Tempo and Dublin Roads was being built around 1953. The building has a steel frame and men building that frame worked on Sundays! This shock news was greeted with a knowing shake of the head and "What else could you expect?" when it became known that they were from Belfast! After the fire station opened, all the young Wickham Drivers became very interested in fire engines and, any time the siren on top of the Town Hall went, we would all race down to the end of the Tempo Road to watch the fun as the firemen appeared from around the town. In those days they either came running, or on bicycles which were abandoned and sent crashing into each other on the wall next Westville. I remember being intrigued at how long the engines were away at the big fire at Florencecourt, home of the Earls of Enniskillen, in March 1955. At one time, fire engines were almost as big a draw as the railway!

From about 1950 onwards, we used the trains quite a lot. Our travel pattern was to go to my mother's home place in the first few days of July and come back in mid-August. Those Sligo holidays were idyllic. We had the run of the farm and helped with all sorts of jobs. We had the sea and a superb beach almost to ourselves (although it was always called a 'strand' then). We came home complete with Sligo accents and a compulsion to say "hello" to everyone we met. This was fair enough in Enniskillen but played not nearly so well once we had moved to Portadown. Those summers also included about ten days in Donegal. These became less frequent after 1953 but the trips to Sligo increased. From 1952 (when we all had had chicken pox and my mother thought we could do with building up) we spent our Easter holidays in Sligo as well. From about then too, I was big enough to go on the one-day visits to Sligo before Christmas to exchange presents. The first of these gave me quite a shock. Compared to the balmy days of summer hay-making, climbing trees and playing in the sand, everywhere was very bare, very cold and very wet!

All of these journeys involved using the train. Getting on to the station platform in Enniskillen seemed something akin to storming a castle, to my young eyes. Guarding the way to the trains was a big door that was slammed shut before departure and then a bell was rung before the guard blew his whistle and the train moved off. One summer, maybe 1954, I was sent up to the station to meet my father's mother who was coming from England. She didn't arrive via Clones but she did arrive shortly afterwards off the Omagh train. And rather than idle about the platform to wait between trains, I sat on the steps outside, in the sun. I sometimes wonder what I missed!

Easter trips to Bundoran always seemed to involve a change at the Junction into Railcar C1. This was relatively easy to do as it did not involve getting bulky suitcases across the footbridge but it was a different matter on the way home.

Railcar C1 on the branch presented something of a tactical problem in that it did not have any 'facilities'. I remember my brother and I getting very excited when we thought that the distaff side of the party was about to be left behind in the ladies' room at the Junction. The railcar was noisy and smelly, I am told. We were oblivious to that but I do remember it being cold. One Good Friday (and it might be as far back as our first Easter trip in 1952), we got as far as Belleek when we set back away from the platform into the short loop and waited for something coming the other way. I cannot recall what that was. It might have been the seemingly never photographed Pettigo permanent way lorry, as a cattle special seems unlikely on that day. Anyway, I clearly remember the long wait and looking across at the Leitrim mountains and seeing them covered in snow. Easter was quite early that year. My mother's comment was "What are we letting ourselves in for?".

Good Friday afternoon in Bundoran was something else in the mid-fifties. The long wait for the connecting Great Northern Derry to Sligo bus, for the final seven miles or so, was like an extra penance. The place was like a graveyard, there was nothing open and the Atlantic wind had something

"If you stood on the seats after leaving the station . . ." A PP class 4-4-0 is seen leaving Ballyshannon for Bundoran. On the right background, amidst the clouds, are the profiles of Benwiskin (far right) and Truskbeg to its left, with the Leitrim mountains above the train itself. *Rev J Parker, Photos from the Fifties*

extra in its cutting edge. The shops had yet to get their fresh coat of paint for the summer trade and a swinging rusty metal sign screeching near the Hollyrood Hotel summed the whole thing up – echoing, deserted, and desolate.

It can now be told, though, that not everything in Bundoran was bolted and shut on that fiercely cold Good Friday. The side door to one bar was open and I remember my mother getting a warming sherry while we got orange minerals. In those days soft drinks were served in very tall and slowly tapering glasses that had huge heavy blobs of glass for bases. And as you drank you left a scattering of orange bits down the glass, unless you swilled them off (a dangerous thing to do) or tried to suck them up with your straw (strangely unsatisfactory). They don't seem to have orange bits these days.

We became quite familiar with the railway, sometimes to the point of embarrassing my mother. Maybe I should mention that we usually travelled without my father. His job meant that he seldom came at Easter and, in the summer, he would join us for the last two weeks before we came home. Once my mother mentioned anything about an approaching customs post, we would set up a chorus about the customs men coming and generally get excited. It wasn't that my mother was ever 'carrying' much (to use the vernacular) that would be of interest to these bogey men. But she got embarrassed when others looked at her askance and seemed to anticipate some fun when the arch interrogators came through the train.

The customs post at Ballyshannon, on the way to Bundoran, was something different, though. If you stood on the seats after leaving the station you eventually got a glimpse of the yellow tops of the huge sandy banks of Tullan strand behind Finner army camp – proof, at last, that we were getting near the sea. The journey was nearly over and the holiday could really begin! I remember being very disappointed in 1957, on our final journey to Bundoran, when we couldn't stand on the seats. There were too many others in the train and, anyway, wasn't I getting a bit big for this?

Other memories of the branch are of those delightful wooden centre corridor carriages with the bevelled circular windows in the intermediate doors that could swing both ways and the knurled door knobs that were just fascinating! Once, though, I can remember looking through broken bits of floor at the grey ballast flying past below. There were landmarks to look out for, too, such as the petrol luggage trolley – 'the bogie' – that banged and echoed its way around the platforms at Bundoran Junction, the glimpse of Lough Erne just before Castlecaldwell or the Fiddler's Stone soon afterwards. The set-back signal cabin at Belleek, with the pottery's disappearing siding, was always intriguing. Belleek also had that tunnel under the main street and the crossing of the Erne.

Bundoran always held the promise that the train would actually run in under the roof rather that stand far out near the engine release crossover. As the biggest child, I had the job of helping lug the huge suitcases off the train, so where we stopped really made a difference! Inside the station, right behind the buffers, was a small Easons bookstall selling papers, magazines, sweets, and cigarettes. We were sometimes

told the story of an engine hitting the buffers so hard that the bookstall fell over, but I've never been able to get any confirmation of this, even from Mrs Kelly who had worked there before moving to Enniskillen.

As I have said, journeys to and from Sligo involved the Great Northern's Derry to Sligo bus. There was always a chance that the bus conductor would be Jimmy McGloin, a neighbour of my mother's family. It was something of a bone of contention, though, that the Derry to Sligo bus left Bundoran at 4.25pm while the 3.00pm from the Junction didn't arrive until 4.36pm! Unless the Derry bus was running late, this meant a wait until 6.30pm. The connection was mercifully better in the opposite direction when all hands were inevitably feeling quite upset. Waiting for a bus at Bundoran often meant hiding from the wind in the glass shelter to the left of the entrance doorway and the bus would simply pick us up by doing a circle in front of the station. Thankfully we seldom had to use the highly inadequate bus

A line up of GNR buses at Ballyshannon garage on Saturday 14 August 1948. From left to right we have No 274 (a 1930 Leyland Lion, originally 119); No 302, a 1934 Leyland, with GNR body, but rebuilt with a Gardner engine; No 218, a similar GNR-built 1937 Gardner; and Nos 434 and 437, both AEC Regent II double deckers, built in 1948 with Park Royal bodies.

JC Gillham

park on the hill overlooking the station. There the shelters were simply V-shaped roofs set about seven feet in the air and nothing else! Whoever designed the place had obviously never been near it on an average day in summer, let alone in the winter. The buses in this park could be something of a variety, for there were visiting UTA green and white buses, alongside GNR buses going to strange places like Carrick on Shannon or Portnoo. I had no idea where either place was but the latter sounded exotic, a place full of pirates and buried treasure. If you know Portnoo, I'll leave you to draw your own conclusions as to how accurate my impressions were!

Very occasionally we got to Bundoran by using the Erne Bus Service, better known as Cassidy's buses. I was at primary school with Maurice Cassidy's son Henry. Cassidy had a route along the southern shore of Lower Lough Erne. I remember once the driver was Johnny Goan and the conductor was Peter Cadden, who later lived in Portadown for a time. The road was very bumpy indeed in those days and there was an emergency stop at one point to allow one of the young Friels to be sick.

Great Northern buses, as well as trains, featured in my childhood. Firstly, during our holidays we went by GNR bus to church in Cliffoney each Sunday morning. This was a Ballyshannon to Sligo working that had the added attraction of usually being a double-decker in both directions! For other journeys to Sligo, to see cousins or to go shopping, we were back to the single deckers. During those long summer holidays, when the roads were much less busy than today, we could hear the distinctive sound of Great Northern buses as they passed on the main road. Even though the main road, aka 'The Coach Road' still, was over half a mile away and over a hill, the heavy throb of a Gardner engine was clearly audible. And so too were the sounds of stopping and starting which might signal the imminent arrival of visitors!

Secondly, there were day trips from Enniskillen to Derrynacreeve, south of Swanlinbar, on the GNR's route to Cavan. My father's mother had come from there originally and my father sometimes went to visit relations on a Saturday, bringing some of us with him. The outward run started at Enniskillen station and went through the town, but I felt lost once we reached the Sligo Road! The return working was a Saturdays-only service which got us back to Enniskillen railway station at 7.25pm. I remember some

of those journeys after dark, with the afterglow of sunset backlighting the Cuilcagh mountains and giving the scene a haunted and spooky feeling.

All of these associations combined to make the sound of a Gardner diesel engine quite nostalgic. Even though I seldom found the silvery wire-covered and hooded Clayton heater provided much in the way of heat, GNR buses had a very solid wooden feel and sound that was sadly absent elsewhere. And I have not since heard the distinctive dull and vibrating buzzing and ringing mixture of sounds produced by the bell in the driver's cab of a GNR bus. The dull creamy yellow and orange glow of the deco-designed light shades only added to their magic.

Another journey from Enniskillen, but by rail this time, was the shopping trip to Blacklion, probably made before I started school. Several wives from Wickham Drive would occasionally head off on the 1.45pm railbus for Sligo and get off at Belcoo. My highlights of the journey were to look out for our house as we passed through the Castlecoole Woods and then the thrill of crossing the Weirs Bridge and looking down into the dark waters or across to the trees where we had played. The Weirs Bridge was much higher than its Belleek counterpart, which seemed so much tamer. Once arrived in Belcoo, we walked across the border to Blacklion and, after visiting a couple of shops, I would find my coat pockets bulging with tea or sugar. I don't know what else was bought. I didn't ask and wasn't told.

These trips were made during the winter and the return from Blacklion to Belcoo was made under the cover of darkness and in total silence. The dreaded customs post was a grey caravan, like the ones used by County Council roadmen and it was parked at the side of the road. I remember that we had to walk in the middle of the road so as not to scrunch the small stones at the side. Once we had successfully tip-toed past this, the rest of the walk to Belcoo station was plain sailing and we made our way to the far platform to wait for the railcar from Sligo. The waiting room was lit by a single oil lamp and I remember one local youth taking great delight in repeatedly running in and blowing it out! After that endurance test, the almost-new Railcar B on the 4.00pm out of Sligo – and another close encounter with a Gardner engine – was most welcome.

In the summer of 1955 there was a break with tradition and I went to Sligo by car. The car was an A35 belonging to a friend of my mother's. I sat on my father's knee in the front passenger seat; how times have changed! I had the job of working the indicator knob which was mounted in the centre of the dashboard near the windscreen. I can't imagine that my services were needed much. The biggest memory of that trip was the approach to Ballyshannon close to what I now know were Camlin gates, where the Bundoran branch was on an embankment and quite close to the road. About a hundred yards on the Belleek side of the gates, we met a train coming out from Bundoran. Again the tall chimney made a strong impression, as did the string of mahogany coaches.

My father's job took us away from Enniskillen in October 1955 when he was transferred to Portadown. The plan had been to travel by train via Clones and Armagh. Unfortunately, on the day, the furniture movers arrived late (another black mark for Belfast men!) and we missed the train. We ended up travelling to Portadown squashed into the cab of the furniture lorry. Thus disappeared my last chance to travel over that part of the Irish North and we never did.

Living in Portadown was very different from Enniskillen. We needed to get a tinny UTA bus to and from school and we had to make new friends. We still looked out for IL (Fermanagh) registered cars, or ones with Topping's labels on the back windows, or lorries heading for the Scottish Wholesale Society. Getting from Portadown to Bundoran now involved using the 11.15am from Belfast and travelling via Omagh to Bundoran Junction. This re-introduced us to the Fintona horse tram. We had seen it before on journeys to Donegal, or on a journey to England in 1952, but now it became part of the regular holiday travels. I remember seeing Dick (the horse) only once. Usually, he was safely in the small stable beside the signal cabin, in accordance with the rules. Sight of the tram was, for the mercenary amongst us, the signal to finally open the packet of custard creams!

Changing at Bundoran Junction at Eastertime, from the Omagh direction, now meant facing that footbridge with suitcases on our way to Bundoran, the reverse of what happened when we started at Enniskillen. Summer travel should have been easier, using one of the Belfast to Bundoran through coaches. Unfortunately the through coach on the 11.15am was usually full by Portadown and we had to change trains in the usual fashion anyway, but this had one compensation. We had seldom encountered Jimmy Kelly on the Bundoran branch but in those final summers of '56

and '57 we travelled behind him between Omagh and the Junction. My mother missed Enniskillen and all her friends there and I remember her having a long chat with Jimmy at the Junction. Probably because I wasn't in the through coach, I have no recollection of the shunt being done at the Junction. Of all my journeys on the branch, I can remember noticing the engine number only once and that was on the final run to Bundoran. The number was 74 and I remember deliberately studying the colours and shading of the numerals on the glistening black cabside.

After the line closed in 1957, we continued to travel to Bundoran by train as far as Omagh where we boarded UTA buses for the rest of the journey. It was melancholic, to say the least, to see the line lying intact in so many places especially at Omagh where the running lines were downgraded to sidings. It was on one of those journeys to Bundoran that I stepped off the bus, in Kesh of all places, to post a letter to the Transport Museum to buy my first-ever railway book – Morton's Standard Gauge Railways in the North of Ireland.

It was some years before the lifting trains began to run and, even then, they ran in Northern Ireland only. Both Bundoran and Ballyshannon were left more or less intact long after the lifting train had finally reached Omagh in 1962. This was something of a blessing in disguise for my brother and I, as we could explore Bundoran station to our hearts' content. We were able to move the turntable and even use the metal name-printing machine in the summer of 1962! In 1964, we were still able to buy GN-printed tickets from Portadown to Bundoran. On the way home I managed to hold on to the return half. But when I told my mother what I had done, she insisted that I go back to the barrier and give it to the ticket collector, Mr Robinson, as she did not want him to get into trouble!

About this time, too, the Railway Bar in Bundoran sported a new illuminated sign. It was a three-quarter view of a CIE A class MetroVick! It made me wonder, not for the first time, whether such machines would still be running through Bundoran if the coastal route to Sligo had ever been built. It is not beyond the bounds of possibility that such a line would still be open to-day, perhaps as far as Ballyshannon!

In the summer of 1965, after the Derry Road had closed, the bus journey began at Portadown station. It was to be my last journey by public transport to Bundoran. I travelled on the Saturday before 12 July and there were so many people that extra buses were hastily summoned. I got a seat right at the front of one of them, a front-entrance vehicle. Then the driver got in and asked "Does anyone know the road to Enniskillen?" I had a job for the morning! During the break in Enniskillen, I headed for the Melvin Cafe which had been our favourite place for ice-cream, though Shaw's in Belmore Street came a close second. Sadly, I didn't see Bridie Pope, who used to preside in the shop, nor did the ice-cream have the distinctive hint of lemon and 'something else' that I remembered so fondly. I have no idea what that 'something else' was; only once have I found something close. That was in northern Italy another seven years later – while photographing steam trains, of course!

Another very late remembrance of Enniskillen came in August 1970 when I had my last trip in SLNCR Railcar B, by then belonging to Coras Iompair Eireann and renumbered 2509. It worked in various places on the CIE system after they bought it and I even managed to photograph it at Portadown in December 1964, while it was being used to familiarise CIE drivers with the GNR main line north of Dundalk. In 1970 it was working in the Rosslare area. A party of us joined an Irish Railway Record Society trip from Rosslare across the South Wexford line to Waterford and then over the goods-only Ballinacourty branch before returning to Waterford. For me it was a splendid farewell to a well-remembered car. The weather was great, the photography was good and the car ran well, even if the gear changing gave some problems. Some of us rode in the driver's cab on the way back from Ballinacourty (it was at the trailing end) and we topped 44 mph a couple of times. The saloon windows in 'B' caught a few people out, though. In most coaches with sliding toplights, you slide a small pane away on each side of the centre to reveal the opening. In Railcar B, though, the opposite applies; the movable panes and openings are in the top right and top left corners of the window. On quite a few occasions on that trip, we saw folk attempt to look out by flinging the toplights apart only to collide violently with the permanent glass beyond! Railcar 2509 has been preserved, and is now at Downpatrick where it is in poor condition. But it is not as bad as first appears and is certainly restorable. The Downpatrick and County Down Railway has launched

an appeal for funds to do just that; consider yourself heartily encouraged to help!

Another Sligo Leitrim vehicle in preservation is, of course, the locomotive Lough Erne, now in the care of the Railway Preservation Society of Ireland at Whitehead. My brother and I had photographed it many times in its UTA and NIR days around Belfast and as we have been involved with the RPSI almost since its inception, have worked on the loco at Whitehead. Naturally we both have a soft spot for an engine going back so far into our roots. John was the fireman when the engine was steamed for what turned out to be its last boiler inspection, in April 1971. On that occasion, it took many hours of hard work and gentle persuasion to bring the steam pressure up to blowing off. John even resorted to emptying the ashpan in an attempt to get the engine to make steam! Later that month Lough Erne carried the Governor of Northern Ireland, Lord Grey, when he visited Whitehead – he was supposed to ride in the brakevan behind, but chose the footplate instead!

So far as I can make out, *Lough Erne* was last used on 8 July 1972 on the Society's Summer Train Rides at the Whitehead site. Since then it has been a static exhibit, needing a lot of money to restore it to full health. One Fermanagh enthusiast, George Stevenson, made a great job of repainting the engine on his visits to Whitehead, before his untimely death.

The Enniskillen wheel turned again in 1986. A friend of mine, Rev John McKegney, was on Ulster Television's advisory panel. During a visit to Fermanagh, the District Council entertained them to afternoon tea in the newly-opened Ardhowen Theatre. John was gazing at the splendid view of the remains of the Weirs Bridge when Gerry Burns, the Council's Chief Executive, passed a comment that it would be great to relive the days of the railway. John, who knew of my connections with Enniskillen, said "I know just the man…" The upshot was that I was asked to present the first of six highly enjoyable railway nights in the Ardhowen. Without John's prompting, a whole cycle of things might not have happened, including this book! The saying about oaks and little acorns is apt, since John is a Derry man.

I hope you enjoy this book as much as I have enjoyed reliving my childhood while compiling it.

THE HISTORY OF FERMANAGH'S RAILWAYS

Norman Johnston

Having set the scene with a personal touch from each of us, it is now appropriate to look in more detail at Fermanagh's railways. We have defined 'Fermanagh' somewhat liberally in this book, rather than stopping dead at the county boundary. Thus the photographic section begins at Clones, an important junction, which was the entry point to Fermanagh for trains from County Monaghan. Likewise Bundoran Junction was, strictly speaking, in County Tyrone, as was Fivemiletown on the Clogher Valley Railway. The Bundoran branch presented a particular problem as it crisscrossed several times between Fermanagh and Donegal. In the end we decided to include the whole branch since it would make no sense to exclude Pettigo, Ballyshannon and Bundoran. After all, Pettigo served the County Fermanagh hamlet of Tullyhommon and Bundoran was the natural holiday destination for Fermanagh folk.

In the 1950s Fermanagh was associated with two railways – the Sligo Leitrim and Northern Counties Railway (SLNCR) and the Great Northern Railway (Ireland). However, the GNR was itself an amalgam of a number of earlier railways and at this point we need to give a brief outline of the history of these earlier lines, as they relate to Fermanagh. Enniskillen must have seemed a very desirable destination for Victorian railway builders because no fewer than three companies aimed to reach there. These were the Londonderry and Enniskillen Railway, the Newry and Enniskillen Railway and the Dundalk and Enniskillen Railway, all three of which were incorporated by Act of Parliament in July 1845. At that time the only public transport available to Fermanagh were the daily Bianconi 'long cars', one of which ran by road from Enniskillen to Dublin via Cavan, Virginia and Navan and the other from Sligo to Omagh via Enniskillen. The county was effectively isolated to all but the most hardened and determined traveller.

The Londonderry and Enniskillen Railway

The LER was the first to reach Enniskillen. The aim of the line's promoters was to tap the potential traffic of Tyrone and Fermanagh to the benefit of the port of Derry/Londonderry. The line was surveyed by none other than the famous Robert Stephenson, son of George Stephenson, the designer of the steam locomotive Rocket which won the Rainhill trials so convincingly in 1829. The company was financed from London but progress was painfully slow. Although Strabane was reached in 1847, it was to be 1852 before the line reached Omagh. The route from Omagh to Enniskillen was opened in stages, the last stretch – from Dromore Road to Enniskillen – being opened on 19 August 1854. The original LER station in Enniskillen was alongside what is now the Irvinestown Road, just opposite Sedan Terrace and north of where the Pound Brae overbridge used to be (see the photographs on page 74 for a view of the general area). The company's finances were in a poor state from the very beginning and it was heavily in debt. Nevertheless it was enterprising in some respects. It was a shareholder in the Lough Erne Steam Navigation Company which operated a paddle steamer Countess of Milan from Enniskillen to Belleek and to Belturbet on alternate days. The LER ran excursions to Enniskillen to connect with these sailings.

The company was plunged into controversy four weeks after it was opened, by the derailment of an Apprentice Boys special at Trillick (Co Tyrone) as it returned from Derry to Enniskillen on 15 September 1854. There were fatalities, and accusations that the derailment was malicious. A number of permanent way men were tried in Omagh but were eventually acquitted for lack of evidence. Trouble in the 'marching season' is nothing new!

The Londonderry and Enniskillen Railway remained isolated from the rest of the railway system until 1859 when the Dundalk and Enniskillen Railway arrived. A year later the LER was leased to the DER with effect from 1 January 1860. This meant that the LER received a guaranteed income from the lease, the DER taking responsibility for running the line and making a profit or loss as the case may be. This lease was taken over by the GNR when it was formed in 1876. The LER remained a separate company until it was bought out by the GNR in 1883.

The Dundalk and Enniskillen Railway

The other two companies which aimed to reach Enniskillen were the Dundalk and Enniskillen Railway and the Newry and Enniskillen Railway. The latter company was to connect the port of Newry to Enniskillen by way of Markethill, Armagh, Monaghan and Clones. The Dundalk and Enniskillen Railway was to connect Dundalk with Clones and to share the responsibility and cost of the remaining 22 miles with the NER. In the event, the NER got no further than Armagh and even that took until 1864! Accepting the inevitable, the company formally abandoned plans to build beyond Armagh in 1857 and renamed itself the Newry and Armagh Railway. The Ulster Railway had already obtained powers to build the Armagh to Clones section, and the DER took full responsibility for the Clones to Enniskillen section.

The Dundalk and Enniskillen Railway, meanwhile, had been constructing its line from Dundalk and had reached Newbliss in 1855. Progress over the next two years was slow and the Newbliss-Clones-Lisnaskea section was not opened until 7 July 1858. Lisnaskea was a temporary terminus for six weeks, the section to Lisbellaw opening on 16 August. Six months later, Enniskillen saw its first train from Clones on 15 February 1859. The station was the later GNR one, at Forthill, roughly where the car park is now. Steps were quickly taken to connect with the LER station. The connecting line was on a 330 ft radius curve which was the tightest on the whole GNR system. The curve took the line through 90° in 200 yds, from the DER station to the LER one, not counting the 60° already negotiated, as the Clones line entered the station. Because of the curve's severity there was a five miles per hour restriction over it. There is some

evidence that the DER was allowed to use the LER station until their own was completed. Shortly after the LER line was leased, Lord Erne (a major shareholder in the LER) said in March 1860 that he wanted trains from Omagh "to stop only at the Dundalk station". The LER station closed soon afterwards and in later years the 'Derry cattle beach' was the only surviving relic of the old station.

From 1860 the Dundalk-Enniskillen-Derry line was operated as one concern, a main line of 121½ miles. In view of its increased responsibilities, the name of the company was changed on 7 July 1862 to the Irish North Western Railway. Although this name only lasted until the formation of the GNR in 1876, the route through Fermanagh was always referred to by railwaymen as 'The Irish North'.

The Belfast connection

The 'Irish North' in 1860 offered Fermanagh residents easy access to both Derry and Dublin (then the capital of the whole island), but as yet the 'Irish North' had connections only at its extremities. To get from Enniskillen to Belfast by rail involved a 62 mile journey to Dundalk and a further 58 miles via the Dublin and Belfast Junction Railway (DBJR) and the Ulster Railway. The Ulster Railway from Belfast had reached Armagh in 1848 and Monaghan in 1858, so a more sensible route from Enniskillen to Belfast, at this time, was 22 miles by rail Enniskillen to Clones (which was not yet a junction), 12 miles by road Clones to Monaghan and 53 miles by rail Monaghan to Belfast.

However the Ulster Railway had plans to provide connections to the 'Irish North' at both Clones and Omagh. First to come was the Omagh connection. The Portadown and Dungannon Junction Railway (worked by the UR) opened in 1858 and, renaming itself the Portadown, Dungannon and Omagh Junction Railway, extended to Omagh in September 1861. From that point Omagh became the most sensible route from Enniskillen to Belfast. Six months later Clones also became a junction when the Clones and Cavan Extension Railway opened on 7 April 1862. This line was financed by four companies (Dublin and Drogheda Railway, DBJR, UR and INWR) but was worked by the INWR (strictly speaking still called the DER until July 1862). The Cavan line made a head-on connection with the Midland Great Western Railway's Cavan branch, thus providing an alternative route to Dublin. Finally, on 2 March 1863, the Ulster Railway opened through to Clones, providing a second connection to Belfast and turning Clones into a railway crossroads. At Clones, the UR built its own engine shed and goods yard, which were just off Rosslea Street, adjacent to the junction with the Dundalk line. The INWR shed was on the site of the later GNR roundhouse shed which replaced both sheds in 1925.

The Bundoran branch

Around 1860 plans were being formulated to build a railway through north Fermanagh to Bundoran. In July 1861 the Enniskillen and Bundoran Railway was incorporated with powers to build a 35 mile line from the LER near Lowtherstown (as Irvinestown was then called) to Bundoran. A year later, in June 1862, this scheme was modified to include an extension to Sligo (23 miles further on) and the company was renamed the Enniskillen, Bundoran and Sligo Railway (EBSR). If this had been built in its entirety, it is much less likely than the Sligo Leitrim line would have been built later. At Sligo the EBSR would have linked up with the north western terminus of the MGWR. The INWR had a significant financial stake in the EBSR and worked the Bundoran line from its opening on 13 June 1866. The plan to extend to Sligo never came to anything and was finally killed off by the opening of the SLNCR in 1881. The Bundoran line had a junction with the INWR at a point between Ballinamallard and Trillick, close to what is now the village of Kilskeery. The junction was initially known as Lowtherstown Road. As Bundoran increased in importance as a holiday resort, the junction was renamed Bundoran Junction, and was one of only a few triangular junctions in Ireland, the layout providing for through running to Bundoran from both Enniskillen and Omagh. Lowtherstown was owned by the D'Arcy Irvines and, shortly after the railway was built, they had its name changed to Irvinestown. Despite the extensive mileage of railway which it now operated, the INWR suffered from the sparse population and comparative poverty in the area that it served. There was little or no industry except in Dundalk and Derry and, in mid-Victorian times, few people had money to spare for leisure travel. The INWR was unable to pay any dividends to its shareholders after 1862. From 1874 the line began to make a loss. It was with some relief that the proprietors of the INWR welcomed the formation of the GNR in 1876.

The Great Northern Railway (Ireland)

The impetus for the creation of the Great Northern Railway stemmed from the fact that the line between Belfast and Dublin was operated by three different companies – the Dublin and Drogheda Railway, the Dublin and Belfast Junction Railway (Drogheda to Portadown) and the Ulster Railway (Portadown to Belfast). Amalgamation would reduce journey times and bring greater efficiency and thus greater profit. It also seemed sensible to bring the INWR into any such amalgamation, to develop traffic between west Ulster

The contractors who built the Bundoran branch, Brassey and Field, used two Manning Wardle 0-6-0 saddle tanks named *Rutland* and *Malvern* to haul the construction trains. This is *Malvern*, which had been built in 1860, in a rare photograph taken during the building of the Worcester to Hereford line. In 1864, sister engine *Rutland* was shipped by boat from Enniskillen to Castlecaldwell where it fell into the Lake but was recovered. Both engines survived and worked at Dundalk until 1892.

Courtesy Industrial Locomotive Society, Frank Jones Collection

and Dublin and Belfast. However the main obstacle was that the highly profitable Ulster Railway valued its independence too much and the equally profitable DDR did not want to proceed without it. An attempt in 1868 failed to reach agreement but, in the end, the DDR decided to proceed anyway. On 1 March 1875 it amalgamated with the DBJR to form the Northern Railway which, on 1 January 1876, was joined by the INWR. The weaker companies had to join on less favourable terms and the loss-making INWR found its shares devalued from £30 to £5 in the process. These moves made the UR look more seriously at amalgamation and so it was that on 1 April 1876 it joined the new combine, the enlarged company adopting the title Great Northern Railway (Ireland). The word 'Ireland' was added to distinguish the company from the already established Great Northern Railway in England.

The creation of the GNR had little immediate impact in Fermanagh, as all the existing railways there were operated by one company in any case. However, gradually the new organisation made itself felt with new locomotives and rolling stock and the loss-making lines in Fermanagh were to some extent subsidised by profit from the other lines. The GNR certainly developed traffic on the Bundoran line, which it purchased from the EBSR in 1897. In 1899 it bought and modernised an hotel in Bundoran, renaming it the Great Northern Hotel.

The Sligo Leitrim

In 1877 a new railway began to become part of the railway scene in Fermanagh. A link between Enniskillen and Sligo had long been on the cards. At one time the LER had considered extending to Sligo, and of course the EBSR had similar plans. Sligo itself had been reached from Dublin by the Midland Great Western Railway in December 1862. The impetus for building the Sligo Leitrim and Northern Counties Railway came from the landowners and prosperous farmers of Sligo and Leitrim. In the late nineteenth century there was a growing trade in the export of live cattle from Ireland to England to provide beef, and the farmers of this region needed a railway to transport cattle to the docks at Dublin, Belfast and Derry. The 42 mile line was authorised by Act of Parliament in 1875 and its promoters planned a route from Enniskillen (where there was a junction with the GNR) via Florencecourt, Belcoo, Manorhamilton and Dromahair to a junction with the MGWR near Collooney

some five miles from Sligo (though with running rights into Sligo).

Construction began in 1877 at the Enniskillen end, the first section – from Enniskillen to Belcoo – opening to goods traffic on 12 February 1879, and to passengers on 18 March. The line was extended by degrees to Glenfarne (1 January 1880), Manorhamilton (1 December 1880) and Collooney (1 September 1881). The junction with the MGWR at Collooney was not finally completed until 7 November 1882, after which through running between Enniskillen and Sligo became possible.

The SLNCR was never a prosperous company and ran its line very much on a shoestring. Its staple traffic was live cattle and it certainly carried far more bovine than human passengers. The opening of the SLNCR greatly increased the amount of traffic from Enniskillen on the GNR. Enniskillen became a staging post for the forwarding of live cattle to Derry and Belfast from the farms of Leitrim, Sligo and even further afield. All this kept the 'Sligo yard' at Enniskillen very busy with constant shunting and transfer of cattle wagons. The SLNCR locomotives were a common sight in Enniskillen and added to the rich variety of locomotives to be seen.

Unusually, if not uniquely, SLNCR locomotives carried names but not numbers, a practice more common on early Victorian railways or on industrial systems. After the withdrawal of the last ex-GNR 0-6-0 tender locomotives in 1949, all the locomotives were 0-6-4Ts, an unusual wheel arrangement. There were three varieties of these – Fermanagh, Leitrim, Lurganboy, Lissadell and Hazlewood dating from 1882-99, Sir Henry, Enniskillen and Lough Gill dating from 1904-17, and Lough Melvin and Lough Erne from 1949 (though not delivered until 1951 as the company could not pay for them, and eventually resorted to a hire purchase deal). Like other lines operating on shoe-string finances, the SLNCR was one of the first to experiment with diesel traction for passenger traffic. From 1935 a railbus was operated and a second added in 1938. These handled all the passenger traffic except a daily mixed steam train. In 1947 the SLNCR purchased a much more substantial articulated diesel railcar from Walkers of Wigan which, with one railbus, operated the passenger service until closure. This railcar still exists and there are plans to have it returned to operational condition.

The Clogher Valley Railway

The last railway to be built in Fermanagh was the Clogher Valley Railway, the only narrow gauge line to operate in the county. It was built to serve the prosperous mixed farming area of the Clogher Valley and ran through a scenic and attractive hinterland. To visitors, the term 'Clogher Valley' seems a bit of a misnomer as it is not that evidently a valley. However, to the north is a range of low mountains which includes Cloghtogle, Topped, Brougher, Ballyness, Knockmany and Slievemore, whilst some four or five miles to the south is another range which includes Slieve Beagh, Essrawer and Culla More. Between these two ranges is the valley shared by the Colebrook River flowing south west

and the Blackwater, flowing north east. The Clogher Valley contains no major towns, but rather a string of small ones. From west to east these are Brookeborough, Fivemiletown, Clogher, Augher and Ballygawley. The purpose of the railway was to link both ends of the valley to the GNR system in a 37 mile line which had no branches. Starting at Maguiresbridge (on the Enniskillen to Clones line) it went to Brookeborough and hence the other villages listed above, leaving the valley at Ballygawley to climb steeply south towards Aughnacloy and Caledon, before rejoining the GNR at Tynan, on the Clones to Portadown line.

The Clogher Valley Railway was essentially a 3'0" gauge roadside steam tramway. It was incorporated by Act of Council in May 1884, under the terms of the Tramway and Public Companies Act of 1883, which allowed any losses incurred in operating the tramway to be made good by the local ratepayers under 'baronial guarantee'. Initially known as the Clogher Valley Tramway, the line was opened on 2 May 1887. Seven years later, in 1894, the company renamed itself the Clogher Valley Railway, the new name carrying more

Above: The Clogher Valley Railway railcar at Aughnacloy on Friday 25 June 1937, in company with brake van No 5. The railcar was numbered 'No 1' and could seat 28. It was built by Walker Bros of Wigan in December 1932 and had a Gardner six-cylinder 6LZ diesel engine. For economy, the rear bogie was second hand from a CVR coach!

HC Casserley, courtesy RM Casserley

Right: 'The Unit', otherwise known as 'No 2'. The lorry body was removable, so it could double as a spare power unit for the railcar. Note the crude repair to the side sheet over the wheels, following an argument with Brookeborough level crossing gates!

Real Photographs Ltd

dignity, it appeared, than 'tramway'. At Maguiresbridge, where the line crossed the road to Lisnaskea, pedestrians waiting at the crossing sometimes asked "When's the tram coming?" to which the crossing keeper would reply irritably, "It's not a tram, it's a train!"

Although the railway followed the public road for most of its length, it had its own trackbed in several places where steep gradients had to be avoided. The most significant of these was a three mile stretch near Maguiresbridge, over what was known locally as 'the Commons', but there were other stretches at Clogher and on either side of Aughnacloy. These perhaps justified the title 'railway' though, on the other hand, at Fivemiletown, Augher and Caledon the CVR trains went along the centre of the main street, a fact which in the 1930s led to congestion and blockages as the number of cars grew.

The majority of passenger trains consisted of a bogie carriage and brake van, hauled by a small tramway type 0-4-2T with side skirts and cow-catcher, running cab first. Some trains ran only between Tynan and Fivemiletown, the Fermanagh end of the line attracting much less traffic. Like the SLNCR, the CVR went over to diesel traction in the 1930s. In 1932 it acquired a Gardner-engined articulated railcar, seating 28, the first of its kind in these islands, if not in the world. The CVR also purchased an additional unit, termed a diesel 'tractor' with no passenger portion. This unit was fitted with a lorry type body, rather like a five plank wagon. It sometimes ran in passenger service hauling a standard coach and brake van. When the line closed in 1941 the County Donegal Railway acquired the railcar, which became No 10 in their fleet. In this form it is now preserved at the Ulster Folk and Transport Museum, Cultra.

The Clogher Valley Railway was largely a Tyrone railway. Only the first eight miles or so were in Fermanagh, and, apart from Maguiresbridge, the only stations in Fermanagh were Brookeborough and Colebrook, the latter station serving Colebrook Estate, owned by Lord Brookborough. After crossing the county boundary into Tyrone near Fivemiletown, the railway remained in Tyrone, apart from the last mile or so, when it crossed into Co Armagh to terminate at Tynan. Between Ballygawley and Tynan it virtually hugged the border with Co Monaghan, but at no time crossed into it, thus avoiding the need for customs stops after partition in 1921.

The CVR stations were very distinctive, consisting of single storey red brick buildings, one end of which usually had a short upper storey. They were ornamented with attractive barge boards and coping tiles, and all still survive in some form or other. Brookeborough station has recently been restored and extended as a cross-community project, with part of the building used by a play group. The platform has been reflagged and a length of track is to be laid. Rather oddly the CVR had no buildings at either Maguiresbridge or Tynan, the GNR facilities there being used by passengers. The company headquarters and workshop facilities were at Aughnacloy, near the eastern end of the line.

Into the Twentieth Century

In terms of construction, the Fermanagh railway map was complete by 1887 and for the next forty years or so the railways had no significant rivals for the provision of transport. Even when motor cars began to appear after 1900, there were relatively few in Fermanagh, apart from those owned by doctors and the wealthy. The state of the roads and the distance to Belfast and Dublin meant that the few cars which existed were largely used for local journeys. The GNR trains used in Fermanagh gradually modernised. In 1876, when the GNR was formed, the passenger trains were made up of a mixture of four and six-wheel carriages, hauled by 2-4-0 locomotives, with some 2-2-2s and the last of the old LER light 2-2-0WTs. By the early 1900s most trains consisted of six-wheelers, and after the First World War, bogie carriages began to appear. By the late 1920s the majority of trains had corridor coaches. The Fermanagh lines were regarded as secondary routes by the GNR management, so the carriages used on them were ones that had been built for the main lines 15-20 years earlier. For example, carriages used on main line expresses in 1900-1905, might find their way to Fermanagh in 1915-25.

In contrast, the steep grades on some of the 'Irish North' lines led to specific engines being designed for them. The first 4-4-0 locomotives built for the GNR, in 1885, were designed for the 'Irish North', and had 5'7" driving wheels. All subsequent GNR passenger tender locomotives were 4-4-0s, but most of them had 6'7" wheels. Other engines designed with the 'Irish North' in mind were the P5'6" class in 1892-5 (added to in 1904-5) and the U class, introduced in 1915, which had 5'9" wheels and were known as the 'Irish

North engines'. In contrast to the small passenger engines used, the Fermanagh lines of the GNR carried heavy goods traffic and justified the use of some of the largest goods engines the company possessed. These included engines in power categories 'C' an 'D'.

Between the Wars

The period immediately before the First World War can justifiably be described as the heyday of railways all over the British Isles. After the war the financial position of Irish railways deteriorated considerably. Some of the reasons for this were shared by railways elsewhere. The introduction of the eight hour day in 1919 led to rising wage costs, as hours over the eight had to be paid at overtime rates. Trade Union power resulted in a rise in the level of wages generally. This was no bad thing if you were a railway worker, but affected the ability of the railways to remain profitable. Ireland had a lower density of traffic than most English railways, which made it particularly difficult to cover operating costs. On the GNR the reality was that the main Belfast-Dublin line was profitable and largely subsidised less economic lines such as those in Fermanagh.

The GNR was further affected by the partition of Ireland in 1921. The creation of Northern Ireland and the Irish Free State affected three lines which each crossed the new international border only once – the SLNCR, the Londonderry and Lough Swilly Railway, and the Dundalk, Newry and Greenore Railway, and one which crossed it twice – the County Donegal Railway. None were disadvantaged like the GNR which crossed the new international border no fewer than 15 times, 10 of these on the Fermanagh border alone. Six of the crossings were between Clones and Cavan but, since there were no stations north of the border on this line, they were disregarded and the line operated as if it were entirely within the Irish Free State. Much more significant was the crossing on the Clones-Enniskillen line which required customs examination at Clones (IFS) and Newtownbutler (NI). Similarly the Bundoran branch crossed into Co Donegal briefly at Pettigo, returning to Fermanagh as far as Belleek, after which it again entered the Free State. There were therefore customs stops at Kesh (NI), Pettigo (IFS), Belleek (NI) and Ballyshannon (IFS). This greatly added to journey times. Travellers between Portadown and Fermanagh faced additional customs stops at Tynan (NI) and Glaslough (IFS) on the Portadown-Clones line.

Apart from the inconvenience to travellers, the border affected the pattern of freight traffic in the long term. Traffic north of the border gradually tended to gravitate towards Belfast and south of the border towards Dublin. Towns on the border itself were affected by changing shopping patterns. Clones, once a thriving town commercially, declined in later years to the advantage of Cavan and Monaghan, and Lisnaskea – a mere village in the 1950s – is now bigger than Clones.

The partition of Ireland also had an impact on the way railway transport was organised. In Britain the government forced the various railway companies to amalgamate into four large companies (the Grouping) in 1923. This was mirrored in the Irish Free State when all railways exclusively within the Free State were amalgamated into the Great Southern Railways in 1925. This amalgamation did not involve the five companies which had lines crossing the border. Within Northern Ireland there was no parallel move, as the only two railways of any significance, which did not cross the border, were the Northern Counties Committee (owned by the LMS in Britain) and the Belfast and County Down Railway. There was little point in amalgamating just these two, since the GNR operated as big a mileage in the North as both put together. The attitude of the Northern Unionist government was not very favourable to the GNR. With its headquarters and management in a 'rival' state, the GNR was viewed with some suspicion, if not hostility.

Enter the Buses

Into this volatile situation a further complication appeared in the 1920s in the shape of bus competition. In looking at this we will focus on Fermanagh, but the problem was universal, affecting all railway companies. The first bus operator in Fermanagh was Hezekiah Appleby who, in February 1926, formed the 'Central Omnibus Company' in direct competition with the Sligo Leitrim. He ran a twice daily bus between Enniskillen and Sligo, charging 5/= (25p) single and 7/6 (37.5p) return. Appleby was actually married to a cousin of my mother's, Jenny Connolly. He was known as 'Hez' for short and was a fun-loving character. In 1929 he started a second route, this time from Enniskillen to Bundoran by Belcoo. This ran only in the summer months, and aimed to siphon off some of the GNR's Bundoran branch traffic. A second operator appeared in 1926 when Captain Merrilies and his son in law William Clarke began an Enniskillen to Derrygonnelly service, adding a route to Derrylin in 1927. These did not directly compete with train services. By 1927 Clarke had taken over the operation and, as Clarke's Blue Bus Services, extended to Fivemiletown and Rosslea and even began a service to Lough Derg for the local pilgrims. This was the main destination of the GNR's 'Bundoran Express' which brought pilgrims, mainly from the Irish Free State.

In 1927 a potentially much more serious competitor entered the field when the largest bus company in Ulster, the newly formed 'Belfast Omnibus Company' (BOC), began a Belfast to Enniskillen service routed through the Clogher Valley. The service had three trips daily and undercut the GNR fare. However, at 4 hours 15 mins for the 93 mile trip, it took considerably longer than the train, so passengers travelled on it if cost was more significant than speed or comfort. The BOC in fact posed more of a threat to the CVR against which it could also compete on speed. Indeed, it opened a bus depot in Fivemiletown. The other early bus operators in Fermanagh can be summarised as follows:

Hard Rocks Motor Service, Lisbellaw, owned by E W McCreary. It operated two buses on an Enniskillen-Tempo service. It also worked to Bundoran in the summer. McCreary was bought out by Clarke in 1933. Fleetwing Bus Service, Omagh, owned by W A Simpson. It ran a service between Omagh and Enniskillen from November 1927, competing with the GNR. By 1934 there were four trips daily, two via Trillick and two via Irvinestown. Dreadnought Motor Service, Omagh, owned by C H Donaghy. It began to compete with Simpson in 1928, but was bought out by the GNR in 1931. Phair Brothers of Belturbet (Co Cavan) ran a service to Enniskillen, via Swanlinbar, twice daily. They too were bought out by the GNR. W E White, in 1928-9, operated a bus from Enniskillen to Longford, via Swanlinbar, with two trips daily. His operation ended abruptly in August 1929 when his bus was wrecked in an accident.

The most enduring of the early operators was Maurice Cassidy, a Fermanagh man who had been a Glasgow tram conductor and a tram driver in New York before coming home in 1928 and setting up the 'Erne Bus Service' in 1929. His familiar brown and cream buses were to be a feature of Fermanagh's roads up to the early 1960s. Cassidy's

main routes were Enniskillen-Clones (five workings), and Enniskillen-Belleek-Bundoran, but he also worked to Rosslea and ran as far afield as Clones-Cavan and Clones-Cootehill. By the mid-1930s he had five buses, (see pages 154-157).

The Northern Ireland Road Transport Board

While all this competition was developing, the Northern Ireland government was coming under strong pressure, particularly from the railways, to bring some order and regulation to the chaos. The railways saw potential in buses as feeders to the railways, but did not want them duplicating their services. The GNR, NCC and BCDR had all adopted a policy of buying out their competitors, Donaghy and Phair Bros being cases in point.

Parallel to the development of bus services, private operators began to purchase lorries and compete with the railways for goods traffic. They managed quite often to capture the more profitable elements of the freight business, leaving the bulkier and less economic traffic to the trains. By 1934 it was estimated that in Northern Ireland more goods were being carried by road than by rail.

In 1934, the Northern Ireland government set up a committee of inquiry into road and rail transport chaired by Sir Felix Pole, a retired manager of the Great Western Railway in Britain. As a result of Pole's report, the Road and Rail Traffic Act (NI) 1935 was passed. This implemented the report's main recommendation by setting up the Northern Ireland Road Transport Board (NIRTB), which was given powers to establish a monopoly for the operation of all bus and road freight services within Northern Ireland. Over the next year or so all private operators operating entirely within Northern Ireland were obliged to sell out to the NIRTB. This included the Omagh based Fleetwing Bus Service, and Clarke's Blue Bus Services, as well as the BOC, which was the core of the new company. Those operators with cross-border routes had to relinquish the Northern Ireland portion of their routes. Thus Hez Appleby had to give up two of his four buses in 1937, and confine himself to the Sligo-Blacklion part of his route. In 1945 Appleby sold his remaining two buses to the SLNCR (see pages 152-3). One exception was that the Erne Bus Service managed to retain its independence, mainly due to the extent of its cross-border operations.

The railways, which by this time were extensive bus and

lorry operators in their own right, had to give up those portions of their fleets which operated within Northern Ireland. The GNR lost 50 of its 171 buses and 126 of its 153 lorries. The NCC and BCDR, being entirely within Northern Ireland, lost their entire fleets. The GNR was able to retain some services which originated in the Free State but terminated north of the border. The companies were compensated with NIRTB shares, but the promised coordination of road and rail was not fulfilled. By the late 1930s the railways in Fermanagh were facing competition from a more efficient and ruthless NIRTB, which now had a major depot in Enniskillen. Worse still, from the railways' point of view, the success of the NIRTB had the effect of convincing the Northern Ireland government that buses and lorries provided a cheap and efficient solution to the province's public transport needs. This resulted in a mind set which, after the war, was unwilling to invest public money in the railways and preferred instead to close them.

Lacking the short branch lines which featured in some areas, the Fermanagh railways avoided any actual closures until 1957, but the CVR, vulnerable to bus competition because of its slow speed, closed for good on 31 December 1941, even its diesel railcar being unable to save it.

The War Years

By 1939, many railways, but particularly the GNR, were facing a bleak future and closures seemed inevitable. Traffic was declining, costs were rising and, as private companies, the railways were not subsidised in any way. Long term prospects were poor as car ownership was rising and roads improving (at public expense) to the advantage of buses and other road users. From this perspective the outbreak of war saved the railways from imminent crisis. Petrol rationing drove private transport off the roads, whilst the needs of war vastly increased traffic on the railways and returned them to profitability. On the GNR the number of passengers carried annually increased from 5 million in 1939 to nearly 11 million by 1944. Goods tonnage increased from about ¾ million tons in 1939 to 1¾ million tons in 1944. Fermanagh played a significant part in the war with the big flying boat base at Castle Archdale and other air bases at St Angelo and Killadeas. These and other military movements required regular troop trains to Fermanagh, routed via Omagh (to avoid violating the Free State's neutrality). The demand for

fresh food for Britain benefited not only Fermanagh farmers, but also those south of the border who dispatched their produce by the Sligo Leitrim, as well as the GNR.

The war had some interesting effects on the cross-border trains of the GNR. The UK during the war operated on double summer time to maximise daylight hours for production, whilst the Free State used ordinary summer time. The Bundoran branch timetable had to show British time at the Fermanagh stations, but Free State time at Pettigo, Ballyshannon and Bundoran. This gave the impression that Down trains were taking 45 minutes from Bundoran Junction to Bundoran whilst the Up trains took 2 hours 45 minutes! A train could leave Kesh at 8.31pm and arrive at Pettigo at 7.41pm!

Before leaving the war years, I must tell a story which I heard from an old soldier who had served in the British Army of the Rhine in the late 1940s. It is a well known fact that Nazi Germany had plans in 1940 to invade Ireland, including Northern Ireland. When the soldier arrived in Germany in 1946, his unit were issued with maps to help them find their way about. These were printed on the back of maps originally issued to the German army. His turned out to be a German map of Ulster, showing the proposed route for an invasion. The plan appeared to involve landing at Ballyshannon and approaching Belfast from the west. Rail transport for soldiers and tanks was a vital part of this plan, but whatever spies the Germans used clearly did not penetrate Fermanagh or Tyrone, because the map showed the Clogher Valley Railway as a major rail artery across south Ulster. The image of the Wehrmacht arriving at Maguiresbridge to requisition ten troop trains and use of the CVR tank transporters is an amusing one!

After the War 1945-53

The end of the Second World War in 1945 did not bring an immediate return to the prewar financial crisis. Although rather run down, the railways were in a strong position because of continued petrol rationing and the difficulty in obtaining new cars, which persisted until about 1950. Profit made during the war allowed the GNR to purchase 15 new steam locomotives in 1947-8. Five of these were a new batch of U class 4-4-0s, Nos 201-205, which were finished in sky blue livery and named *Meath*, *Louth*, *Armagh*, *Antrim* and *Down* respectively. They were unusual in having rectangular

GNR No 203 *Armagh,* one of the five new U class 4-4-0s built by Beyer Peacock in 1948 and, oddly, the least photographed of this class.

Real Photographs Ltd

windows in the cab sides instead of the usual curved cut outs. They were regulars on the Bundoran Express and other Fermanagh trains. They were also the first blue engines in Fermanagh, and the first named GNR engines in Fermanagh since the period of the First World War. They were soon complemented by the 1915 batch (196-200) which were painted blue as they went through the works and also given names – *Lough Gill, Lough Neagh, Lough Swilly, Lough Derg* and *Lough Melvin*. These ten engines, though not confined to Fermanagh, added much needed colour to the trains of the county over the next ten years. In 1950 the GNR also purchased ten three-coach diesel trains which were the first of their type in either Britain or Ireland. Built by Park Royal and using AEC engines, each train had two power cars with an unpowered intermediate. One of the new trains was used to operate a direct Belfast-Enniskillen diesel service, via Clones, from 1953.

The UTA

Meanwhile railways in general were facing a new phase of reorganisation. In Britain the 'big four' were nationalised in 1948 to create British Railways. This was mirrored in the Irish Free State by the creation of Córas Iompair Éireann in 1945 and its nationalisation three years later. CIE controlled all rail and road transport, including Dublin buses and trams. Following this trend, the Northern Ireland government, in 1948, created the Ulster Transport Authority and brought the BCDR, NCC and NIRTB (though not Belfast Corporation Transport) all under one management. However this left the GNR and the other four cross-border railways out in the cold with an uncertain future.

The UTA reflected the government's attitude towards railways by pruning their railway network drastically in 1950. The remaining lines were dieselised fairly cheaply in the 1950s by rebuilding existing coaches as diesel railcars, with a minimum of new build. In contrast, the 1950s saw considerable investment in new buses with front entrances and in road improvements.

The Great Northern Railway Board

Meanwhile the GNR struggled on as an independent company with no prospect of remaining profitable and no resources to modernise. The crisis point was reached in late 1950, after the company had made a loss over the previous financial year. On 6 January 1951 the GNR announced its intention to close the system in mid-February 1952 but, on the 8th, served one week's notice on its employees. Faced with the sudden and complete loss of all rail services in the Great Northern's area, the two governments stepped in to negotiate with the company.

The outcome was that, after meeting the company's current deficits as an interim measure, the governments of Northern Ireland and the Irish Republic purchased the GNR for £4.5M, as from 1 October 1953, each paying half the cost. This created the unique situation of the GNR being effectively nationalised, but owned by two separate states. To administer the company, a board was created called the Great Northern Railway Board, with ten members – five nominated by the Republic's Minister for Industry and Commerce and five by the Northern Minister for Commerce. The chairmanship was rotated annually. This board was responsible for decisions about investment in rolling stock and infrastructure as well as actual operation of the line. It was also charged with meeting operating costs out of revenue as soon as possible. Writing from the vantage point of an age when there is much discussion about the need for cross-border bodies, it is interesting to look at the operation of a cross-border body that existed forty-five years ago!

To the general public there was no visible change, especially as the day to day running of the trains remained with the GNR management. Only the appearance of the word 'Board' in place of 'Ireland' in the company crest and GNRB on cap badges betrayed the new ownership. The main problem faced by the Board was that to meet operating costs out of revenue there had to be investment in new equipment, but that investment had to be agreed and financed by the two governments. In sharing the purchase of the GNR equally the Northern Ireland government got the better part of the bargain, in that more than 50% of the GNR mileage lay within Northern Ireland, but the downside was that it also had to pay 50% of any investment or losses.

Instinctively the Northern Ireland government wanted rid of the GNR as soon as possible. In a period when the two governments rarely communicated with each other about anything, it resented having to cooperate with the Irish Republic over transport policy. The Board wanted to invest over £500,000 in new diesel trains, but it took until mid-1955 before this was approved, and another two years

before the first of the new trains was ready. By that time it was just too late to save Fermanagh's railways. Further proposals for new investment met a wall of procrastination and indifference. Essentially the problem stemmed from the differing attitudes of the two governments to transport. The government of the Irish Republic saw railways as an essential part of future transport needs and wanted to invest and save the railways. The Northern Ireland government saw the GNR as an albatross and wanted to save money by replacing trains with buses, except for the Belfast-Dublin main line.

Closure Proposals

Whilst the legislation setting up the GNRB required joint decisions on matters of investment, it also allowed either minister to make unilateral decisions affecting the lines within his specific jurisdiction. Thus the GNR operating management were hostages to fortune after 1953. Decisions about the future of the GNR system could be made without reference to them. This situation allowed the Northern Ireland government to force the closure of certain branch lines inside Northern Ireland in 1955-56 (Banbridge-Scarva, Banbridge-Newcastle, Banbridge-Knockmore Junction, and the Cookstown branch). Fermanagh was a more difficult proposition as most of its routes were cross-border, and closure ought therefore to have required a joint decision by the two governments. It came as quite a shock therefore when the Northern Ireland government proposed in 1956 that it was going to close the lines from Omagh to Newtownbutler, Portadown to Tynan and Bundoran Junction to Belleek. This proposal was all the more surprising for the people of Fermanagh in that the Prime Minister of Northern Ireland at this time, Lord Brookeborough, was a Fermanagh man.

The proposed closures involved 97¼ route miles, but their knock-on effects would be catastrophic. If the GNR Fermanagh lines closed, the SLNCR, already near the end of its financial resources, would be forced to close – a further 42¾ miles. Similarly the Belleek-Bundoran section could not survive in isolation, likewise Tynan to Monaghan and Newtownbutler to Clones could not remain open – another 22½ miles. It was also unlikely that the GNRB could sustain services on the Cavan-Monaghan and Clones-Dundalk sections once their connections had gone, ultimately affecting yet another 77½ miles. All told therefore these closures were going to eliminate 240 miles of railway line, the largest closures in one sweep up to that time in Ireland.

At meetings of the GNR Board there was deadlock, with the Northern Ireland Chairman recommending complete closure and his counterpart recommending continued financial support. On 5 June 1957 the Northern Ireland government unilaterally told the GNRB that all services on the disputed lines within Northern Ireland were to end on 30 September. Meanwhile the Operating and Civil Engineering departments carried on as if this was not really going to happen. Throughout the summer of 1957, extensive ballasting and relaying was carried out on the Bundoran branch and elsewhere, pointless work if the line was about to close.

The Enniskillen-Belfast Diesel Express

In the Spring of 1957, the first of the long-awaited second batch of eight new diesel trains was almost ready. These were built at Dundalk but this time with BUT engines and became known as the BUT railcars. On 19 June the first eight-coach train entered service on the Belfast based 'Enterprise' Belfast-Dublin express. This train had four power cars (701-704) and four non-powered cars. The next train was to be of six cars and was intended for the Belfast-Derry service. However with power car 705 ready but idle, the GNR hit on the idea of using it on a service to Enniskillen to demonstrate the potential of the new trains. Thus it was that on 22 July 1957 a new fast Enniskillen-Belfast service was introduced. The train consisted of power car 705 plus class D3 brake second coach 396, together seating a maximum of 96. The train left Enniskillen at 8.50am, stopped briefly at Bundoran Junction to connect with the 7.35am ex-Bundoran, and reached Omagh at 9.35am. After running round its coach,

it left Omagh at 9.45am and, stopping only at Carrickmore to cross a down train, reached Belfast at 11.20am, thus cutting 65 minutes off the usual schedule.

The return trip left Belfast at 7.00pm and ran non stop to Omagh (8.26pm) where it met the 7.00pm from Derry. It left Omagh at 8.36pm and ran non-stop to Enniskillen arriving at 9.05pm. With 2 hours 5 minutes for the whole trip, this was a remarkably fast service. Two photographs of this rare working are reproduced. The train gave a foretaste of how the new trains could have transformed services on the Fermanagh lines if the closures had not been pushed through so soon. The matter was debated in the Northern Ireland Senate, where the new service was praised for its speed and comfort. Senator O'Hare urged the government to grant a two year suspension of the closure and claimed that fifty people had used the service when he travelled. However the debate centred less on the potential of the new service than on the fact that, in the photograph of the train in that morning's Northern Whig, the Government's Lord Lt Col Gordon could only see twelve passengers! Be that as it may, the train was an undoubted success and, in the last week of the service, Enniskillen sold 257 day return to Belfast tickets for this train.

The Enniskillen-Belfast express approaching Bundoran Junction in August 1957.

NC Simmons, Photos from the Fifties

The express diesel just north of Portadown, at Cumo level crossing. Notice that the trailer is now facing the opposite way after changing direction at Omagh.

Colin Hogg

A Mystery

There is another intriguing aspect to the circumstances surrounding the closure. It is perhaps not fully realised that most of the passengers on the 'Bundoran Express' travelled, not to Bundoran, but to Pettigo. Pettigo was the railhead for a pilgrimage to Lough Derg, a few miles away, buses being used for the last part of the journey. An island in Lough Derg was the renowned site of St Patrick's Purgatory, and was the oldest religious site in Ireland. The pilgrims who used the 'Bundoran Express' mostly came from the Republic of Ireland, from Dublin, Drogheda, Dundalk, Clones, etc, and the train ran non-stop through Northern Ireland to avoid customs delays. This train ran during the pilgrimage season (1 June–15 August) and was very important to the people of the South.

The late Tom McDevette MBE told me that on one occasion in 1957 he was at Bundoran Junction and spoke to a signalman there. Commenting on the pending closure he said "Isn't it dreadful about the railway going to close," to which the signalman replied, "Sure it's not going to close. Lot of nonsense. If it was going to close why would they be fixing the track up? Anyway isn't the Southern Government going to pay them to keep it open so that the 'Pilgrim train' can run?" (This may not be the exact conversation, but certainly the gist of it.) Tom put this down to the man being misinformed but, in more recent years, he was talking to a CIE official in Dublin and mentioned this incident. To his surprise the man said "There might be something in that because in the archives at Connolly Station (the old Amiens St terminus of the GNR) there is a file of correspondence between the Southern and Northern governments over that very subject." It would be intriguing to know more about this because, if it is true, the whole story of the closures has not yet been told and it may be that the government of the Irish Republic was prepared to go to remarkable lengths to keep the GNR open, and the Northern Ireland government equally determined to close it.

FERMANAGH'S RAILWAYS IN PICTURES

Charles P Friel

We begin our pictorial coverage of Fermanagh's railways in County Monaghan, naturally enough! Clones lies very close to the south-eastern corner of Fermanagh and, before 1921, was the nearest big town for much of south Fermanagh. For the rail traveller it was often the point of access to the county and it would be highly inappropriate to omit this interesting and, occasionally, very busy junction.

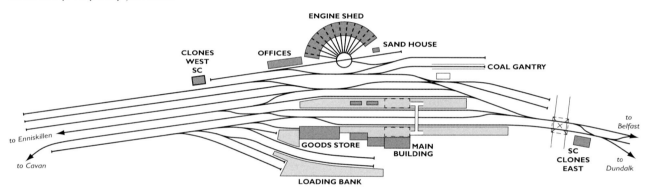

Laft: Our first photo shows a train from Dundalk arriving past Clones East signal cabin and making its way into the back of the island platform. The locomotive is 1915 built U class 4-4-0 No 200 *Lough Melvin,* here in the GNR's passenger livery of lined blue. The three coaches are led by a J4 brake composite and, typical of the line, there is a long tail of vans at the back of the train. The first two are 20 ton capacity P vans. Their working was strictly rostered and we may guess that this is the 10.45am from Dundalk.

Photographer unknown

Opposite top: Our second view of Clones is from the same vantage point as the first but now looking west through the passenger station where the Up 'Bundoran Express' is waiting to leave for Dundalk and Dublin. The main station building is on the left and the island platform on the right. Most GNR footbridges were closed-in affairs with a rounded roof of corrugated iron, but Clones' footbridge was quite open and flat roofed. This is 11 August 1957, a Sunday, so the time must be about 3.40pm. The locomotive is one of the 1948-built U class 4-4-0s – No 204 *Antrim*. To the extreme right is a glimpse of the roof of Clones engine shed – a partial roundhouse, built in 1924 just after Portadown's similar structure. Unlike Portadown though, Clones shed is still standing and in use. Note the six-coach rake at Platform 2.

HB Priestley, courtesy CP Friel

Opposite bottom: Looking east from platform 1, we see the shunting engine, AL class 0-6-0 No 140, resting between duties in the middle road below the footbridge and alongside the AEC diesel railcar set which has just worked the 7.45am from Belfast. The distinctive spire of the Roman Catholic church is visible in this May 1956 view.

RH Barr

Above: At the west end of platform 1 we see P6'6" class 4-4-0 No 72 with a two coach train for Cavan on Monday 18 April 1955.

HC Casserley, courtesy RM Casserley

Opposite top: SG3 class 0-6-0 No 49 pauses in the middle road with a goods train consisting mostly of 8 ton open wagons. Fifteen of these heavy goods locomotives were built in 1920-21.

HB Priestley, courtesy CP Friel

Opposite bottom: Our final view of Clones is of PP class 4-4-0 No 74 storming away with a long excursion train for Bundoran on Sunday 25 July 1954. To the left of the train is the water tower and, behind it, the coaling gantry where wagons of coal, on a siding about eight feet above the running line, fed coal to the waiting engines.

A Donaldson, courtesy WT Scott

Above: This is one of the oldest photographs in the book and was taken from an Enniskillen-bound train stopped at Newtownbutler in October 1897. The cameraman was no less than L J Watson, the GNR(I)'s chief locomotive draughtsman, who was in effect the designer of some of Ireland's most successful locomotives. He was a keen photographer and, although using glass negatives for locomotive portraits, had bought a roll-film camera in Dublin earlier that month. This view is from the first film he took with it. Newtownbutler station building was designed by W G Murray in the Gothic revival style, and is still inhabited. Note the enamelled advertisements for Tylers boots and Lifebuoy soap. If you look closely you can just see a wee boy being brought up to see the engine!

CP Friel collection

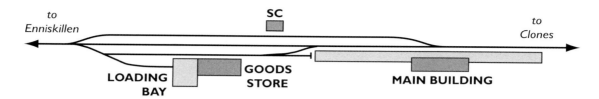

to Enniskillen — **SC** — **LOADING BAY** — **GOODS STORE** — **MAIN BUILDING** — *to Clones*

Opposite top: Another view of an Enniskillen-bound passenger train, this time dating from Monday 18 April 1955. The locomotive is 197 *Lough Neagh*, one of the 1915 batch. The loop to the left could hold up to 38 wagons and a locomotive but had no passenger platform. The grounded six-wheel carriage body on the right was Johnny McLoughlin's office.

HC Casserley, courtesy RM Casserley

Opposite bottom: Newtownbutler's signal cabin was at the west end of the station with the loop just in front of it and the running line nearer the camera. The goods yard is to the right. At the platform is UG class 0-6-0 No 147 with the 4.30pm Dundalk to Enniskillen passenger train, due here between 5.17 and 5.22pm. The date is Monday 8 July 1957.

RM Arnold

LISNASKEA

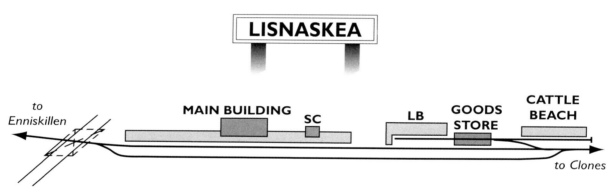

to Enniskillen — **MAIN BUILDING** — **SC** — **LB** — **GOODS STORE** — **CATTLE BEACH** — *to Clones*

Right: A group of railway men beside Lisnaskea signal cabin in 1930. From the left they are William Smith, William Symington, Oliver Ramsey, James Elliott, C Collins, the Stationmaster J Scott and his son Teddy. This view is looking towards Clones and shows the goods shed with an open wagon in the doorway. To the extreme right, beyond the Up starting signal, is the cattle loading bank – or 'beach' to railwaymen.

Photographer unknown

Opposite top: Lisnaskea, like Newtownbutler, had a passing loop (mainly for use by goods trains) but only one passenger platform. In this view we are looking west past the signal cabin to where U class 4-4-0 No 198 *Lough Swilly* has the 1.25pm from Londonderry (Foyle Road) to Dundalk (arriving here at 5.36pm, and not due in Dundalk until 7.24pm!) The date is Easter Monday, 2 April 1956. The jet of steam below the bufferbeam is a leak from the train heating which took steam, at 40 psi, into pipes beneath the seats. The level crossing gates are visible in the distance.

RM Arnold

Opposite bottom: U class 4-4-0 No 204 *Antrim* pauses at Lisnaskea with a Clones to Enniskillen passenger train in 1957. The guard and the station porter seem to be taking particular care in loading a lady's bicycle into the guards van.

A Donaldson, courtesy WT Scott

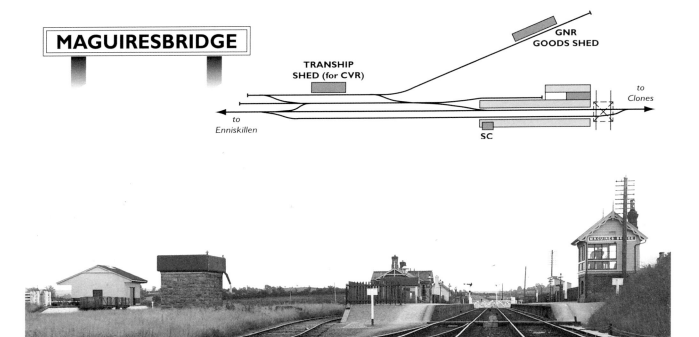

Above: Maguiresbridge looking east towards Clones. The signal cabin is to the right at the Enniskillen end of the Down platform with the white level crossing gates marking where the road crosses the line. The Down platform had a small waiting shelter but the main station building is at the Up platform in the middle of the picture. This picture dates from after the closure of the Clogher Valley Railway and shows grass where the 3ft gauge CVR tracks used to be, to the left of the main station building (see page 47). Two GNR open wagons are at the goods store to the extreme left.

Real Photographs Ltd

Above: This delightful view of Maguiresbridge is looking towards Enniskillen on Saturday 18 July 1953. Here P6'6" class 4-4-0 No 73 waits, on the right, while working the 1.15pm from Clones to Enniskillen. This was usually a railbus duty. Coming the other way is PP class 4-4-0 No 12 with a Bundoran to Belfast special composed, it seems, entirely of low elliptical roofed coaches. Note the way 'Maguiresbridge' appears on the signal cabin, where signalman Wilson Haire supervises proceedings.

RM Arnold

Above and right: These two photographs were taken at Maguiresbridge about 1920 and come to us courtesy of Mrs Patricia Dolan of Enniskillen. Mrs Dolan's paternal grandfather, Edward Smith, was the head porter here at the time and he is seated on the right of the lower picture. All of the staff have the full uniform including waistcoats and caps and there is no shortage of watch chains! Mrs Dolan's father was another Edward Smith who was a driver in Enniskillen. In the upper picture, looking towards Enniskillen, the staff were joined by some of their families and a passenger or two. In the upper picture, a flourishing goods yard has both GNR and Clogher Valley goods wagons down at the interchange shed. And the whole place is spic and span!

Both Patricia Dolan,
courtesy Headhunters' Museum

Opposite bottom: An unusual locomotive in these parts was Q class 4-4-0 No 133, seen here approaching Maguiresbridge from Enniskillen. These larger 4-4-0s did not often work south of Enniskillen but this photograph was taken on Saturday 28 September 1946, at the time when trains between Omagh and Portadown were diverted via Enniskillen. This was because the line was closed by a landslip at Gortavoy between Pomeroy and Donaghmore on 6 September. We know that the photograph was taken at 12.15pm so this is the diverted 9.25am from Londonderry to Belfast. The wagons in the sidings to the right include an engineer's six-wheel three-plank open wagon with a load of ballast is coupled to a 25-ton goods brake van, one of a batch built in Belgium just before World War One.

RM Arnold

THE CLOGHER VALLEY RAILWAY

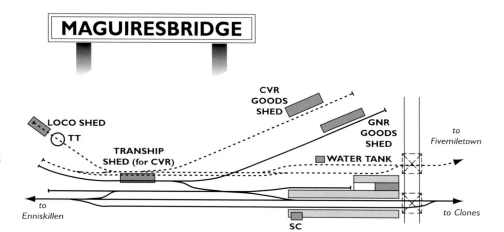

Maguiresbridge in 1937 showing the Clogher Valley lines

Above: Maguiresbridge in 1939. On the right we can see the GNR siding which terminates before the platform. On the extreme right the fence obscures a view of the GNR broad gauge platform. The narrow gauge platform and lines are to the left. No 6 *Erne*, having arrived earlier from Fivemiletown, has now turned and is taking water, prior to making the return journey.

Real Photographs Ltd

Above: Looking in the opposite direction in 1937, we get a clearer view of the narrow gauge side of the station. The main passenger building is on the left and the Clogher Valley's water tower on the right. In the distance is the transshipment shed, where goods traffic was exchanged between broad gauge GNR wagons on the left and narrow gauge CVR ones on the right. The wicker hampers on the platform may well contain fresh bread.

Real Photographs Ltd

Right: On 14 May 1920, No 3 *Blackwater* has arrived with the 11.30am mixed train from Fivemiletown. This is a particularly significant picture for my co-author Norman, as his grandfather William Johnston was still Station Master when it was taken, and his father and uncle were small boys living at the station. No 3 still has the original large headlamp and further down the platform, a porter is unloading luggage onto a hand trolley.

Ken Nunn collection, LCGB

Bottom left: In July 1941, the Clogher Valley assembled this monster train at Maguiresbridge to bring the brethren, their banners and their bands to the demonstration field. Here we see a passenger brake van to the left and no fewer than 11 bogie carriages – the CVR only ever had 13 of these!

Bottom right: The CVR closed on the last day of 1941 though the final railcar did not leave Fivemiletown for Tynan until ten past midnight on New Year's Day 1942. That was a Thursday and this photograph was taken at Maguiresbridge the following Saturday when the railcar, not usually seen south of Fivemiletown, made a final round trip to pay off the staff. The two boys on the left are the sons of Canon Fleming. The wee girl standing on the step of the railbus is Dora Fleming, their sister? The small man on the right is Bobby Symington. Also included is Wilson Haire who was the GNR signalman at Maguiresbridge. The taller man was the railbus driver, Hugh Murphy. Also included is Mrs Tutty and Betty Tutty – Mr Tutty was GNR stationmaster at Maguiresbirdge at the time.

Both Betty Tutty, courtesy of Headhunters' Museum

Opposite top: A train for Fivemiletown is seen at Maguiresbridge in 1933. The locomotive is No 6 *Erne*, one of six identical 0-4-2T locomotives built for the opening of the line in 1887. Because of the roadside tramway nature of much of the CVR track, the locomotives had sheet metal cow-catchers and side skirts to hide the wheels and motion. For safety reasons, the locomotives ran cab first and had a large acetylene lamp to help at night. The water was carried in side tanks and the coal in a bunker placed across the top of the firebox. The leading vehicle in the train is third class bogie No 15, which accommodated 40 passengers on longitudinally placed seats that were originally bare wood, but which had been upholstered about 1930. The coach has verandah ends. Behind the coach is brake van No 2, one of six such vehicles. It too has a verandah at one end and a large sliding door on each side to accommodate the mails and parcels traffic. At the rear of the train is one of the line's thirty cattle wagons. They, like the coach and the locomotive, were built for the opening in 1887.

Real Photographs Ltd

Opposite bottom: A close up of the transship shed in 1937. The 5'3" gauge lines of the GNR are to the left and the 3'0" gauge Clogher Valley lines to the right. As you can see, there wasn't much shelter and, the growth of weeds suggests, not much use either! The CVR's seldom photographed engine shed is visible in the right background.

Real Photographs Ltd

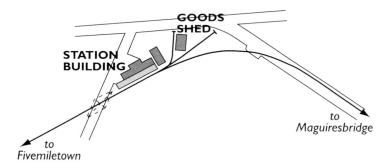

to Fivemiletown

to Maguiresbridge

Right: Brookeborough, the first station out of Maguiresbridge, had a substantial passenger building and two goods sidings but no loop. Here we are looking east, towards Fivemiletown, on 29 June 1937. The Station Master (or agent) lived in the two-storey part of the building, where the station nameboard was mounted. The level crossing gates, at the far end of the station, were a fairly recent, and lightweight, replacement for the originals, which were demolished one Sunday morning when diesel rail tractor No 2 ran away. The driver, Joe Murphy, escaped injury by retreating into the train well before impact! 'The Unit' carried a permanent reminder of the crash when the damage was repaired by cutting away its lower cab-sheets (see page 26).

Real Photographs Ltd

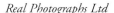

Below: Colebrooke station as it is today. The line ran on the far side of the building. This station was built to serve the Colebrooke Estate, owned by the Brooke family to this day. Sir Basil Brooke, later Lord Brookeborough, was Prime Minister of Northern Ireland from 1943 to 1963. The station ceased to feature in CVR timetables in the 1930s and became an unstaffed halt.

MJ Pollard

Opposite top: Stonepark halt was situated at a crossroads on the Fivemiletown side of Brookeborough, quite close to Colebrooke station. In this view, No 6 *Erne* is heading towards Maguiresbridge on 25 June 1937. The guard is probably studying the photographer, Henry Casserley, to ascertain whether or not he wants the train to stop.

HC Casserley, courtesy RM Casserley

Right: A builder's photograph of No 5 *Colebrooke* showing the locomotive in its original condition, with condenser. We can see that the cow-catcher was fitted at one end only. The huge original oil lamp can be seen on the backplate, its chimney rising above the line of the cab. Below the side tanks are four hinged and two sliding inspection doors. Comparing with the picture of No 6 (on page 48) we can see some changes. The original doors were too light and rattled a lot. They were replaced with a heavier gauge of metal and more substantial hinges. The ones below the cab door and alongside the cylinders were dispensed with. Looking higher up, we can see that there is as yet no coal bunker. The whistle is mounted on the cab roof, and the Ramsbottom safely valves on top of the dome, which is placed quite far back. Alongside the chimney can be seen the condensing pipes which fed the exhaust steam into the side tanks. The condensing steam caused problems with the engines' injectors which preferred cold water. Note too, the bell, mounted on top of the boiler and the large maker's plate on the smokebox – Sharp Stewart & Co, Limited, Atlas Works, 3373 – 1887 Manchester. 3373 was the maker's number. The photo has been embossed by the North British Locomotive Company who took over Sharp Stewart in 1903.

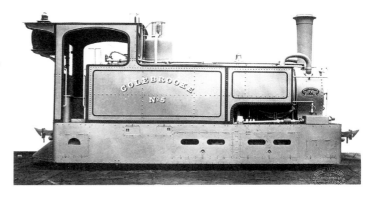

Real Photographs Ltd

Above: Corralongford halt was in Fermanagh and was located two miles west of Fivemiletown. Like other CVR halts, its facilities were minimal, consisting of a bench seat, a nameboard and a noticeboard for timetables and posters. This view shows well the CVR trackbed, usually running on the verge to one side of the road.

Real Photographs Ltd

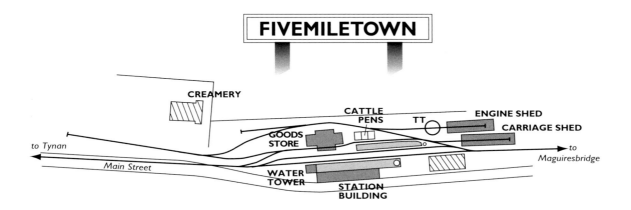

Opposite top: A Tynan-bound train at Fivemiletown is here in the charge of No 6 and may well be the same train that we saw earlier at Maguiresbridge. Here the coach, brake van and cattle wagon have been joined by two further cattle wagons. One of the cattle wagons is higher than the others – it was one of six that could be used for conveying horses. All the other cattle wagons could be converted to carry goods traffic by closing the ventilators below the roof.

Real Photographs Ltd

Above: Fivemiletown station with an as yet engine-less train for Tynan at the platform. In keeping with CVR architecture, Fivemiletown's Station Master had two storey accommodation. The ticket office was behind the glazed wooden screen, though its clock is absent. The water tower is just visible on the right, while, to the left, is the goods store with a van alongside.

H Fayle, courtesy IRRS

Above: We finish our coverage of Fivemiletown with a look in the Maguiresbridge direction, sometime in 1933. The building to the left is the engine shed with its turntable. Alongside is a carriage shed. Notice that its wall, next the running line, is not carried down to the ground. This was to provide ventilation and to help vehicles dry out in wet weather. Note the water column, with its leather bag blowing in the wind, and the high operating handle, so that the firemen could control the watering operation while standing on top of the locomotive's tanks.

Real Photographs Ltd

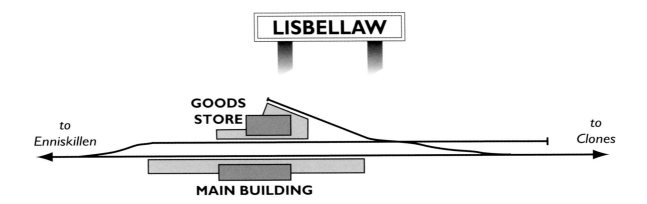

LISBELLAW

GOODS STORE

to Enniskillen

to Clones

MAIN BUILDING

Above: We return to the Great Northern to continue our progress towards Enniskillen. Lisbellaw was another one-platform station with a loop alongside. On Saturday 7 April 1956 No 198 *Lough Swilly* sweeps in with the 10.45am passenger train from Dundalk to Omagh, while those waiting to board the train get ready to look for seats. Behind the three coaches is another string of vans for all the parcels traffic, mails and perishable sundries. To the left we see the first of several station names set out in six foot tall concrete letters. They were also to be seen at Lisnaskea, Enniskillen, Trillick and Dromore Road stations.

RM Arnold

Above: Going the other way is PP class 4-4-0 No 106 with the 4.00pm Enniskillen to Clones passenger train on Easter Monday, 2 April 1956. The splendid four-coach train would normally be a 'mixed' – ie with goods wagons on the tail and a brake van at the end. Maybe during a holiday there was no goods traffic.
RM Arnold

Below: Lisbellaw's main station building is seen looking back from the cab of U class 4-4-0 No 196 on the 10.45am from Dundalk to Enniskillen on Saturday 7 September 1957.
A Burges

Above: A driver's eye view from the cab of U class 4-4-0 No 196 *Lough Gill* as it restarts the 10.45 from Dundalk to Enniskillen away from Lisbellaw on Saturday 7 September 1957. Today the A4 main road occupies the trackbed at this point.

A Burges

Opposite: This intriguing view of Enniskillen dates from about 1952 – after the Taylor Woods factory arrived but before the Fire Station was built at the junction of the Dublin and Tempo roads. The railway line from Bundoran Junction enters at the bottom of the picture and gently curves alongside the Irvinestown Road towards the bridge at the Pound Brae. The sidings to the right of the line mark where the Londonderry and Enniskillen Railway's original station was; it was later known as the Derry Cattle Beach and was used to load cattle from the nearby cattle mart at the Fair Green. Beyond the Pound Brae, the line curves sharply to the left, with the goods yard to the right and continues to the passenger station. Part of the SLNCR's yard is visible at the extreme left with just a glimpse of the GNR's engine shed visible below the County Hospital. The Weirs Bridge is just visible near the top left corner and the Sligo Leitrim track hugs the further bank of the River Erne as it heads for Belcoo.

Aerofilms, courtesy Ethel Dixon

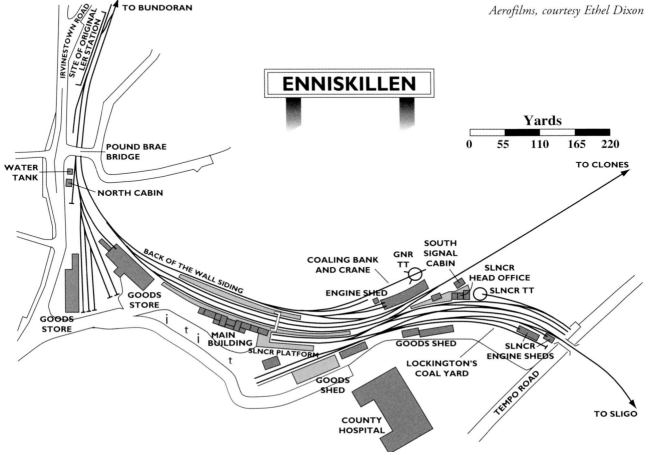

Opposite: A delightful study of PP class 4-4-0 No 42 departing with the 7.40pm to Bundoran at the west end of Enniskillen on Tuesday 20 July 1954.

Colin Hogg

Right: Enniskillen South on Tuesday 24 May 1953. No 197 *Lough Neagh* and Jimmy Kelly wait by the shed as No 198 *Lough Swilly* arrives from Dundalk. Is that *Hazelwood* in the Sligo yard?

NW Sprinks

Above: A general view looking east from the passenger platform as U class 4-4-0 No 205 *Down* arrived with the 10.45am from Dundalk on Wednesday 19 June 1957. To the extreme left is the crane for adding coal to the engines' tenders and the turntable beyond it. To its right is the water tower and then the engine shed itself with an engine at the right-hand road. To the right of No 205 is the SLNCR yard with their Brake Van No 1 at the tail of what will be the 2.30pm goods train for Sligo.

Brian Connell, Photos from the Fifties

Opposite top: P class 4-4-0 No 73, of 1895 vintage, departs for Clones with at least three coaches. On the right, SG3 class 0-6-0 No 8 seems to be attached by a tow rope to PP class 4-4-0 No 46, the latter being in light steam. Note the two SLNCR clerestory bogies in the bay on the left. Note the two signal arms on the tall signal post in the centre of the picture. The upper signal was for trains running through the station, such as the Bundoran Express, and was visible from alongside the goods store. The lower repeater arm was for trains starting from the platform. Because of the footbridge, this lower arm was only visible from almost half way along the platform.

RM Arnold

Opposite bottom: Another general view from opposite the engine shed shows PP class 4-4-0 No 12 in company with one of Derry's LQG class 0-6-0s, No 161, while another engine shunts a wagon seemingly involved in gathering up loco ash, clinkers and so on. Mr Boland ran a tidy ship! The date was Friday 23 December 1955. The passenger carriages in the middle road (to the left) formed a pre-Christmas extra that ran each evening that week. It left Enniskillen for Omagh at 7.40pm as a continuation of the 4.30pm from Dundalk and came back at 10.00pm, taking a connection out of the 7.30pm from Belfast to Londonderry. The train arrived here at 10.55pm and lay over in the middle road, as seen here. The second carriage is the only K29 class Third, No 484. It entered traffic on 9 December 1949 as the last of the 19 ex-LNWR carriages which the GNR bought in 1947-49.

EM Patterson

Above: This scene is looking into Enniskillen station from the Clones end of No 1 platform in May 1950. The short canopy on the extreme left marks where the Sligo Leitrim had its passenger platform. Below the footbridge PP class 4-4-0 No 46 waits to leave with a train for Clones. To the right the fireman is sitting down as AL class 0-6-0 No 32 propels cattle wagons into the 'back of the wall' siding. The train is probably the Enniskillen Shipper which left at 11.00am daily and ran to Belfast (Maysfields) via Clones and Portadown with (mostly) cattle for live export to England and Scotland. The traffic was so valuable that the train was often given precedence over passenger trains leaving Portadown. Other livestock trains from here brought animals to Derry, Dublin or Greenore for export, cattle to the plains of Meath for fattening or sheep and lambs to Carrickmacross. Those who know Enniskillen can get their bearings from Cole's monument, just at the right of the Up starting signal.

GW Sharpe

Opposite top: The time should be 11.37am because this picture shows, on the right, the arrival of the AEC diesel train from Belfast via Clones. Power car 603 is leading and 602 is at the other end. The train on the left, at platform 1, is the stock for the 12 noon to Omagh – its engine has yet to come from the shed. The wagon nearest the camera has a bread container.

NC Simmons, Photos from the Fifties

Opposite bottom: Enniskillen shed on Saturday 11 August 1951, with at least three locomotives 'on shed'. To the left is a very clean SG3 class 0-6-0 No 117, probably for that evening's goods to Derry at 9.40pm. The engine to the right is PP class 4-4-0 No 44. The tender between them belongs to LQG 0-6-0 No 160. To the extreme left is the grounded six-wheel coach body that was used as sleeping quarters by some engine crews. Beyond that is the crane used for coaling engines. The turntable is hidden behind 117's right hand lamp bracket. The wagons on the right are being shunted to the SLNCR yard.

HB Priestley, courtesy CP Friel

Above: A closer view of Enniskillen shed in late September 1957 and a lovely portrait of P6'6" class 4-4-0 No 73. Modellers will want to note how the shed curved to follow the Clones line on the right. The cutting beyond the back of shed survives today as a footpath.

NC Simmons, Photos from the Fifties

Above: H class 2-4-0 No 87 moves forward after bringing in a train from Omagh on Tuesday 12 September 1898. To the extreme right, another engine waits to back down and take 87's place at the head of the train. Another engine is in the left-hand shed road.

Ken Nunn collection, LCGB

Right: Railbus 4 is seen here working the 6.20pm to Clones on Tuesday 20 July 1954. This railbus dates from 1935 and was built at Dundalk for service on the Dundalk, Newry and Greenore Railway. It was sold back to the GNR in 1947. Just visible at the back of the bus are the steps used to enter and leave the vehicle at level crossings.

Colin Hogg

Opposite bottom: On Wednesday 18 July 1952, U class 4-4-0 No 203 *Armagh* is departing on the 2.10pm to Dundalk, while LQG 0-6-0s Nos 158 and 9 sit on shed. In the distance is SLNCR 0-6-4T *Lough Gill*.

RM Arnold

Above: In this 1955 view, looking north west from platform 1, a train from Omagh is sitting at platform 2 and AL 0-6-0 No 59 is sitting in the middle road with bread containers. Clearly visible next the engine is a Brewster container and, on the same wagon, a Stevenson container is partially visible.

M Batley, courtesy HA Nelson

Opposite top: At the north end of Enniskillen, PP class 4-4-0 No 12 waits to depart for Bundoran Junction on Monday 8 June 1953.

John H Price

Opposite bottom: Every Spring, Dundalk overhauled two of the newer U class 4-4-0s for working the Bundoran Express between Dundalk and Bundoran. They also 'did up' several road buses for duty at Pettigo, bringing pilgrims to and from Lough Derg. Here, on Tuesday 24 June 1953, two Gardner-engined buses are waiting in the middle road before being worked to Pettigo, probably on tomorrow morning's goods train. The GN had four of these six-wheeled Omnibus Trucks, clearly labelled "Return to Dundalk". These wagons had a 33 foot 6 inches long deck and had timber truck binding chains at each end. The nearer bus is No 258 (ZC 5472) on wagon 8504 while the further one, No 257 (ZC 4735), is on wagon No 8497. The buses were GNR-bodied Gardner-engined 35-seaters built at Dundalk in July 1938 and withdrawn in 1955. Although numbered sequentially, the buses have some livery variations.

Bluebell Railway Museum - JJ Smith Collection

Above: For this picture, we have to roll back the calendar to 1914. The photograph was taken by James Ray who had been born 'James Wray' in Donegal in 1860. He emigrated to Boston in 1880 and changed his name to Ray before setting up the successful Ray Detective Agency. He came home in 1914 to visit his family and, on this day, was about to leave Enniskillen for Dublin. You will have already noticed the proliferation of advertising on the station wall. Did you see the hawker on the platform, with the wide leather belt over one shoulder supporting his tray of sweets, papers, cigarettes and, probably, button holes?

James Ray, courtesy Valerie Nelson

Opposite top: Photographs of the exterior of Enniskillen seem to be quite rare – maybe the photographers were all too busy inside! This view is taken from the path up from Westville, with the goods yard and the Pound Brae away to the left. The large board beside the door under the awning gives a list of arrival and departure times.

CP Friel collection

Opposite bottom: This was the view from the top of Cole's Monument one day in 1927. In the foreground, the goods yard is, unusually, home to two short bogie coaches, suggesting that this is a holiday time and these are being held to strengthen a special train, perhaps for the Twelfth. In the siding nearest us, drover's vans are at the buffers and at the bottom left corner – these were used to accompany livestock trains of cattle or horses, for instance. In the passenger station, an engine's exhaust hangs in the air as a train leaves for Bundoran Junction. The Sligo Leitrim's yard forms much of the backdrop and seems to be very busy.

Courtesy Headhunters' Museum

Above: U class 4-4-0 No 204 *Antrim* arrives in from the Bundoran direction past the famous name set into the bank on Tuesday 24 May 1955. The man walking along the path on the left is Gerry Molloy, a foreman painter.

NW Sprinks

Opposite top: Railcar C3 waits, with trailer 847, at the up platform before working the 6.20pm to Clones on Tuesday 26 May 1953. This view shows the unusual valence along the canopy roof and the arched windows opening onto the 'Back of the Wall' siding. Three of these single-cabbed and articulated railcars were built at Dundalk in 1934-36 when C (later renumbered C1) worked between here and Bundoran during the winter timetables. C needed to be turned after each trip and Bundoran's turntable had the rails extended to accommodate the new technology. When the later cars, C2 and C3, were working Dublin suburban trains, they worked back to back with one car towing the other. Larger railcars took over this work after World War Two and the three cars ran as single units, as C3 is here.

Opposite bottom: Railcar C3 waits to leave with the 8.45am for Bundoran on Wednesday 25 May 1955. Beside the railcar's cab are Fireman Billy Hawthorn and Driver Birdie Rankin. To the right, U class 4-4-0 No 204 *Antrim* has arrived with the 7.50am from Clones and waits to move off to the shed; the train will work forward to Omagh at 9.25am.

Both NW Sprinks

Above: The 2.10pm combined train for Bundoran and Omagh leaves Enniskillen in late September 1957. From other pictures taken that day we can surmise that the locomotives are PP class No 44 piloting P class No 73. The train is in the cutting alongside the goods shed and is traversing the most sharply curved running line on the GNR. The track was laid a half an inch wider – at 5'3½" – to allow trains an easier passage and this was safe enough at such slow speeds as the 5 mph allowed here. Enniskillen North signal cabin is partially hidden by the bank beyond the concrete name.

NC Simmons, Photos from the Fifties

Opposite top: On Sunday 31 July 1955, PP class 4-4-0 No 43 gets a break from its usual passenger duties to take charge of a permanent way train. The view is looking north from the end of the up platform. Note that No 43 is coupled to one of the new 2500 gallon tenders built the previous year.

A Donaldson, courtesy WT Scott

Opposite bottom: A familiar sight to many Enniskillen railwaymen was AL class 0-6-0 No 59, for long the regular shunting engine here. Delivered on New Year's Day 1894, the engine was rebuilt as shown in April 1915. She is seen here sitting near the Pound Brae bridge on an unknown date in 1956. Coupled to 59 is 20-ton Brake Van No 90, built at Dundalk in November 1950. There were 45 of these vans and No 81 of 1945 has just been fully restored by the youth wing of the Railway Preservation Society of Ireland at its Whitehead headquarters. The van on the left, No 492, could take up to 9 tons of goods; it was built at Dundalk in November 1941. Behind the wagons is Enniskillen North signal cabin. The water tank to the right was used for watering the engines and providing water for the cattle being loaded at the cattle beach on the other side of the Pound Brae bridge.

NW Sprinks

Above: Nothing has come down to us to identify why the picture was taken or when. The line-up of 18 men include railway uniforms and an odd mixture of civilian attire, with an inconsistent mixture of headgear. The only clue as to date is that the licensee named above the Refreshment Room door is one Henry Plews. He had been the Irish North's manager here for 23 years before becoming GNR Secretary in 1890 and then General Manager from February 1896 until his retirement in November 1911, when he was co-opted as a Director. This would suggest 1911 as the latest date for this picture.

Courtesy Headhunters' Museum

Upper: Another view from the Henry Cole monument in 1927, this time looking across the Irvinestown road towards the Pound Brae and Cooper's Crescent. The goods store is on the right. Between it and the North signal cabin, a U class 4-4-0 steams towards the bridge.

Courtesy Headhunters' Museum

Lower: In this photograph, the photographer has swung his camera further left to show the line disappearing, alongside the Irvinestown road, towards Ballinamallard. There are several wagons parked at the Derry cattle beach on the site of the original Londonderry and Enniskillen Railway's terminus. The water to the left is Race Course Lough.

Courtesy Headhunters' Museum

Above: Heading away from Enniskillen is PP class 4-4-0 No 44 working a train for Omagh on Tuesday 24 May 1955. Note the leading vehicle, a W1 six-wheel clerestory brake. At this point the line ran parallel to the Irvinestown Road, visible in the background. Alongside No 44 is a long rake of cattle wagons, perhaps awaiting cattle for export. The hall in the right background is a gospel hall.

NW Sprinks

Below: Leaving Enniskillen in the Omagh direction is this double-headed goods train. The leading locomotive is Q class 4-4-0 No 130 and the train engine appears to be a PP. The location is Drumclay, a short distance out of Enniskillen.

RM Arnold

Above: In the opposite direction, at the same location, we see PP class 4-4-0 No 106 with the 1.25pm Derry to Dundalk train on Wednesday 2 June 1954. This train waited at Omagh from 3.02pm until 4.17pm! It was due in Enniskillen at 5.08pm and Dundalk at 7.42pm. The four passenger carriages are followed by a motley collection including two four-wheel passenger vans, a piped van and two cattle wagons. Curiously, the locomotive has only one headlamp and it is over the engine's left buffer rather than at the chimney.

NW Sprinks

GORTALOUGHAN

Right: Gortaloughan halt was 2½ miles west of Enniskillen. It had one platform, sixty-five feet long, on the Up side and opened on Monday 23 September 1940. No trains were timetabled to stop here though four Omagh - Enniskillen and five in the other direction could stop on request on weekdays. The Bundoran Expresses were excepted, of course, as were the 7.15am and 12 noon from Enniskillen to Omagh. Trains stopped most often for the few days at the start of July when there was a religious convention at nearby Crocknacrieve for members of the sect nicknamed 'The Cooneyites'. Approaching here is the 11.20am goods from Bundoran to Enniskillen which was due to pass here about 6.00pm. Gortaloughan had no goods facilities, so this train was not stopping. The locomotive is P6'6" class 4-4-0 No 73 and the photograph dates from August 1957.

RM Arnold

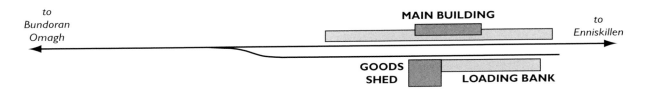

to
*Bundoran
Omagh*

MAIN BUILDING

to
Enniskillen

**GOODS
SHED**

LOADING BANK

Above: Ballinamallard was another station with just one passenger platform though, despite having a goods siding, it had no loop and was not a block post. Here 4-4-0 No 73 arrives with a train from Bundoran to Enniskillen on Tuesday 3 July 1956. There are two enthusiasts on the platform, the further one being the photographer Drew Donaldson, who took some of the photographs in this book.

RM Arnold

Left: UG class 0-6-0 No 79 pauses at Ballinamallard while working a Sunday excursion from Cavan to Bundoran on 8 September 1957. Like all GN excursions, the handbill would have advised "No itinerant musicians or fruit sellers allowed. Hand luggage only." The signal post on the left, also visible in the previous picture, was bi-directional. Ballinamallard had no cabin and both arms seemed to be normally in the off position, except perhaps when the siding was being shunted. They were controlled by a ground frame. The trap point, preventing anything from the siding getting on to the main line, is clearly visible on the right foreground.

RM Arnold

Above: PP class 4-4-0 No 12 arrives at Ballinamallard on a Down passenger train, probably for Omagh. The main station building is to the left while an open wagon and a van occupy the siding alongside the goods store to the right. The store has recently been tastefully converted for use as a community hall.

WT Scott

Above: Coming in the opposite direction to No 12, Q class 4-4-0 No 132 arrives from Omagh. The goods store is to the left with a trap point to keep runaway wagons off the main line. On the right a horsebox body sits on the platform.

Courtesy Headhunters' Museum

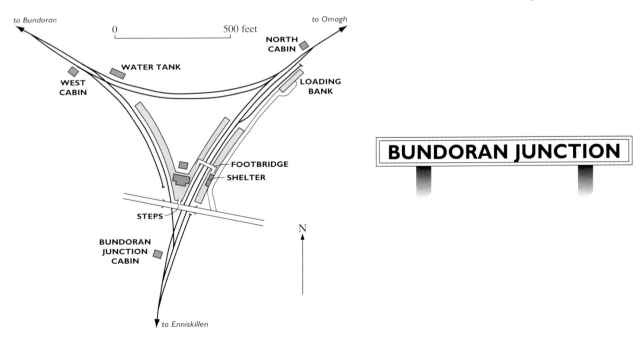

Opposite top: Passing Bundoran Junction South signal box is PP class 4-4-0 No 50 with the 12 noon from Enniskillen to Omagh on Wednesday 2 June 1954. The train has the usual empty bread container at the back of the train – probably collected at Ballinamallard.

Opposite bottom: Bundoran Junction on the same day, a view looking north from the Enniskillen side of the overbridge. Through the left-hand arch of the bridge, we see the 10.30am from Bundoran in charge of PP class 4-4-0 No 42. You should be just able to see that, in addition to the usual passenger van, the train includes two shorter vans next the engine. This train was due here at 12.03pm and will work to Enniskillen at 12.44pm, arriving there at 1.00pm. Through the right-hand arch we see the tail of the 12 noon Enniskillen to Omagh train.

Both NW Sprinks

Above: Bundoran Junction on Saturday 8 June 1957. This is the view from the Kilskeery Road bridge and behind the nameboard are the steps leading down to the platform. Prominent is the very pleasant, glazed, Refreshment Room, built on to the front of the Station Master's house about 1910, which was under the management of Mrs Gray. The train visible is the 10.30am ex-Bundoran, with a passenger van at this end, waiting to continue as the 12.44pm to Enniskillen. Note the water tank in the distance. A motorised luggage trolley was used to convey luggage between the Bundoran platform and the Omagh one in the foreground.

L King

Opposite top: A busy time at Bundoran Junction, as seen from the footbridge. On the left is the 1.45pm Omagh to Enniskillen, due away from here at 2.20pm. In the foreground is the last coach of the 2.05pm Enniskillen to Omagh which will leave at 2.36pm and is headed by P class No 73 (out of view). Visible through the bridge is the 2.35pm for Bundoran with PP class 4-4-0 No 44. This engine had probably piloted the 2.05pm which ran as a combined train from Enniskillen to Bundoran Junction. This train stopped short of the turnout for the Bundoran branch, whereupon No 44 would have run up the branch to allow No 73 to work the Omagh section forward to its platform. Then 44 would have reversed back off the branch to collect the Bundoran coaches and vans and bring them to the branch platform. The train behind 44 has seven empty cattle wagons on the tail – these might be empties being worked for a fair next day along the branch. On the other hand, if they were Omagh-bound, the locomotive on the Omagh to Enniskillen train was conveniently placed to do the honours. Busy times indeed! The signals visible here present a contrast. The signal on the left is on a white painted post of planed timber but the one beside the stone steps is a telegraph pole type made of creosoted timber. The bridge number – 178 – is visible just to the left of the Enniskillen-bound locomotive. Each bridge was given a unique number, in this case numbered from '1' at Dundalk. The Bundoran branch had its own series, beginning with '1' at Bundoran Junction.

NC Simmons, Photos from the Fifties

Opposite bottom: The Bundoran goods passes the Junction on Friday 20 July 1956, hauled by PG class 0-6-0 No 11. This goods had left Bundoran at 11.20am and, after serving Ballyshannon, waited at Belleek for both Bundoran Expresses to pass. Getting away from Belleek at 1.40pm, it then got to Pettigo where it had to wait to cross the 2.35pm from the Junction. It then served both there and Irvinestown before running non-stop to Enniskillen. It was due to pass Bundoran Junction at 4.35pm and arrive in Enniskillen at 4.55pm.

A Donaldson, courtesy WT Scott

Above: PP class 4-4-0 No 74 arrives with an early morning Enniskillen to Omagh goods train in September 1957.

Noel Craig

Below: We are now at the north end of the layout, with the Omagh-Enniskillen platforms visible to the left. We can see PP class 4-4-0 No 42 approaching the North cabin on the curve that linked the North and West cabins. Here No 42 is about to shunt a van off the back of its train and leave it at the Enniskillen platform; it will be shunted onto the back of the 12 noon to Omagh. The link gave Bundoran Junction a triangular layout, something rare in Ireland and was most often used on Sundays to allow Omagh to Bundoran excursions (and their return workings) to run through without the nuisance of reversing. The siding on the left was used for goods traffic but here houses a six-wheel carriage in connection with permanent way and signalling work.

N W Sprinks

Opposite top. At the Enniskillen to Omagh platform on Wednesday 2 June 1954 we see PP class 4-4-0 No 50 blowing off while working the 12 noon from Enniskillen to Omagh. On the extreme right, at the back of the platform, is milepost 70, the distance measured from zero at Dundalk.

NW Sprinks

Right: On 2 June 1954 PP class 4-4-0 No 50 passes Bundoran Junction North cabin with the 12.00 Enniskillen to Omagh.

NW Sprinks

Above: The Bundoran line platform, also on 2 June 1954. Here we see No 42 arriving with the 10.30am from Bundoran. It will continue as the 12.44pm to Enniskillen. In months other than June, July and August, this train would leave the Junction at 12.30pm. In the siding on the left are at least seventeen wagons of what looks like used ballast.

NW Sprinks

Opposite top: PP class 4-4-0 No 44 waits to leave Bundoran Junction on Thursday 12 September 1957. The train is the Bundoran portion of the 2.05pm from Enniskillen to Omagh seen several times already. This was a continuation of the 10.45am ex-Dundalk and the first northbound train of the day scheduled to stop at Gortaloughan, if requested.

Colin Hogg

Opposite bottom: Bundoran Junction West signal box was at the Bundoran end of the triangular layout. On 2 June 1954 we see No 42 arriving with the 10.30am from Bundoran, seen with a varied collection of vacuum-fitted vehicles next the locomotive – a cattle wagon, a van, a Y class four-wheel passenger van with sliding doors and an older W class six-wheel van with double doors.

NW Sprinks

Above: Just beyond Bundoran Junction West cabin, we see PP class 4-4-0 No 74 with the two-coach 11.10am Enniskillen to Pettigo on 2 June 1954. This train provided a service for pilgrims to Lough Derg from all stations between Enniskillen and Pettigo, arriving there at 12.22pm. It ran from 1 June until 15 August, when Saint Patrick's Purgatory at Lough Derg closed its doors. The locomotive is running tender first as there was no turntable at Pettigo and there was no path available to run back the 15 miles to the Junction to turn.

NW Sprinks

Opposite top: PP class 4-4-0 No 42 is seen here passing the West cabin (on the left) and taking the line linking it to the North cabin. The date is Saturday 29 June 1957 and the train is the 1.35pm from Pettigo to Omagh, due here at 2.10pm. In the 1956 and 1957 Summer timetables, this train ran from Pettigo to Omagh rather than back to Enniskillen as in previous years. At the North cabin, the train will reverse to the Down (Enniskillen to Omagh) platform and wait to cross the 1.45pm from Omagh before leaving at 2.36pm for Omagh. This train ran during the Lough Derg season only, from 1 June to 15 August. The leftmost track in the foreground is a siding which trailed back to the Kilskeery road bridge. Note, too, the water tank on the right.

Bluebell Railway Museum, JJ Smith Collection

Opposite bottom: This is Tague's level crossing with No 42 on the 10.30am from Bundoran on a wet 28 September 1957, the Saturday before the line closed. This crossing was a stopping place for several trains, as required, but latterly the only one shown in the timetables was the first train towards Bundoran, the 9.13am (later 9.30am) from the Junction.

A Donaldson, courtesy WT Scott

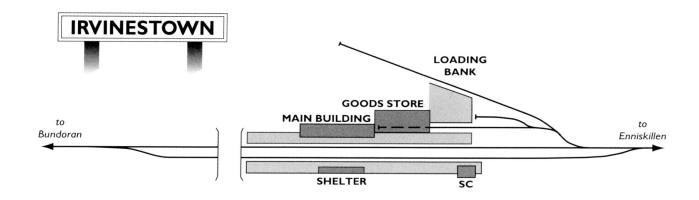

Left: This view, from a Bundoran-bound train rolling into Irvinestown on Friday 30 August 1957, gives a fine impression of this well-kept station. We can see the metal bridge carrying the road from Enniskillen across the line, towards the town, away to our right. The main station buildings are on the up platform on the right – you can see that the large door of the goods store is open. Nearer the camera is a bread wagon with two containers, for McCombs and Hughes bakeries in Belfast. Each of these containers, I was once told, could hold 28 dozen loaves!

A Burges

Opposite top: Under the road bridge at Irvinestown comes PP class 4-4-0 No 46, working the goods from Bundoran, due here at 2.15pm, but running late in this May 1956 photograph. Marshalled just behind the locomotive are three of the distinctive bread containers which are now empty and being returned to Belfast or Londonderry. Just visible on the right is the smokebox of the locomotive (74) working the 2.35pm passenger from the Junction to Bundoran.   *RH Barr*

Opposite bottom: The goods from Bundoran reached Irvinestown at 2.15pm and, after shunting the yard, waited for the 2.35pm from the Junction, part of the 2.05pm from Enniskillen, Before leaving at 2.55pm, some railwaymen posed for the photographer. On the running plate of PP class 4-4-0 No 50, at the smokebox, are Driver Freddie Rankin and his Fireman Kevin Love. Standing below are Stationmaster Owen Kelly, to the left, and the train's guard Tommy Hadden. At the front of the train are the empty bread containers gathered up from Belleek, Kesh and here. To the right is the start of the long siding that served the cattle beach. Irvinestown's fair, on the 8th of each month, used to generate a 12.10pm stock special to Londonderry, worked by a Derry engine and crew.   *RM Arnold*

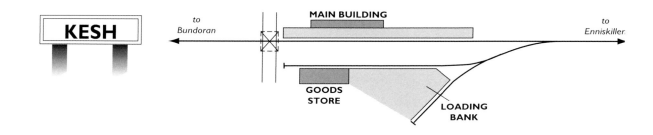

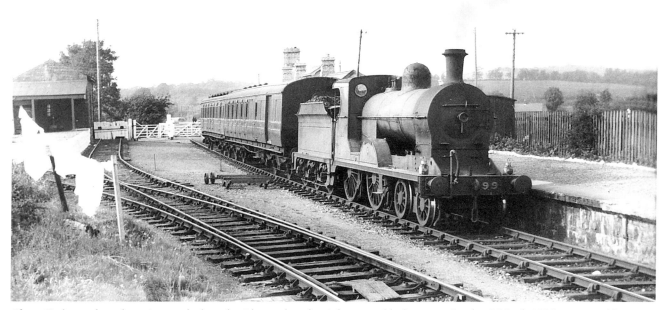

Above: Kesh was the only station on the branch without a loop but it became a block post on Sunday 8 March 1936; trains could cross by using the siding (if there was room, of course). The pointwork was controlled by a ground frame at the Enniskillen end of the station; another controlled the level crossing. Kesh had just two sidings and both are visible on the left. In this view No 199 *Lough Derg* has the 5.25pm Bundoran to Enniskillen on Saturday 21 June 1952. Kesh was downgraded from a station to a halt on 1 May 1953 when it came under the control of Irvinestown.

RM Arnold

Opposite top: Kesh, this time on a wet day. The village is to our right and the level crossing carries the road to Derry and Omagh (the route of the Omagh to Bundoran bus after 1957). Here PP class 4-4-0 No 74 has the Bundoran portion of the 2.10pm ex Enniskillen on Wednesday 4 April 1956.

RM Arnold

Opposite bottom: This is an old commercial postcard of Kesh, dating from about 1930; we are looking towards Pettigo.

CP Friel collection

Above: PP class 4-4-0 No 50 pauses with a passenger train from Bundoran at some time in the 1950s. The grounded six-wheel carriage body on the platform provided accommodation for HM Customs.

Lens of Sutton

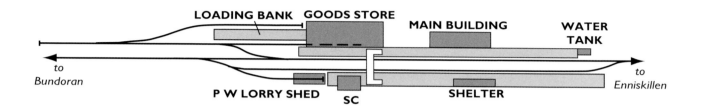

Above: This is an old commercial postcard of Pettigo, taken looking east from the Bundoran end. It was one of a series published for Guest & Neville, Merchants, of Pettigo by the Doo-Well Publishing Co, Ballymena. Curiously, it was printed in Saxony (Germany). Like Irvinestown and Ballyshannon, Pettigo's goods store was part of the station buildings on the up side. Near the store are a couple of permanent way bogies and sleepers, some of them large, suggesting a re-sleepering of a turnout. The station has yet to acquire its footbridge, the extension to the Up platform, or the protective awnings on the Up platform seen in the following pictures.

CP Friel collection

Right: The Up (Bundoran to Dublin) 'Bundoran Express', hauled by No 204 *Antrim*, arrives at Pettigo to stop alongside its Dublin to Bundoran counterpart. The far platform is very busy with those who have made the pilgrimage, or 'done the island' in the vernacular, and two porters are keeping passengers back from the platform edge. The protective awning of corrugated asbestos was erected just after the last war and gave some shelter to the pilgrims, who by this time were on their third day of fasting with virtually no sleep. In 1952 a record of almost 22,000 pilgrims used this busy station. In 1957 this was still 18,000.

P McKeown

Below: Pettigo was a very busy spot on any weekday in the summer between about 1.04 and 1.23pm. This is the view from the footbridge on Thursday 18 June 1953, looking towards Bundoran. Just departed is the Down Express – a five-carriage train hauled by 199 *Lough Derg*. The carriages at the platform form the Up Express hauled by 202 *Louth*. The coach nearest the camera is a modern F16 corridor composite and it is followed by a clerestory-roofed M1 bogie van. The rear coach is a brake compo, the through coach for Belfast. Waiting in the background is the 11.10am from Enniskillen headed by a third U class locomotive, this time No 198 *Lough Swilly*. It will return as the 1.35pm to Enniskillen. The concrete block shed to the left was built to house the permanent way lorry that was once stationed here. In more recent times, it was used by local ganger Joe McFadden. But each summer Gerry McAuley from the bus garage at Donegal Town would set up shop here while supervising and maintaining the GNR buses used for the shuttle to and from Lough Derg.

L King

Above: After the departure of the other trains, the 1.35pm passenger for Omagh would move up to the platform. On Saturday 22 June 1957 the locomotive is PP class 4-4-0 No 44. Standing proudly in the cab is Driver Douglas Armstrong of Enniskillen. The first coach is a J4 brake composite. Pilgrims from south Fermanagh stations could use the 7.50am ex Clones to join the 11.10am Enniskillen to Pettigo. On the homeward leg they could use the 1.35pm as far as the Junction where they could change into 1.45pm from Omagh to Enniskillen, arriving at 2.46pm, and then wait for the 4.00pm 'mixed' thence. They must have been hardy souls! Two nursing colleagues of my mother, who were going to Lough Derg, once used the 11.10 service, but they got into such a deep conversation that they lost all contact with the real world and only realised what was happening when they saw Kesh for the second time that day! Somehow the shunt at Pettigo, and the layover in the siding from 12.12pm until 1.35pm, totally escaped their notice! No 44 had been Dan Sweeney's engine; he even named his greyhound *Engine 44*.

RM Arnold

Left: The title 'Bundoran Express' first appeared in June 1931. That Express started from Clones where one carriage from Dublin and one from Dundalk were combined with two carriages and a passenger van from Belfast. The train then ran non-stop to Pettigo. This arrangement continued until the summer of 1947 when the Express acquired its formal title and the arrangements that many of us knew came into operation. This photograph was taken on Tuesday 16 June 1937 and shows U class 4-4-0 No 199, then in black livery and unnamed, arriving at the end of its non-stop run from Clones. Is that a priest from the Island waiting for his pilgrims?

Tom Middlemass

Below right: The location is Ross Harbour, about a mile east of Castlecaldwell, with the picturesque Lower Lough Erne alongside. Nowadays the road occupies the trackbed and the old road is a very pleasant lay-by. At the further end of the leading coach is a board reminding drivers to reduce speed at the permanent 30 mph slack between mileposts 20½ and 21¾. Castlecaldwell was at milepost 22¾, measured from the Junction. Here, on 8 September 1957, we see U class 4-4-0 No 197 *Lough Neagh* at the head of the regular Sunday excursion from Derry to Bundoran.

Leaving Derry (Foyle Road) at 12.50pm, the five coach train served Strabane, Sion Mills, Victoria Bridge, Newtownstewart and Omagh. After stopping at Fintona Junction, Dromore Road and Trillick, the train then took the direct curve at Bundoran Junction. It stopped at every station on the line, except Castlecaldwell and Belleek, before arriving in Bundoran at 3.52pm. The return working was at 8.33pm, though, wisely, it was advertised as departing 10 minutes earlier. Eventual arrival in Derry was at 11.46pm. According to one of my father's sisters, who often used this train, the time in Bundoran was spent in open-air dancing near the Roguey Rocks.

RM Arnold

This is Ross Harbour again, but fairly soon after 26 September 1956 – the clothes suggest a Sunday, the 30 September perhaps. On 26 September part of the embankment collapsed into Lower Lough Erne. A bus service replaced the trains between Pettigo and Bundoran between 27 September and the reopening of the line on 18 October 1956. The line-up of cars and motorcycles is impressive for its time.

RM Arnold

CASTLECALDWELL

GOODS STORE

to
Bundoran

to
Enniskillen

WAITING ROOM

Above: Castlecaldwell as seen from a Bundoran-bound train on Saturday 30 August 1957. Like Kesh, this station became a block post on Sunday 8 March 1936. Like Kesh, it did not have a signal cabin though it already had a very useful loop. Like some stations south of Enniskillen, the loop was normally used only for goods traffic and had a short goods platform but see next picture. The loop was fairly short but could hold a 20 wagon train.

A Burges

Opposite bottom: Unusually here is a passenger train using the goods loop at Castlecaldwell. P6'6" class 4-4-0 No 73 is working the 10.30am from Bundoran on Monday 1 August 1955. The reason for this rare occurrence has not been recorded. Before the Second World War, the loop was sometimes used by empty trains waiting to pick up parties of pilgrims at Pettigo. Near the station nameboard, to the left, can be seen two sets of wooden steps which were used to cross fences at some level crossings. They were probably made at Dundalk and deposited here by the Down goods around 9.00am. Judging by the passenger train, the time in this photograph is about 11.10am.

RM Arnold

Right: Looking from the Bundoran end of the main platform, we see U class 4-4-0 No 205 *Down* working the 12.10pm Sundays Only from Enniskillen to Bundoran on 8 September 1957. Leaning from the cab, holding the staff, is driver Paddy Martin. The guard is too far away to be identified but the other man on the platform is permanent way man Bob Watson, carrying a track hammer.

RM Arnold

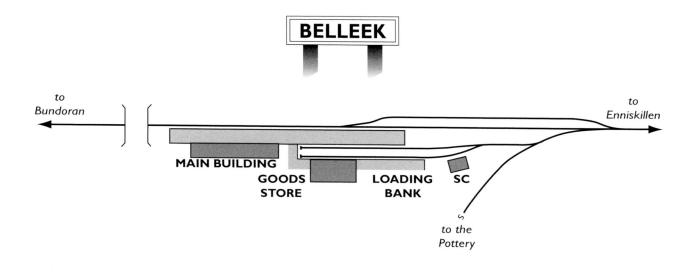

BELLEEK

to Bundoran

to Enniskillen

MAIN BUILDING

GOODS STORE

LOADING BANK

SC

to the Pottery

Above: This is the 10.30am from Bundoran, hauled by PP class 4-4-0 No 50, enduring the Customs men at Belleek on Friday 30 August 1957; indeed the engine crew are taking a break from the footplate during the stop. The goods store and loading bank are to the left and, in the foreground, is the turnout for the short loop.

A Burges

Left: Going the same way at Belleek is this 'Hills of Donegal' excursion on Saturday 30 May 1953. Starting at Belfast, the train ran first to Strabane, where the passengers changed to a County Donegal narrow gauge train for the journey to Ballyshannon, via Stranorlar and Donegal town. After walking though Ballyshannon to the GNR station, the passengers found their train waiting to take them on to the heady delights of Bundoran. This is the return train en route to Belfast, via Omagh, hauled by UG class 0-6-0 No 80, built in 1937. The left hand figure is driver Barney McGirr.

RM Arnold

Above:. This is the viaduct over the Erne, just west of Belleek, on Saturday 22 June 1957, when PP class 4-4-0 No 42 was working the 10.30am from Bundoran to the Junction, typically with two passenger vans coupled next to the locomotive. The photographer is on the County Fermanagh bank of the Erne, but the train is in County Donegal. The bridge was renewed in March 1953, after which the restriction on double-heading across the bridge was lifted. The contractors were Dorman and Long and it was said that if you didn't work hard enough for Dorman, you wouldn't work for Long!

RM Arnold

Opposite top: Percy Wray, on the platform, bids farewell to the driver of U class 4-4-0 No 203 *Armagh* as the train leaves Belleek on the 8.45am from Enniskillen to Bundoran on Saturday 22 June 1957.

RM Arnold

Opposite bottom: A healthy gathering of passengers are assembled at Belleek in this postcard dating from the early 1900s. The goods store is to the left and the station master's house is on the hill to the right, above the passenger shelter, where the woman of the house watches our unknown photographer at work.

CP Friel collection

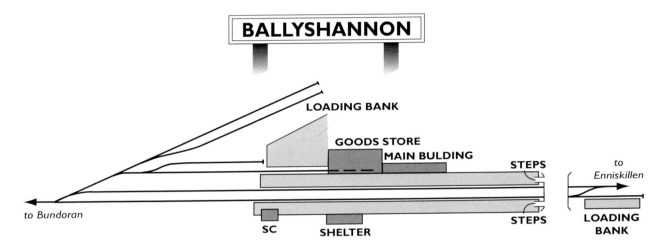

Left: We move now beyond the boundaries of County Fermanagh to complete our coverage of the Bundoran branch. At Ballyshannon's Down platform on Thursday 2 August 1956, PP class 4-4-0 No 74 waits at the head of the 2.10pm from Enniskillen. Driver John Kerrigan, from Bundoran, stands near the front van and keeps his distance from the gaggle of passengers having their luggage rummaged by the white-capped Customs man on the table by the van at the far end of the train.

RM Arnold

Below: A general view of Ballyshannon looking west from the road overbridge, probably in September 1957. In the bottom left corner is the gate that sealed off the Down platform for customs work. Beyond the station nameboard and the noticeboard is the customs hut and trestle table. Beyond that again are the shelter and signal cabin, seen in a previous picture. On the Up platform are the main station buildings with the goods store beyond the Gents.

Rev J Parker, Photos from the Fifties

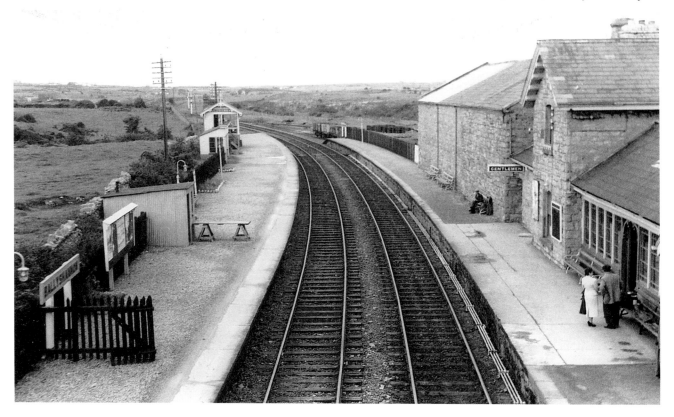

Opposite top: This is the approach to Ballyshannon from the east looking down from the road overbridge. Here we see PP class 4-4-0 No 107 approaching with the 2.40pm from Bundoran Junction on Wednesday 18 May 1954. In the left background is the distribution part of the hydro-electric power station at the Assaroe or Cathleen's Falls on the River Erne. The three sidings to the left of the locomotive were brought into use on Monday 2 December 1946. They were used to bring in stone, cement and other supplies for Cementation Company, builders of the dam and generating house. Being 350 yards from the signal cabin, the connection was controlled by a ground frame which was released by a key on the end of the Belleek-Ballyshannon staff. The contractors had their own 2'6" gauge railway but, so far as we know, all transporting form the siding was by road lorry. In the short siding to the right are two cattle wagons at the loading pens. *SC Nash*

Right: The Franciscan Friary at Rossnowlagh was formally opened on Sunday 29 June 1952 when the President Sean T O'Ceallaigh and the Taoiseach Eamonn DeValera both attended along with about 5000 others. The choir from the Franciscan Friary at Merchant Quay in Dublin travelled for the occasion in this special railcar. It is a two-year-old four-piece AEC railcar with a K23 Buffet Car included. Leaving Dublin at a challenging 6.00am and Clones at 8.25am, the railcar ran non-stop from there to Ballyshannon, arriving at 10.18am. After lying over in Bundoran, the return train left here at 6.30pm and reached Dublin just before 11.00pm. Here the choir spills off the train, escorted by one of the community, while the white-capped Customs man stands back (for a change!).

Courtesy Franciscan Friary

Above: PG class 0-6-0 No 10, long a regular performer on the branch goods trains, leaves for Enniskillen on an unknown date with the daily goods which includes a number of permanent way wagons. The Cementation sidings diverge to the right of the engine; the controlling ground frame was behind the photographer on this side of the lines. *RM Arnold*

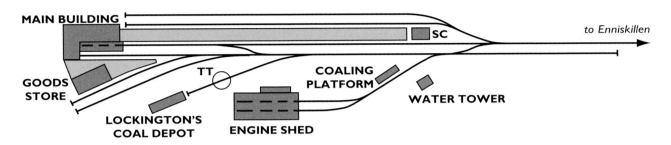

MAIN BUILDING

SC

to Enniskillen

GOODS STORE

TT

COALING PLATFORM

WATER TOWER

LOCKINGTON'S COAL DEPOT

ENGINE SHED

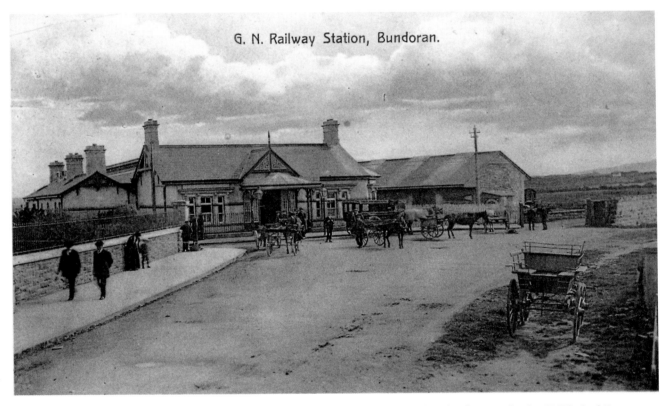

G. N. Railway Station, Bundoran.

Above: Bundoran's passenger building was the only one on the branch in the yellow brick style of WH Mills, the GNR's Civil Engineer. In this unattributed postcard, posted from Bundoran on 4 July 1921, four sidecars and their drivers seem to be waiting for customers off an arriving train. To the right of the main door is the two horse, four-wheel horse bus for the Great Northern Hotel. This ran until the summer of 1929. The building to the right is Bundoran's rarely-photographed goods store.

CP Friel collection

Above: Inside Bundoran's one platform train shed in its last summer.

Stations UK

Right: An early 20th century scene showing J class 4-4-0 No 18, after arriving at Bundoran with a passenger train, though the headlamps suggest an empty coaching stock train. Unfortunately no details have survived. This locomotive was named *Hollyhock* before 1914. It was built in 1885, one of a class of twelve and the first of a long line of GNR 4-4-0 locomotives. At one time they were common in Fermanagh and were mostly withdrawn in 1924-9. The exceptions were Nos 118 and 119, which were sold to the Sligo Leitrim in 1921. There they were named *Blacklion* and *Glencar* respectively. *Glencar* was broken up in August 1928 but its boiler survived in *Blacklion* until its withdrawal in 1931. It wasn't actually broken up until June 1937.

CP Friel collection

Opposite top: We have to thank the intrepid Ken Nunn, from the south of England, for this rare nineteenth century view of Bundoran. Here we see H class 2-4-0 No 84 with a train of six six wheelers. The guard's raised look-out on the rear vehicle is just visible. The date was 11 September 1898 when the locomotive was just 17 years old. Note the burnished buffers and smokebox straps. The locomotive was later rebuilt and lasted until 1932. It may be that 84 had arrived under the station roof but then set back to clear the engine release crossover. Cattle wagon No 3452, in the sidings on the right, is open all round above shoulder height but, unlike many of its predecessors, it has a roof. Note the fence dividing Bundoran's long finger platform, with the cabin at the far end.

Ken Nunn, courtesy LCGB

Opposite bottom: P6'6" class 4-4-0 No 73 seems to be about to run round its train after arriving in Bundoran on Saturday 14 September 1957 with the 10.45am Down. The leading coach is a tricomposite brake, followed by an ex-LNWR corridor third, one of a batch purchased from the LMS in 1947. Two passenger vans complete the train. The two tracks in the bottom right corner are sidings whilst the turnout along the right edge leads to the 44-foot diameter turntable. The three bracket signal controlling the approaches to Bundoran is just visible in the extreme right background.

Colin Hogg

Above: This could have been 10.30am on any summer's morning but this wet morning is in late September 1957 and scenes such as this were not to be repeated many more times. On the right, U class 4-4-0 No 199 *Lough Derg* has just arrived with the 9.10am from the Junction (scheduled 10.29am) and has run up to the buffers of No 2 platform. Note the K22 clerestory third, originally 2nd/3rd. On the left PP class 4-4-0 No 50 blows off, impatient to be away with the 10.30am to Enniskillen, which has a cattle wagon coupled behind the engine. The two men in the right centre of the picture are Benny Nolan and a plumber called Lynn from Enniskillen. Driver Paddy Gallagher is just discernable in 199's cab.

NC Simmons, Photos from the Fifties

Opposite top: We turn the clock back to about 1900 for this view of a train of six-wheelers, with a birdcage brake at the rear, arriving at Bundoran. The locomotive is ex-Ulster Railway K class 0-4-2 No 106 *Tornado*. The engine was built by the Ulster at Belfast in 1872 and was rebuilt, as seen here, by the GNR(I) in 1889. It was renumbered 106A in 1906 when a new PP class 4-4-0 took the name and number. The engine was scrapped the following year. Typical of the time, the engine has burnished smokebox handrail and straps and buffers – even the cylinder covers are bright! The platform to the right was used for coaling engine tenders.

C P Friel collection

Opposite bottom: An interesting Edwardian view at Bundoran showing passengers just arrived on an excursion from Greenore, comprising six-wheel Dundalk, Newry and Greenore Railway stock in LNWR livery. Note what appears to be a large picnic hamper on the platform and the elaborate carriage board.

Courtesy J Richardson

Above: The Great Northern Hotel in Bundoran as seen in the Great Northern's *Magic Miles in Ireland* tourist booklet of 1934, though the cars suggest the photo was taken about five years earlier. The present owner/manager of the much-extended hotel is Brian McEniff who was captain of the first Donegal GAA football team to win the Ulster Championship in 1972 and managed the county team to its first All-Ireland Football title in 1992. From our point view, though, it is just as interesting that he competed in the All-Ireland Go-Kart championships in Ardee in 1956 with his aptly-named go-kart 'The Bundoran Express'.

Opposite top: This delightful scene has been published before but fully deserves another airing. The date is Thursday 3 June 1954 and shows railcar C3 and No 204 *Antrim* outside Bundoran shed, with AL class 0-6-0 No 59 visible beyond the shed. The railcar has worked in on the 9.10am from the Junction and will return on the 2.25pm to Enniskillen, calling, as required, at several crossings. These were Crowe's, Castle Archdale and Johnston's, between Kesh and Irvinestown and Tague's, in the Irvinestown to Bundoran Junction section. In addition, the railcar will stop at Legg's Crossing, between Pettigo and Castlecaldwell, for mails only. As indicated by the nameboard, 204 will work the Up 'Bundoran Express' (due away at 12.20pm) The 0-6-0 had arrived with the 5.50am goods from Enniskillen, due here at 10.20am. After shunting, 59 has been turned and is sitting in the siding off the turntable, probably to have its fire cleaned before leaving at 11.50am on the goods for Enniskillen, where it wasn't due until 6.12pm. A couple of passenger vans are just visible at the loading bank, alongside the passenger train shed.

NW Sprinks

Opposite bottom: Bundoran shed on Friday 6 August 1937 with P class 4-4-0 No 72 and the branch goods engine, AL class 0-6-0 No 58, on shed. In the centre background, the Church of the Immaculate Conception appears above the engines while, to the right, we have a glimpse of the turntable and Lockington's coal store beyond. Charles Clifford, who went on to design the GNR's outstanding S class 4-4-0s, was once the Loco Foreman here.

WA Camwell

Above: Bundoran looks busy in this Sunday evening view, taken on 8 July 1956, showing PP class 4-4-0 No 106 ready to leave with a 'Hills of Donegal' excursion returning to Belfast. The seven or eight coach train includes a modern flush panelled buffet car. In the left background, visible in the siding alongside the train shed, is a four coach train with roof boards, probably the stock of the 'Bundoran Express'. At platform 2, and the siding behind are at least three separate trains – probably excursions waiting to leave later that evening. The coach on the right is a class J6 brake composite, with centre corridor accommodation in the third class end and side corridor for first. Just visible, in the right background, is a large corrugated iron and wood pavilion towering above the bus depot. The pavilion was used by some excursions for picnic lunches. In the last summer (1957), some 40,000 day trippers arrived in Bundoran.

DTR Henderson

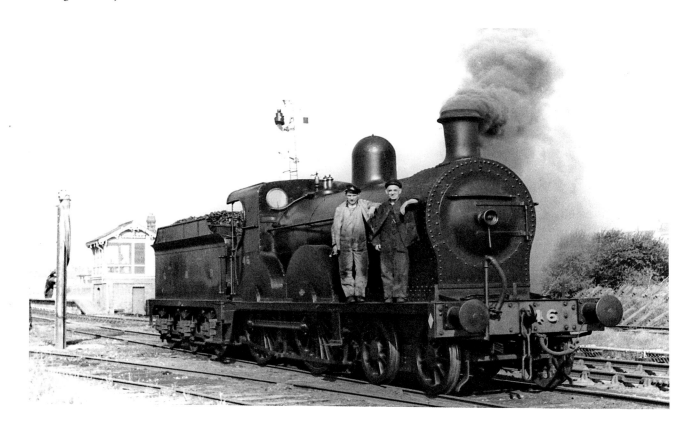

Opposite top: A classic posed shot of Fireman Frank Carty (left) and Driver Paddy Martin on the running board of PP class 4-4-0 No 46 on Wednesday 22 April 1953. The locomotive is sitting on the loop and has probably just taken water from the column on the extreme left. The lazy black smoke suggests that the locomotive is brewing up before working the 10.30am to Enniskillen. Bundoran cabin is visible behind the tender.

HC Casserley, courtesy RM Casserley

Opposite bottom: This picture came to light just as we were finalising the book. It is a scene that I often wondered if anyone had photographed. The mountains to the right are, left to right, Benwiskin, Truskbeg and Ben Bulben; they dominate the scene at my mother's home place as mentioned in Charles Remembers. Here we are about a mile out of Bundoran, beyond Drumcrin. It is Sunday 30 June 1957 and there have been excursions into Bundoran from Clones and Derry and a four-piece AEC from Dublin, as well as the usual Expresses. This train, though, did not appear in the weekly circular. U class 4-4-0 No 201 *Meath* had worked a remarkably short three-coach Express into Bundoran in the early afternoon. Rather than retire until next morning, she and the Express carriages were 'borrowed' for this special to Irvinestown which left at 9.00pm, long after all the others had gone home! Marshalled next the engine, and still carrying its Express board, is the Belfast through coach, L11 Brake Third No 11, dating from 1913. Then come the two more modern Dublin coaches, an F16 Corridor Composite and an L12 Brake Third. Driver Paddy Martin looks to be well pleased with himself! This picture makes a most fitting farewell to Bundoran.

Bluebell Railway Museum, JJ Smith Collection

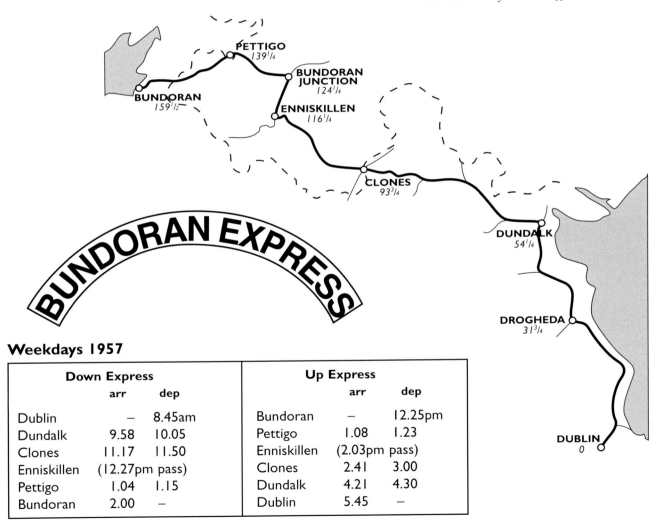

Weekdays 1957

Down Express			Up Express		
	arr	dep		arr	dep
Dublin	–	8.45am	Bundoran	–	12.25pm
Dundalk	9.58	10.05	Pettigo	1.08	1.23
Clones	11.17	11.50	Enniskillen	(2.03pm pass)	
Enniskillen	(12.27pm pass)		Clones	2.41	3.00
Pettigo	1.04	1.15	Dundalk	4.21	4.30
Bundoran	2.00	–	Dublin	5.45	–

Left: S2 class 4-4-0 No 191 *Croaghpatrick* waits at Dublin's Platform 1 with the down Bundoran Express on Saturday 12 June 1954.

Brian Green

Below: Just north of Fairview, S class 4-4-0 No 173 *Galteemore* has a big train well under way as she heads for Dundalk on Friday 29 April 1955, the first day for the Express that year.

NW Sprinks

Right: VS class 3-cylinder 4-4-0 No 206 *Liffey* passing Harmonstown, on the outskirts of Dublin, with the Down 'Bundoran Express', probably in 1956. Unusually the train is only three coaches long and does not include any refreshment vehicle. The train may be a relief (a second portion following the main train).

A Donaldson, courtesy WT Scott

Below: The Down 'Bundoran Express' waits at Clones on Saturday 10 June 1955. Emphasising the variety of motive power on this train, the locomotive is UG class 0-6-0 No 148, built in 1948, and the load is the more usual seven bogies. The leading vehicle is an M1 full brake, followed by several modern flush panelled coaches – four K15 thirds and an F16 composite. At the tail of the train is the brake composite from Belfast, added here in place of the buffet car, which had come on the train from Dublin and was now detached to await the Up 'Express', due at 3.00pm. This layover of the buffet car would be frowned upon by today's accountants. However, to change the buffet car over at Pettigo would have been operationally difficult, with three trains in the station. Standing alongside the leading van is the wheeltapper with his long-handled hammer.

A Donaldson, courtesy WT Scott

Opposite top: This has for long been one of my favourite photographs; it brings back so much and I feel I could just walk into the scene. It is Monday 31 May 1954 and No 204 *Antrim* drifts in with the Down 'Express'. The driver is Paddy McKeown and the fireman, holding the staff, is Denis Cosgrove. Neil Sprinks was fortunate to get this superb shot, as the Lough Derg season had commenced the previous Saturday that year, instead of the normal 1 June. Being so early in the season, the train is another lightweight – an M1 van, an F16 compo, a K15 third and a brake compo. As the 'Express' was not supposed to stop in Northern Ireland precautions were needed to avoid a signal check. Sometimes the Lisbellaw signalman tied a luggage label to the staff saying, "Take your time – Enniskillen not ready." The label, of course, went in the firebox! On a personal note, the Tempo Road is visible behind the telegraph poles and the sharp-eyed may just make out the Killynure siding just right of the signal pole, with a string of cattle wagons in it.

Opposite bottom: U class No 196 *Lough Gill* passes Enniskillen South with the down Express on Sunday 30 May 1954.

Both NW Sprinks

Above: The Down 'Bundoran Express' eases through Enniskillen in August 1957 hauled by No 204. On the left is the diesel train from Belfast which had arrived at 11.37am. This is about 12.27pm. The diesel was booked to depart to Belfast at 12.30pm after the 'Express' had cleared the Lisbellaw-Enniskillen section.

Courtesy Headhunters' Museum

Above: With steam to spare, P class 4-4-0 No 73 has a lightweight 'Express' well in hand as it passes Ballinamallard en route to Bundoran in June 1957.

N W Sprinks

Opposite top: Kesh at 12.55pm on Saturday 1 September 1956, with the Down 'Bundoran Express' coming through – non-stop of course. The signalman on the platform is holding up the staff for the Kesh-Pettigo section for the fireman while, further down the platform, the local Customs man has helpfully taken the Irvinestown-Kesh staff while keeping an eye for contraband being thrown from the train. The scene is being watched by a couple of boys on the station seat. Next the engine are a J11 tricompo-brake and an F16 composite.

A Donaldson, courtesy WT Scott

Left: From just south of the overbridge at Bundoran Junction we see U class 4-4-0 No 201 *Meath* diverge on to the branch with the Down 'Bundoran Express' on Saturday 8 June 1957. Despite the almost inevitable closure of the line a mere sixteen weeks later, we can see a newly-laid turnout below the locomotive and incompletely ballasted track on both the lines to Omagh and Bundoran. An Engineer's tool van (No 8168, converted from a passenger van) is in the siding on the extreme left. Notice the sleepers and chairs scattered about on the same siding.

L King

Above: U class 4-4-0 No 198 *Lough Swilly* takes water at Pettigo while the pilgrims leave the Down Express. At the other platform, the Up Express was headed by PP class 4-4-0 No 107. Away to the left is the cattle pen on the goods platform.

RM Arnold

Above: This is Belleek, as seen from the bridge carrying the main street across the line. The train is the Down 'Bundoran Express' on Bank Holiday Monday, 5 August 1957, hauled by U class 4-4-0 No 201 *Meath*. The train is of six bogies, the first four of which are modern – a J11, an F16 and two K15 thirds. On the left a single van occupies Belleek's goods loop – the shortest on the line and capable of holding just fifteen wagons and a locomotive. The siding to the Belleek Pottery factory passed behind the signal cabin and ran for about 160 yards down a steep gradient before reaching the Pottery gates. The siding brought in coal, clay and other new materials, while the outward traffic was, of course, the Pottery's famous porcelain.

A Donaldson, courtesy WT Scott

Right: On a Sunday in August 1957, U class 4-4-0 No 201 *Meath* has arrived at Bundoran with the 'Express' and has set back to clear the engine release crossover – the driver seems to be winding the engine into forward gear again so that it can move forward to run round. *Meath* will shunt the train to the siding behind platform 2 and then go to the shed to be turned, serviced and 'put to bed' until its next turn of duty, which will be the following day's Up 'Express', which she will work to Dundalk. The left is dominated by Bundoran UDC's water tank.

ColourRail

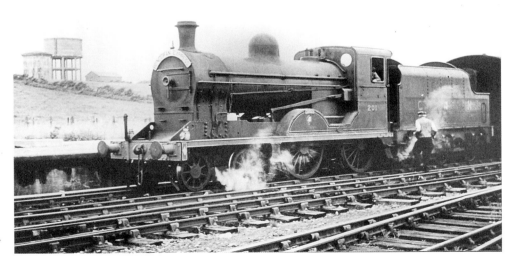

Opposite bottom: In this view of Irvinestown we are observing the approach of the Up 'Bundoran Express' headed by No 201 *Meath*. On the left is the Down platform with the typical GNR shelter. Behind the Up platform, the door of the goods store is closed as it is a Sunday.

RM Arnold

Above: Pettigo with the Up and Down Expresses crossing on Saturday 1 September 1956. The Dublin-bound Up Express is in the charge of U class 4-4-0 No 202 *Louth* which is taking water before setting out on its 45½ mile run though Fermanagh (and a bit of Tyrone) en route to Clones. The steam below the bufferbeam is from the cylinder drain cocks and suggests that No 202 is about to get her train under way. The border was at the next bridge where the Termon river ran under the line, about 200 yards behind the photographer.

A Donaldson, courtesy WT Scott

Opposite top: On the Lisbellaw side of Enniskillen, No 204 *Antrim* is working the Up 'Bundoran Express' on Wednesday 10 July 1957 and is seen here alongside the Tempo Road, just visible on the left. To the right is the Killynure siding, empty on this occasion. The express is made up of just five carriages; often it was longer. The through coach for Belfast is at the back of the train.

RM Arnold

Opposite bottom: Having re-entered the Irish Republic near Clones, and taken water, the 'Bundoran Express' is seen here pulling out of Clones to head for Dundalk, hauled by U class 4-4-0 No 198 *Lough Swilly*. The coach to the right is an ex Dundalk, Newry and Greenore Railway 6-wheel brake – a classic LNWR designed vehicle. This line, originally owned by the LNWR, used the old pre-1923 London North Western livery right up to the 1950s.

RM Arnold

Above: Journey – and pilgrimage too, perhaps – almost over. An Up 'Bundoran Express' rolls into Dublin (Amiens Street) behind QL class 4-4-0 No 128 at an unknown date in the 1950s. On this side of the engine the fireman has time for a cigarette, the hard work now behind him. The K12 buffet car is immediately behind the locomotive and one of its attendants, his work also done, is leaning from a window.

CP Friel collection

The Sunday 'Bundoran Expresses' ran for the last time on Sunday 18 August. The last 'Bundoran Express' from Dublin to Bundoran ran on Saturday 31 August, returning from Bundoran on Monday 2 September 1957, worked by No 203 *Armagh* with Driver David Vennard and Fireman Kevin Love. And that was that!

THE SLIGO LEITRIM AND NORTHERN COUNTIES RAILWAY

Above: It is now time to retrace our steps to Fermanagh's county town and examine the Sligo Leitrim and Northern Counties. We begin near the Great Northern's Enniskillen South signal cabin, seen here on the left. Below it, the GNR line from Clones is in the cutting, with an oil lamp marking the spot where the single line staff for the section to or from Lisbellaw was handed over. The building in the centre of the picture is the Sligo Leitrim's Head Office including the General Manager's office. It was made of unpretentious corrugated iron and usually painted a brownish red colour. It appears in some SLNCR documents as 'Chief Office'. There is some evidence to suggest that the platform on which the Head Office sits was the Sligo Leitrim's original passenger station, but the best verdict seems to be 'case not proven'. The track past this platform was the only connection between the GNR and SLNCR tracks – note the change from chaired track to flat-bottom rail. In the centre foreground is a remarkable movable diamond crossing, a rare item of trackwork. This picture dates from about 1932.

Real Photographs Ltd

Opposite top: This is a rare view of the inside of the SLNCR's headquarters, showing the Inspector, Thomas Algeo (left, with bowler) in the General Office. The young lad working the typewriter is David Lunny, a clerk. The window blind behind Mr Algeo has been pulled down for the photograph but the magnesium flare has cast a shadow from the chimney of the stove on the right. From the calendars on the wall, the date would appear to be January 1904 but sometimes a calendar was left up for some time if the picture was an attractive one! Mr Algeo was later Mayor of Enniskillen and died, aged 89, in 1960.

Courtesy Headhunters' Museum

Below: This is a view from the South cabin on Friday 6 August 1937. The track in the bottom left corner of the picture leads to the SLNCR turntable. In the sidings in the distance, seven-ton open wagons 139 and 76 flank a train of three six-wheel carriages. The six-wheel brake coach in the foreground is an ex GNR vehicle. Above it the SLNCR main line can be seen curving past the two Sligo Leitrim engine sheds, one of which contains *Lough Gill*. The bridge over the Tempo Road was immediately past the further shed. The white painted signal, seen here, was beyond the bridge. Another signal in the right background marks where the SLNCR curved away to the south en route for Castlecoole and Sligo. The nearer engine shed – known as the 'large shed' – was another corrugated iron structure. The coal unloading bank, mentioned in 'Charles Remembers' was the siding running behind the large shed.

WA Camwell

Opposite top: On Wednesday 21 July 1954, 0-6-4T *Lough Melvin* shunts a train of six-wheelers at the SLNCR yard. The carriages appear to be Nos 2, 3 and 4, in order from the locomotive. This was the stock of the 4.00pm from Sligo, with steam substituting for Railcar B which had failed at Florencecourt earlier that day (see page 146). The gentleman on the right is Mr E W (Ernie) Monahan, the SLNCR's Accountant who added General Manager to his duties in early 1956. The GNR line from Clones is on the left and, again, the Sligo Leitrim's Head Office is on the short platform which had been the SLNCR's station between opening of the line in 1879 and the enlargement of the GNR station in 1883.

Colin Hogg

Opposite bottom: An interesting view across the Great Northern towards the Sligo Leitrim yard on Saturday 15 June 1957. To the left, at the shed, is GNR PG class 0-6-0 No 151. Across the tracks, the SLNCR's *Hazelwood* is shunting brake compo carriage No 9 for that evening's 7.20pm mixed to Sligo. The Sligo Leitrim had three bogie carriages, Nos 9, 10 and 11. They were funded by the Free State government as compensation for 8 six-wheel carriages that were lost in the Civil War. They were ordered in September 1924 from Hurst Nelson and were delivered to Belfast. They ran thence via Clones but they ran hot at Tynan and lay there for some time awaiting attention.

Michael Davis, Photos from the Fifties

Above: At the top end of the passenger platform, one of the 'Lough' class locos pauses while a rake of cattle wagons (on the left) is being transferred on to the Great Northern for onward despatch to Belfast or, maybe, Derry. In the foreground, the collection of bicycles clustered around the signal post belong to GN railwaymen whose shed is across the tracks to our left. In the distance, to the left of the signal, Railbus A and trailer are reversing towards the turntable. On the extreme right is the SLNCR goods store which was destined to be last railway building still standing in Enniskillen (though it succumbed in 2008).

Photographer unknown

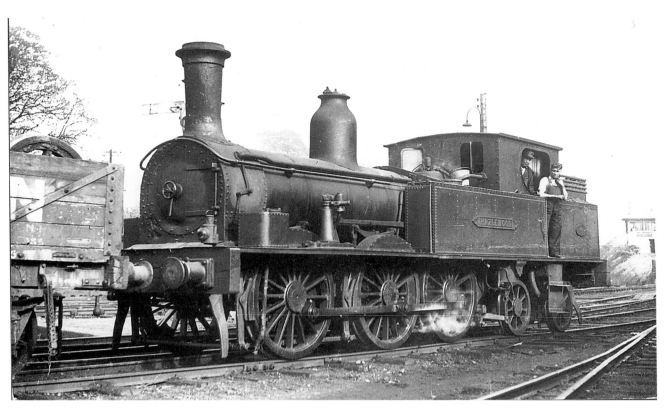

Opposite top: *Hazlewood* was built in 1899. It was the last of the five 'Leitrim' class 0-6-4T locomotives to be built and the only one to survive until 1957. Apart from the addition of coal rails, the only visible change since its construction was a different cab shape, resulting from a malicious derailment in 1923, during the Irish Civil War. The cylinder visible below the water tank, above the leading bogie wheel, was one of two that operated the locomotive's steam brake. The wheel arrangement was an unusual choice in Ireland for main line use; almost all other classes of 0-6-4T were built for shunting in goods yards or dock lines. The Sligo Leitrim had ten locomotives with this wheel arrangement and seemed to have little reason to try anything else. If anything, the two ex-Great Northern 4-4-0s used on the line in the 1920s were not suited to the job in hand.

Real Photographs Ltd

Opposite bottom: *Lissadell* waits to leave Enniskillen with six-wheel coach No 3 on Wednesday 17 May 1950. Unfortunately no other details of this interesting working have survived. At the GNR platform, to the right, are a cattle wagon and horsebox. *Lissadell*, also built in 1899, was a sister of *Hazlewood*, seen in the previous picture. Members of the class were unofficially called 'Small Tanks'.

GW Sharpe, courtesy CP Friel

Above: A side view of *Sir Henry* in 1948 on the turntable at Enniskillen. Incidentally this was the only turntable owned by the SLNCR, since Manorhamilton did not have one and the GSR/CIE table was used at Sligo. The building to the left is the SLNCR's Head Office. Enniskillen South cabin was unusual in being glazed on all four sides rather than the more usual three. This was because it controlled Sligo trains as well as GNR ones and an all-round view was essential. *Sir Henry* was built in 1904 and reboilered in 1929. He and his sisters – *Enniskillen* and *Lough Gill* – were known as 'Large Tanks'.

Real Photographs Ltd

Above: *Lough Erne* and *Lough Melvin* were the last conventional steam engines built for Ireland. *Lough Erne* had only been in service for about six weeks when this photograph was taken on Thursday 6 September 1951 in the Sligo yard at Enniskillen. Here on the running plate are (left) Driver Tommy Gilloway, who had come from the Castlederg and Victoria Bridge, and his Fireman Joe Nolan.

EM Patterson

Left: The plate on the back of *Lough Melvin*'s coal bunker indicating that the locomotive was still the property of the builders Beyer Peacock. *Lough Melvin* and *Lough Erne* were built in 1949 but the Sligo Leitrim could not afford to buy them. The eventual compromise was that the engines were bought on a hire-purchase basis and duly arrived in June and July 1951. Gerry Lambe and Vicky Holland, from the shops in Manorhamilton, were sent to Belfast to help with the assembly and testing of the two engines before they were worked to Enniskillen, probably via Omagh.

Photographer unknown

Left: The SLNCR used railbuses for many of its passenger services. The first was Railbus A, delivered to the Sligo Leitrim on 20 June 1935 and converted from an older GNR Associated Daimler Type 413 road bus, with an AEC petrol engine. Like many buses from this manufacturer, the vehicle had a full width cab. It was fitted with Howden-Meredith patent wheels. This type of wheel, devised at Dundalk, allowed the bus to retain its pneumatic road tyres but now inside a railway profiled tyre. This allowed the bus to retain all the characteristics of road suspension. Above each wheel rim was a detector that would activate the brakes if the pneumatic tyre deflated. In 1938 it was fitted with a Gardner 4LW diesel engine.

Real Photographs Ltd

Above: The original Railbus A had only been converted to diesel propulsion for about a year when, on 7 March 1939, it was runner-up in a tussle with a steam locomotive. Its replacement was an even older railbus (Ex-GNR D1), dating from 1926. The diesel engine of the original 'A' was reused. It is seen at Manorhamilton en route to Sligo with its high trailer in tow.

Kelland Collection, Bournemouth Railway Club

Left: By December 1950 a replacement body for Railbus A was required and another GNR bus body was pressed into service on the same chassis. With this body, the revitalised 'A' is seen on Enniskillen's turntable, along with its luggage trailer. The trailer was built at Manorhamilton in 1942 using the bogie off a scrapped Great Southern Railway Sentinel steam railcar.

CP Friel collection

Below: This is Railbus 2A, another Dundalk conversion of a GNR road bus, but this time with a Gardner diesel engine from the start. It arrived on the line in early 1938 with a new body and, although similar to the last metamorphosis of 'A', had many detail differences. In these pictures you can see 2A's outward sweep at the bottom of the side panels, compared to A's inward sweep, as well as many differences around the fronts of the vehicles. In the dock platform, on the left, is one of the 1924 bogie coaches. Most likely it is No 10, the coach that worked on the 10.20am Sligo to Enniskillen and the 1.40pm return. As it always, therefore, ran during daylight hours, it wasn't equipped with any form of lighting! Latterly a coach stabled here would have been for the 7.20pm mixed to Sligo.

Rev J Parker, Photos from the Fifties

Above: The pride of the line was Railcar B. Built by Walkers of Wigan, 'B' was an articulated vehicle after the style of the GNR 'C' cars or the pioneer Clogher Valley Railcar 1 seen earlier (page 26). This is the powered end, with a spacious driver's cab and engine, carried on a 4-wheel bogie. The passenger section included a sizable area for luggage and parcels accessed by the double doors. The door at the further end included retractable steps for use at level crossings. The radiator for the diesel engine was carried on the roof at this end. Railcar B cost 1½p a mile to run, compared to 12½p for a steam train. With its own luggage compartment, it didn't require a trailer and didn't need to be turned.

P McKeown

Left: We begin our journey along the Sligo Leitrim with this view of Railcar B in the bay platform at Enniskillen, as seen from under the footbridge. Railcar B made two round trips to Sligo each day and here it has arrived with the 9.30am from Sligo, due at 11.40am. Across the platform, to the left, is the GNR's 12 noon to Omagh with the station pilot adding empty bread containers to the tail of the clerestory-roofed carriage.

Photographer unknown

Opposite top: The SLNCR's passenger platform is to the left in this view of *Lough Gill* which has brought a cattle wagon to the platform alongside the HM Customs office. The device beyond the wagon is a loading gauge which was used to measure whether any loads would be too high for the line's overbridges. The wagon to the left of *Lough Gill* is a tank wagon; these were used to transport oil, petrol, diesel and paraffin.

RM Arnold

Opposite bottom: The 7.20pm mixed was the only regular way to travel behind steam over the Sligo Leitrim. 'Mixed' meant that there was a passenger coach at the front of the train with goods wagons (with brake van) on the rear. Here *Hazelwood* is preparing to leave on Tuesday 24 May 1955 but the crew take time to pose for the visitor. On the platform are Porter John Howe and Foreman Jimmy McHugh while, in the loco cab are Fireman Bertie Hegarty and Driver Tommie Marren. The coal looks a bit small for the job and the carriage, clerestory bogie No 11, could do with some attention.

NW Sprinks

Above: *Lough Erne* has just arrived in Enniskillen with the 6.30am goods from Sligo (due here at 10.00am) on Monday 31 May 1954 and is starting to shunt the train back into the sidings that have access to the GNR. The GNR engine shed is on the extreme left and the roof of Enniskillen South cabin is just visible above the first wagon. *Lough Erne* was built in 1949 and was one of the last two engines built for the SLNCR, its sister being *Lough Melvin*.

NW Sprinks

Opposite top: The elderly *Hazelwood* takes water in Enniskillen yard; the passenger station is away to our right.

Courtesy Headhunters' Museum

Opposite bottom: In September 1957, looking from the Sligo Leitrim yard towards the station, we see *Sir Henry* between duties and waiting at the Head Office platform. In the background a Great Northern train has arrived from Clones, whilst SLNCR railbus 2A waits to leave, probably on the 12 noon to Sligo. The wagon on the extreme left, with the corrugated ends, was for transporting bagged cement from the factory at Drogheda.

NC Simmons, Photos from the Fifties

Above: This view is almost back to back with the previous picture. Here *Enniskillen* – built in 1905 and the second of three 'Sir Henry' class engines – is shunting in the Sligo Leitrim yard on Friday 27 September 1957. Immediately behind the locomotive is 7-ton brake van No 6, followed by brake composite coach No 9, two cattle wagons and two loaded open wagons. Part of the County Hospital (see 'Charles Remembers') is visible above *Enniskillen*'s chimney.

SC Nash

Opposite top: Lough Erne is seen here getting away from Enniskillen with the 7.20pm mixed to Sligo on Monday 31 May 1954. Bogie brake compo No 9 was a regular feature on this train and is followed by four cattle wagons (one of them unroofed), two open wagons and a brake van. On the extreme right is the SLNCR turntable, with what looks like a diesel fuel pump on the embankment.

SC Nash

Opposite bottom: The Sligo Leitrim had two engine sheds at Enniskillen, as we have already seen. This brick-built shed housed the steam engine based here. On Tuesday 24 June 1937 the locomotive in residence was *Sligo*, the first of two engines to carry the name. This locomotive had been GNR A class 0-6-0 No 49 until 1931, when the Sligo Leitrim bought it. It was replaced in 1941 by sister locomotive No 69 which was also named *Sligo*. Note the brickwork on the corner of the shed, stepped to clear the loading gauge of the nearby running lines. The very small metal bridge over the Tempo Road (SLNCR bridge No 1) is visible behind and to the left of the shed. The longer corrugated iron shed, on the right, was later the overnight stabling point for Railcar B.

HC Casserley, courtesy RM Casserley

Above: It is about 10.00am on Wednesday 2 June 1954, and Driver Tommy McKernan is bringing the 6.30am goods from Sligo along the edge of the woods at Castlecoole, on the Enniskillen side of the Dublin road bridge. The loco is *Lough Melvin* and the train is mostly cattle wagons, of course.

NW Sprinks

Opposite top: This photograph was taken on Wednesday 25 July 1934 when the swimming pool on the right was officially opened. Wednesday was half-day closing for many of Enniskillen's shops so there were many locals present for a swimming gala that included a display of diving, swimming and water games. The attention of everyone has turned to the Weirs Bridge where a train is approaching from Sligo. The train is a mixture of carriages from the SLNCR, GNR and GSR. It must be the empty stock for the following Sunday's Garland Sunday excursion to Sligo when the SLNCR traditionally borrowed stock from its neighbours. The excursion was the only reliably steam-hauled passenger train on the line. It brought pilgrims to the Holy Well at Tobernalt near Carraroe outside Sligo town. The engine is one of the two surviving Leitrim class locos (see page 130), more likely to be *Hazelwood* since *Lissadell* was withdrawn in that year.

Courtesy of Headhunters Museum

Opposite bottom: This view is from the opposite, or southern, end of the bridge and shows *Sir Henry* setting out for Sligo with the 2.00pm goods on Friday 20 July 1956. The wagon next the engine is a horse box, while the first, lighter coloured, van in the middle of the bridge is a Great Northern cement van, based in Drogheda. Between the piers can be seen a bucket dredger and other plant used in deepening the river to help alleviate flooding.

A Donaldson, courtesy WT Scott

Above: Yet another delightful scene from the camera of Neil Sprinks. We are at the south end of the Weirs Bridge as *Lough Erne*, with a lightly loaded 7.20pm mixed train for Sligo crosses on Monday 31 May 1954. The train was known as a 'mixed' because it conveyed both passengers and goods. Here the passenger accommodation (as always) is provided by bogie brake composite No 9. There must not have been any goods wagons needing to be moved from Enniskillen that evening, so the train is completed by only a goods brake van. Note the bridge number painted on the masonry pier to the left.

NW Sprinks

Opposite top: This is near level crossing No 2 – or 'No 2 gates' to the railwaymen – where the line crossed the minor road to Drumkeen and Stinson's Bridge. The train is the 6.30am goods from Sligo, made up of covered vans from CIE, the GNR and some from the SLNCR. The locomotive is *Sir Henry* and the date was Wednesday 26 June 1957. High on a hill above the back of the train is the signal guarding No 3 gates at Mullaghy on the Enniskillen to Swanlinbar road.

NW Sprinks

Opposite bottom: *Lough Erne* is seen here stopped near Florencecourt while working a goods from Enniskillen to Sligo on Monday 18 April 1955. The second wagon contains stone ballast and this is being shovelled over the side for later use on the track. While this saved the expense of working a separate ballast train (as on most other railways), it had an adverse effect on timekeeping.

HC Casserley, courtesy RM Casserley

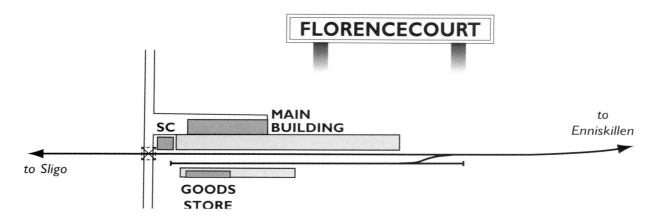

Left: This is Florencecourt looking towards Belcoo in 1956. There was one passenger platform, with the signal cabin at the far end controlling a level crossing. Access to the siding on the left, with its goods store, was from the Enniskillen end of the station. Visitors arriving here to visit Florencecourt House would have discovered it was almost three miles away!

Stations UK

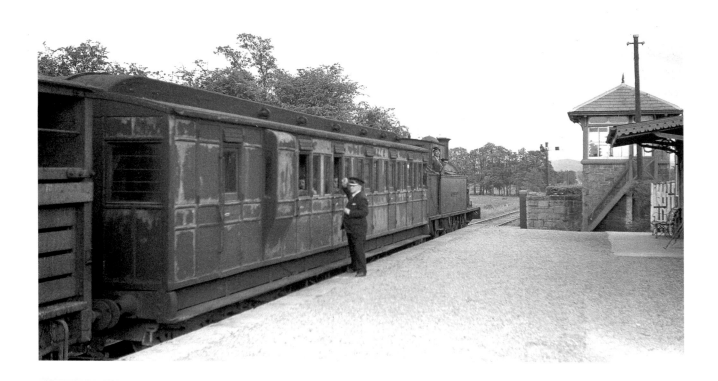

Opposite top: Stopped at Florencecourt platform is the 7.20pm mixed from Enniskillen to Sligo on Monday 16 June 1952. The smartly-attired Guard is busy with the passengers in Brake Composite No 9, while the crew of Lough Gill keep an eye on our photographer. Note the signal cabin on the right and the awning on the station building.

JJ Smith, courtesy of Bluebell Railway Collection

Opposite bottom: An interesting view, taken on Wednesday 21 July 1954, showing Railcar B, which was working the 12 noon to Sligo. The brakes of the railcar had seized at a level crossing just beyond Florencecourt and *Lough Melvin*, sent from Enniskillen, has hauled it back to Florencecourt. The passengers have been obliged to disgorge both their luggage and themselves so that the railcar can be shunted to a siding; the passengers had to squeeze into the following railbus.

Colin Hogg

Above: This is Neil Sprinks' famous picture of a Sligo Leitrim mixed train leaving Florencecourt. Neil sent a print to Mr Monahan, the SLNCR's Accountant and General Manager who was so impressed that he put it on the cover of the line's last Public Timetable. The train was the 7.20pm to Sligo on Wednesday 2 June 1954. The engine is *Lough Erne* and the leading carriage is No 9. The line is on a down grade of 1 in 66 here which undoubtedly helped the engine get away in such fine style.

NW Sprinks

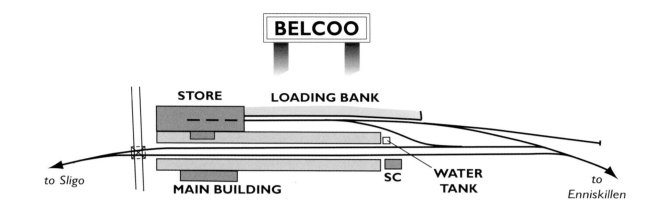

BELCOO

STORE · LOADING BANK

to Sligo · MAIN BUILDING · SC · WATER TANK · to Enniskillen

Left: Belcoo, in 1956, looking towards Enniskillen. Railcar B is probably on the 9.30am ex-Sligo. In this view we can see the main station building with its awning on the Down platform. On the extreme left is the goods store and the waiting room on the Up platform.

Stations UK

Right: This second view, looking in the same direction, but from the opposite side of the line, allows us to look along the Down platform towards the signal cabin. On the Up side the water tower is now visible and the goods yard is occupied by some cattle trucks and an open wagon. The Railcar is on a special working from Sligo to Enniskillen for a party from the Reading Enthusiasts' Club who spent a week on threatened Irish lines in late September 1957. Here, one of the party is boarding on the non-platform side into the luggage compartment.

NC Simmons, Photos from the Fifties

Above: The Enniskillen end of Belcoo on Thursday 26 September 1957. *Enniskillen,* with the 9.00am goods from Sligo, is taking water from the tank on the left. The coach is again bogie compo No 9 and is being worked empty to Enniskillen for use on the 7.20pm mixed. Beyond the locomotive is part of the goods yard, which handled considerable Free to Free goods traffic. This was an arrangement arrived at in 1936, whereby goods from the Irish Free State could be shipped through Northern Ireland in sealed wagons for delivery to customers in another part of the Irish Free State – hence the name. Belcoo was, of course, the railhead for Blacklion in County Leitrim. Belcoo's signal cabin, main station building and Down platform have recently been restored by their proud owner, Miss Mairead O'Dolan.

Hugh Davies, Photos from the Fifties

Left: The 7.20pm Sligo-bound mixed train pauses at Belcoo on Wednesday 21 July 1954. The locomotive is *Lough Melvin* and the train is composed of two six-wheelers, bogie coach No 9, a couple of cattle wagons and a brake van. The six-wheelers were being returned to Sligo after use on the 4.00pm Up train, when the failure of Railcar B resulted in a steam substitution (see page 146). Some goods wagons are visible in the goods yard in the left background, and the home signal is still in the off position.

Colin Hogg

Above: Railbus 2A pauses at Belcoo with the 1.45pm from Enniskillen to Sligo. The goods store dominates the background, with its extension at the Glenfarne end. Railbus 2A and trailer are working the 1.45pm from Enniskillen to Sligo and here, at Belcoo, is crossing a goods being shunted for the British Customs at the other platform. The goods store dominates the background with its modern extension at the Glenfarne end. Every November and December, the shed was a hive of hectic activity as hundreds of turkeys (and quite a few geese) were killed and plucked before despatch to Christmas tables far and wide but mostly in Scotland. Surprisingly, no-one has yet identified the lady on the platform, the wee boy – or the dog!

Derek Young collection

Left: Belcoo signal cabin on a quiet Sunday 30 May 1954.

NW Sprinks

Above: This is Belcoo as seen from the level crossing on Tuesday 23 June 1953 when *Lough Melvin* paused here while working the 2.15pm goods from Enniskillen to Sligo. The large goods store is to the left and a small corrugated-iron lean-to serves as the passenger waiting room on the Up platform. On the extreme right is another corrugated iron building, partly obscuring the main station building. This was the Post Office which was convenient for Freddie Monahan who was both Station Master and Post Master.

Bluebell Railway Museum, JJ Smith Collection

Left: Looking the other way from the water tower at the Enniskillen end of the up platform on Friday 23 December 1955.

EM Patterson

151

FERMANAGH BUS SERVICES

Our bus section covers the operations of four bus companies which operated in or into Fermanagh. We begin with the SLNCR and specifically with the last two buses operated by Hezekiah Appleby, who was related to my co-author Norman.

Left: On this page are the two buses taken over from Appleby on 2 April 1945. This is the Fermanagh-registered IL 2058, a 20-seater Bedford WLB built in 1932. The photograph was taken on Friday 13 April 1948 at Manorhamilton. Towards the end of that year, this bus and the one in the lower picture were replaced by new Commers.

JC Gillham

Left: This is Manorhamilton garage, where the SLNCR buses were serviced and maintained. On Monday 8 June 1953, Sligo-registered EI 5040 is inside the garage. This was a 1948 32-seater Commer Commando with a diesel engine which replaced one of the Appleby buses. On the left is SLNCR lorry and bus driver John Roche and on the right is mechanic Sean Loughlin.

JC Gillham

Opposite bottom: On Monday 3 August 1948 we see another ex-Appleby bus at Manorhamilton. This is EI 3905, a 29-seater 1938 Bedford. It has been lettered 'SL&NCR' below the windows, although it is otherwise still in Appleby's livery.

JC Gillham

Right: The other new Commer of 1948 was EI 4907, also a 32 seater Commando, and seen on the same date at Manorhamilton. The SLNCR livery was of dark and light green.

JC Gillham

Below right: A more complete view of the second 1948 Commer, EI 5040, at Manorhamilton on Friday 23 December 1955.

EM Patterson

Left: Two Erne buses are visible in this Wednesday 18 August 1948 view at the Diamond, near Enniskillen's Town Hall. Nearer the camera is ZI 8748, a 1932-3 built Leyland Lion LT4, purchased second hand from CIE. On the opposite side of High Street is sister Leyland ZI 8744. The rear of this vehicle shows the attractive Erne Bus Service scrolling, the livery of this fleet being cream and brown. Beyond the Leylands is Galligan's clothes shop which used rolling balls on a sort of overhead railway to send cash from each counter to a central cash office – and bring back the change. It fascinated the young Friels on every visit!

JC Gillham

Above: Bundoran, on Saturday 14 August 1948, with the Atlantic as a backdrop. ZI 8744, still with its original GSR rear entrance body, is waiting for its return trip to Enniskillen. The steeply raked driver's windscreen and low roof profile were very typical of early 1930s bus design. Note the starting handle, which was designed to rest in a 'handle down' position when not in use and remained like this even while the vehicle was in motion.

JC Gillham

Left: This more modern looking vehicle is in fact another early 1930s Leyland Lion which has been fitted with a new front entrance body. It was originally built for the Great Southern Railways and is seen here at Bundoran on Saturday 14 August 1948.

JC Gillham

Above: IL 5698, a 1952 front entrance Leyland Royal Tiger PSU with Saunders-Roe body, was the most modern bus in the Erne fleet. In this 1957 view we see it at Custom House Quay, Dublin, when it was on private hire duty, along with IL 5414, a 1951 front entrance Leyland Comet. Behind the Erne buses is a UTA Leyland Tiger Cub dual-purpose bus, with high-backed seats.

NC Simmons, Photos from the Fifties

155

Opposite top: The Erne Bus Service's garage at Enniskillen was in Quay Lane, opposite the gasworks. Here, in this Monday 8 June 1953 view, we see a rear aspect of IL 5698. By this date, the two oldest Tigers – ZI 8744 and ZI 8748 – were lying derelict outside the garage.

JC Gillham

Opposite bottom: A line-up of Erne buses pose for the photographer on the Shore Road at Carrickreagh (aka Carracreagh), just west of Ely Lodge on the southern side of Lower Lough Erne, en route to Bundoran. The leading vehicle is IL 5561, a front entrance Leyland Comet. Then comes the Royal Tiger coach (see below) and IL 5609, a Saunders Roe-bodied Royal Tiger. The photographer (a Mr McCabe from Clones) was probably on the roof of another Erne bus!

Courtesy Soinbhe Lally

Above: Maurice Cassidy took great pride in keeping up with the latest developments in the bus world. 1954 brought this zenith of style, a Burlingham Seagull-bodied Leyland Royal Tiger that was the pride of the fleet. Fermanagh-registered IL 7077 had an unusual centre entrance and was proudly known to us Enniskillen schoolboys as 'The Coach'. It was far superior to any UTA vehicle for, apart from the very comfortable seats and splendidly large windows, it had both a heater and a wireless! It became 205 in the UTA fleet in October 1957. It later became No 598 and was painted in Ulsterbus colours before withdrawal in 1968. It achieved a sort of immortality when modelled in this form by Corgi in 2006. Always too good for everyday use, it specialised in hire work and is here posed alongside Lower Lough Erne, when new, with friends and family. Left to right, behind, are driver Johnny Goan, Sonny Harron and Paddy Cadden. The tall man is Ned Maguire who operated the Erne Bus Service in Carrigallen in county Leitrim. The middle row has company Secretary Lena Corrigan with Maura Cassidy, Eileen Ovens, Maurice Cassidy and Maud Cassidy. In front are Patricia, Sheila and Art Cassidy with baby Maurice Corrigan completing the picture.

Courtesy Soinbhe Lally

Above: GNR No 242 (ZC 4102), another single deck Gardner, parked at Enniskillen station on Thursday 18 May 1950. No 242 was built in 1938 and had a GNR body. The building in the left background had been built as the Victoria Hotel in anticipation of the line from Clones which was supposed to have its terminal in the Fair Green. Sadly, the ground proved to be too soft and the railway had to keep to the higher ground. The building later became Victoria Buildings and, for a while, part of it housed an RIC barracks. After the last war, the ground floor housed Creighton's furniture shop but the building has now been demolished.

HC Casserley, courtesy RM Casserley

Left: GNR single deck Gardner-engined bus No 368 (IY 6182) in Railway Street, Enniskillen, parked outside the station. This bus was built in 1949 with a Harkness body. Note the layout of the windows in comparison to No 242.

B Boyle

Above: Pettigo was divided by a river, out of sight to the left, which also marked the political border between the Irish Free State and Northern Ireland after 1921. That part of the town that was in Northern Ireland was called Tullyhommon. Here three Leyland PS1s, on private hire, are waiting close to the border on Wednesday 2 August 1950. They may be waiting to pick up a party of pilgrims visiting Lough Derg, near Pettigo. At the front is MZ 1809, built in 1948, one of the last to be completed in NIRTB colours.

JC Gillham

Right: At the old UTA bus depot at Eden Street, Enniskillen, the main subject of this photo is L 300, a Commer Beadle demonstrator, a one off, built in 1957, and just arrived in from Belfast. Also visible is Z 772 a 1946 Leyland PS1, about to set out for Fivemiletown. The bus behind L 300 is probably another PS1.

B Boyle

THE LAST DAY AND ITS AFTERMATH

As mentioned on pages 32 and 33, the Northern Ireland government had announced, on 30 April 1956, that it intended to close Omagh to Newtownbutler, and Bundoran Junction to Belleek as well as Portadown to Tynan. This would leave the Republic of Ireland with remnants of lines and Transport Tribunals were set up in both Belfast and Dublin. The Belfast Chairman was Sir Anthony Babbington who was joined by three people from the UTA and only one from the GNRB. The Dublin Chairman was Dr Beddy. The GNR's General Manager, JF McCormick, appealed for monies to dieselise the system but, significantly, the Northern Ireland government was not represented at all! Figures produced showed that the closure would affect 120 jobs in Northern Ireland and 400 in the Republic. It would also affect 141 jobs on the SLNCR (35 of whom were in Northern Ireland). The SLNCR was credited with moving 70,000 head of cattle in 1955, some 10% of the Republic's exports.

The Tribunals' reports were issued in September 1956 and recommended closure north of the border but retention of services in the Republic and offered a supporting grant of £15,000 to the Sligo Leitrim but only until the end of September 1957. On 5 June 1957, the Stormont Minister of Commerce, Lord Glentoran, announced that the GNR lines north of the border would close on 30 September 1957. The Dublin government was dismayed but unable to do much.

As late as 6 September 1957, the Ulster Farmers' Union tried to persuade the Stormont government to

Top: PP class 4-4-0 No 50 raises steam at Bundoran shed. Driver Paddy Martin stands by the tender while the Fireman, Bob (or Roddy) McCordy is on the footplate. Paddy Martin had a daughter being christened that day but duty had to come first!

SC Nash

Above: PP class 4-4-0 No 42 had arrived into Bundoran at 10.30 with the 8.45am from Enniskillen and, a couple of minutes later, we see sister engine No 50 storming out of Bundoran with the 10.31am to Enniskillen.

SC Nash

keep open the Enniskillen to Omagh line as a long siding and thus give the SLNCR an outlet to the ports. The Dublin government promised to continue its £15,000 grant to the SLNCR if that siding came to be.

The GNR Board had a meeting with the NI government on 18 September and it was only then that all hope was finally lost and the closure on Monday 30 September 1957 was accepted as inevitable. Two days later, on September

20, the SLNCR formally announced its intention to stop running on Monday 30 September 1957 though staff would be retained until Saturday 5 October.

So it was that Monday 30 September saw the last public trains in the area of our book. We should be especially grateful to Sid Nash and John J Smith from the South of England, who travelled to Bundoran on the Sunday. Their pictures help us to illustrate that last day.

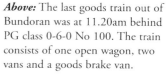

Above: The last goods train out of Bundoran was at 11.20am behind PG class 0-6-0 No 100. The train consists of one open wagon, two vans and a goods brake van.

SC Nash

Left: No 42 returned Enniskillen on the 2.25pm from Bundoran. Here the train is stopped at Pettigo with Driver Davy Armstrong and Fireman Paddy Love in charge. On the left, P class 4-4-0 No 73 is leaving with the last train into Bundoran, the Bundoran portion of the 2.05pm from Enniskillen.

SC Nash

Right: The newspaper photographers lined up this picture of PP class 4-4-0 No 71 before it left with the 3.50pm to Londonderry. Driver Arthur Darragh and Fireman Billy Hawthorne pose on the footplate. On the platform, the Guard Thomas Hilliard (left) shakes hands with Station Master Albert Trenier. Enniskillen shed was long famous for its clean engines but, for once, No 71's number needed a wipe from an oily rag and someone has written 'Loving memory' on the none-too-clean tender. How were the mighty fallen! *Photographer unknown*

Below: PP class 4-4-0 No 71 arrives past Bundoran Junction South signal cabin with the three bogies and tail of vans that formed the 3.50pm from Enniskillen to Londonderry. Note the spray of flowers on the smokebox door of No 71; several engines carried bunches of anemones (the flower of remembrance) or huge sprigs of heather on this last sad day.

SC Nash

Bottom: At Bundoran Junction, No 42 arrived with the 2.25pm from Bundoran and waited in the branch platform. After No 71's arrival, Q class 4-4-0 No 136 departed with the 1.35pm from Londonderry to Enniskillen. No 136's smokebox has a clean patch where anemones had been placed earlier. No 42 will follow at 4.28pm.

SC Nash

Right: Still at Enniskillen, SLNCR Driver Paddy Nevin and Guard Richard Rooney of Sligo brought in Railcar B on the last 4.00pm from Sligo. Watched by Portora schoolboys, Paddy posed in the cab for the local press after the arrival at 6.15pm. Railcar B was known as to everyone as 'Paddy Nevin's railcar'; he regularly came to Enniskillen station on his days off to make sure that B was well!

Photographer unknown

Bottom: The last train from Enniskillen to Clones was at 6.20pm. It was due to be worked by U class 4-4-0 No 199 *Lough Derg* (which had a 1954 F type tender) with Driver Gussie Kelly and Fireman Cecil Haire, son of the Maguiresbridge signalman. Two Light Engines, LQG class 0-6-0 No 160 and PP class 4-4-0 No 50, were meant to run ahead of this train at 4.30pm en route to Dundalk. But somehow they were coupled on the front of the 6.45pm. Wiser counsels prevailed everyone was reminded that three engines would have the bridges down! In the event, the two leading engines ran ahead and No 199 was left in sole charge of the train. In a final twist, Driver Gussie Kelly said to his fireman "Here, son, you'll not get another chance. You take her" and insisted that Cecil drove as far as Newtownbutler where they handed over to Clones men. They came home on the 4.30 from Clones. It comprised No 196 *Lough Gill* hauling two bogies, a wagon and a van; the Driver was Charlie Armstrong.

Photographer unknown

Left: The last train from Enniskillen to Omagh was the 6.40pm to Omagh which was to be worked by PP class 4-4-0 No 74. Before departure, though, it was decided that QG class 0-6-0 No 150 would also work the train. No 150 was crewed by Driver Barney McGirr and Fireman Peter Judge. No 74 had Driver Arthur Darragh and Fireman Billy Hawthorn. The Guard was Fred Cshill from Ballinamallard. This photograph shows the final train to Omagh and was taken while the 6.20pm to Clones was still in the up platform.

S C Nash

To complete the record of the last day, let us recall some of the other movements. The last trains on the Bundoran branch appear in the pictures. After working the last train into Bundoran, PP class 4-4-0 No 73 worked the train Empty Carriages to Omagh. They left Bundoran at 4.05pm and ran via the back line at the Junction to arrive in Omagh at 5.30pm. The guard on this train was instructed to retain the Electric Train Staff for each section on the branch and deliver them to the Agent in Omagh.

Meanwhile, back in Enniskillen the final 3.50pm mixed to Clones was a massive five bogies and twelve cattle wagons. The identity of the loco is not known but we do know that the Driver was Jimmy Redpath and the Fireman Eric Irwin with Jimmy Reid as Guard. At 5.30pm, Q class 4-4-0 No 136 worked the final Portadown goods out of Enniskillen.

The final passenger trains out of Enniskillen to Clones and to Omagh are covered in the pictures as is the final arrival from Sligo. Enniskillen sold a total of 254 tickets for the trains to Clones and Omagh!

One wee boy, who was brought up to the station at Enniskillen to witness the final departure to Omagh, was overcome with grief. In the silence between the blowing of whistles and the engines moving off, a very shrill young voice pierced the night air with the heartfelt cry "I hate Lord Glentoran!" His mother glowed with embarrassment but he got a cheer from the subdued and disbelieving crowd.

There were some spectators on the platform at Enniskillen when the 5.30pm from Londonderry arrived at about 8.15pm. The train was hauled by U class 4-4-0 No 197 *Lough Neagh*. The crew were Driver Freddie Rankin and Fireman Norman Brown with Guard Herbert Wilson. There

was an Empty Coach train from Enniskillen to Clones at 8.45pm but no record of it seems to have survived.

There were only a few waiting to welcome the two final arrivals into Enniskillen. At 9.25pm there came the final arrival from Omagh, the connection out of the new railcar service mentioned on page 33. On this night, the power car, BUT No 705, continued to Londonderry where it was used to strengthen a railcar set already working from there to Belfast. The Brake Second coach was worked by steam from Omagh to Enniskillen on the last night. The train was meant to be worked by No 150, which had piloted the 6.40pm from Enniskillen. Fireman Billy Hawthorne described her as a 'rattle box' which might be why U class 4-4-0 No 197 *Lough Neagh* worked the final 8.45pm from Omagh. That train comprised the Brake Second and two other carriages and, crewed by Driver Arthur Darragh with Fireman Billy Hawthorne, arrived into Enniskillen at 9.25pm. They brought the engine to the almost deserted shed where only Paddy McGinn, the steam raiser, was on duty. Arthur and Billy handed the engine over to him before they shook hands – and that was the last they saw of each other until 2002!

Once that train had arrived, the section was clear for the final 9.30pm goods from Enniskillen to Omagh. Again, no-one seems to have noticed the departure or who worked it. The final movement of all on this long day was the 9.45pm from Clones. It was due at 10.33pm but arrived six minutes late amid much whistling. Bringing down the curtain on 98½ years of trains between Clones and Enniskillen was U class 4-4-0 No 196 *Lough Gill* with Driver Jimmy Armstrong, Fireman Victor Coulter and Guard Thomas Hilliard. engines and a steam crane in residence!

Left: This is one of very few known pictures of the final 7.20pm mixed to Sligo and which came to light in the nick of time for this book. Here *Lough Melvin* has a small audience as the crew of Driver Gerry O'Connor and Fireman Bertie Hegarty prepare to leave Enniskillen for the last time. In anticipation of many wanting to travel, there were two carriages, Nos 9 and 11, as well as a goods brake van (carriage No 10 could not be used as it had never had lights fitted!). The final ensemble reached Sligo at 10.35pm, an hour late.

Bluebell Railway Museum,
JJ Smith Collection

Aftermath of Closure

Fermanagh's stations fell eerily quiet on the night of 30 September 1957. For many of the older men, it was the end of their railway careers. Many of the younger men saw little future in railways, left the job and, sadly many had to take the emigrant boat. The men who stayed were transferred to Omagh, Derry, Portadown or Belfast.

The passengers did not fare much better. Before the closure, a journey from Bundoran to Dublin took 5¼ hours but now it took 8¼ hours. Similarly a rail trip from Bundoran to Belfast that used to take 4¾ hours (on a bad day) now took a numbing 6 hours by bus. Also on the buses, a monthly ticket between Enniskillen and Clones that had cost £3.90 was now a thought-provoking £5.96, a 53% increase.

The railway was not totally dead, however. Next morning, at 8.30am, PP class 4-4-0 No 44 left light engine and ran to Fintona where it collected the famous horse tram. Leaving Fintona at 10.15am, the tram was worked via Omagh and Portadown to arrive in Belfast at 3.35pm. The tram was destined for the Belfast Transport Museum and is now on display as part of the Irish Railway Collection at the Ulster Folk and Transport Museum, Cultra near Holywood.

A sadder job that day was the ensemble that left Enniskillen at 11.00am when one engine hauled two dead engines to Clones.

Along the lines, some staff remained to do the sad job of packing up all sorts of moveable items such as furniture, signs, clocks, weighing scales and so on into vans for despatch to a store in Dundalk. Then keys were turned in locks and the place fell silent and ghostly – dead but not yet buried.

Then, on the Thursday 3 October, an engine and van left Clones at 9.00am and called at every station to collect redundant wagons. Not all of the wagons were empty, though. Each station had to carefully pack up the full contents of the offices, everything moveable on the platforms, in the signal cabins, lamp rooms, goods stores, engine sheds and permanent way stores. Everything had to be accounted for, packed into clearly labelled boxes and loaded into vans for despatch to the stores in Dundalk. It seemed that the Board was keeping open the option of reopening and would be able to do so with the treasure trove held in Dundalk. This working was in Enniskillen from 11.05am to 12.25pm at and reached Omagh at 2.20pm before finally arriving into Portadown at 6.00pm. The guard on this train had the melancholic job of retaining the electric train staff for each section after Newtownbutler and delivering the lot to the Agent in Omagh.

On the Sligo Leitrim, too, things were being run down. The bus services had been immediately taken over by CIE but the redundancy notices for SLNCR staff did not take effect until the Saturday after closure. Like on the GNR, staff busied themselves moving stuff into goods stores for safekeeping – and eventual auction.

On the Wednesday, *Lough Melvin* was steamed in Sligo and worked goods wagons to Enniskillen. Next day, *Lough Erne* repeated the exercise and, finally, *Enniskillen* worked the last wagons to Enniskillen on Friday 4 October. The SLNCR wagons on each train were deposited at either Collooney, Manorhamilton or Enniskillen where they would eventually be auctioned off. The train also worked any GNR wagons to Enniskillen for onward transmission to Omagh and the brave new world of the UTA.

These movements left *Enniskillen* and both of the new engines in Enniskillen where they took up residence in the deserted GNR engine shed. Of the other SLNCR locos, *Sir Henry* and *Hazelwood* had finally come to rest in Manorhamilton and were sold for scrap there despite rumours that *Hazelwood* was going to the new Belfast Transport Museum. The other Sligo Leitrim engine, *Lough*

Gill, was at Dundalk. It had gone there in April 1956 to await a repair that never happened and it remained there until auctioned with the two engines in Manorhamilton for a mere £910.

But back to the final SLNCR movements. Railbus 2A ran from Sligo to Manorhamilton on the Wednesday. On Thursday 3 October, Railbus A did a round trip from Enniskillen. The final movement took place on Saturday 5 October when Railbus A and trailer ran from Enniskillen to Sligo. On the way back to Enniskillen, the staff at each station were finally paid off and a way of life was over.

A winding-up meeting of Sligo Leitrim shareholders was held in Dublin on 14 November 1957 and on 17 December 1957 a new company was formed. The SL&NCR Co Ltd would oversee the disposal of assets in due time.

And that was that – or was it? There is an unconfirmed story that Frank Morgan of Ballyshannon arranged for a coal train to run from Derry to Ballyshannon in November 1957.

Apparently there were six of the 15-ton loco coal wagons hauled by a PG class engine and driven by Enniskillen Driver Birdie Rankin. Reportedly, he, the fireman and the guard had a terrible time dismantling temporary fences south of Omagh. The tale does not include any information on the return working, if there was anything other than an Engine and Van movement. Even after more than 50 years, any information would be very welcome!

The following January was a hard one with many roads closed or made very difficult by

Above: A derelict Enniskillen, exactly one year after the closure, photographed by John Gillham on 1 October 1958, the first day of UTA ownership. This was also the day of the public auction of the movable assets of the SLNCR at Enniskillen, probably taking place immediately behind the photographer.

Right: The Sligo yard at Enniskillen on the same date. The wagons in the background, along with Railbus A, Railcar B and 0-6-4Ts *Lough Erne, Lough Melvin* and *Enniskillen*, were being auctioned, the latter fetching £475 scrap value. Apart from the weeds, little has changed from the similar view five years earlier, on page 59.

Both JC Gillham

snow and ice that refused to thaw. Mails and deliveries of bread were particularly badly affected and there were calls in Stormont for relief trains to be run from Omagh over the closed lines. These appeals, of course, fell on deaf ears.

Even the GNR itself was itself wound up. It ceased to exist on 1 October 1958 when all of its assets were divided, more or less equally, between CIE and the UTA. Each government had subscribed half of the £4.5million purchase and so it was, for instance, that each company inherited 83 locomotives.

None of this really had much impact on Fermanagh but, on the same day, the SLNCR's property in Fermanagh came under the auctioneer's hammer. The auction was held in the Head Office and the items auctioned included the three engines, Railbus 2A, and 35 goods wagons (all lying at Enniskillen). Also auctioned off were the bridges, water tanks, the permanent way, gates, telegraph poles and the signals as well as the contents of the offices but none of the buildings were included.

A bid of £1075 for *Lough Melvin* and *Lough Erne* was refused but the UTA began negotiations with Beyer Peacock. The track in Enniskillen yard fetched £625 while the Tempo Road bridge went for a mere £20. There were no bids for the Weirs bridge. Railbus A and trailer went for £36 while *Enniskillen* was bought by Eastwoods of Belfast for £475. It is interesting that the three engines in Enniskillen were in good order when the line closed. *Lough Melvin* and *Lough Erne* had been a mere six years in traffic and *Enniskillen* not long back from a heavy overhaul in Dundalk. Some believe

that *Enniskillen* was in the best order of the three; maybe the UTA should have bid for her too?

Within a couple of hours, most of the Sligo Leitrim in Fermanagh had changed hands for under £20,000 and all of the tracks had been lifted by the end of the year.

Railcar B was not part of the auction as it has been sold privately to CIE. On the day of the auction, it was safely locked in the long shed at Enniskillen. On 31 October 1958, under its own power, it picked its way over the disused railway to Omagh and reached Dublin via Portadown. This was a strange retracing of its arrival from Wigan via the same route when new. Then its windows had posters advertising its builders and the van carried the motorbikes of the three fitters who travelled with her; they had a motor bike holiday in Connemara after B was commissioned. In CIE hands, Railcar B became 2509 and was soon painted in the CIE green livery. It was used on several short workings such as between Limerick and Nenagh or to bring ferry passengers to and from the boats at Rosslare. It was withdrawn in late 1970 but was not scrapped. It is currently at Downpatrick awaiting restoration, for which an appeal has been launched.

In December 1959, the purchase of *Lough Melvin* and *Lough Erne* was finalised and they were hauled dead from Enniskillen to Omagh by LQG class 0-6-0 No 111. It was running tender first and the tender became derailed at the north end of Fintona Junction. The steam crane had to be brought from Adelaide shed in Belfast to put things right. So, over two years after closure, Fintona Junction had four steam engines and a steam crane in residence!

167

Left: SLNCR loco *Enniskillen* was sold for scrap while lying in the GN shed at Enniskillen. This most poignant of photographs was taken on Sunday 12 October 1958. In the ten days since the auction, the loco had been somehow dragged from the shed and then reduced to these more manageable chunks of metal. The most recognisable parts are the cylinder block ahead of the wheels and frames with the copper inner firebox above and behind them and the rear bogie separated from the rest. Other recognisable parts of the loco lie nearby in the debris field. There are no fewer than 13 oxygen cylinders and three acetylene cylindersamongst the remains of a once-proud engine. Even this long after closure, the buildings and track at Enniskillen were almost intact.

Bluebell Railway Museum,
JJ Smith Collection

Above: Already overgrown with weeds, Enniskillen is seen prior to lifting, on 22 August 1959.

Roger Joanes

Lough Melvin and *Lough Erne* became UTA Nos 26 and 27 respectively, of class Z, and retained their nameplates but they were soon repainted in UTA livery with the nameplates in polished brass letters on a red ground. The engines were used for various shunting jobs around Belfast's goods yards and they worked the trains of loco coal from the docks to Adelaide shed and to York Road. Latterly, they were the only engines able to work on the sharply-curved lines of the Belfast Harbour Commissioners and one of 27's last duties was to rescue a new diesel-hydraulic engine that had got itself stuck! No 26 was withdrawn in 1965 but No 27 remained in traffic until June 1970 when she was bought privately by the then Chairman of the Railway Preservation Society of Ireland, Roy Grayson, and moved to Whitehead. She has not been steamed since 8 July 1972 and needs a lot of work to restore her.

But back to Fermanagh. It was not until early 1960 that the UTA broke the line at the border near Clones and began to lift the rails and recover the sleepers. An engine was based in Enniskillen and it worked trains of recovered materials to Omagh for possible reuse. The lifting gangs reached Lisnaskea during the summer holidays and Enniskillen before Hallowe'en. One eight year old Enniskillen schoolboy spent his summer holidays on the lifting train – heading east

in the morning with bag of sandwiches, apple and bottle of milk and then spending the day with the train and getting home about teatime. What his parents did not know was that he continued doing this for a whole fortnight after school had resumed!

The track gangs had passed Enniskillen about December 1960 and, after reaching Bundoran Junction, turned their attention to the branch. Lifting began at the border bridge at Belleek and had reached Kesh in June 1961. A few months later, the last materials train left Bundoran Junction and Omagh was finally reached in early 1962.

Could Fermanagh's railways have survived?

Today, looking back, it is interesting to speculate as to what would have happened to the railways in Fermanagh if political considerations had not forced their closure in 1957. Certainly the SLNCR could not have lasted much longer. Even if the two governments had decided to take it over or subsidise it, the live cattle trade was in decline anyway. The spread of refrigeration meant that by the late 1960s most cattle were slaughtered locally and then transported as meat. In both Ireland and Britain the movement of live cattle by

Above: Sallaghy level crossing was on the Newtownbutler side of Lisnaskea, where the road to Crom crossed the line. Here, on Thursday 19 May 1960, the UTA lifting train is seen heading towards Enniskillen with a train of recovered rails and sleepers. The loco is SG2 class 0-6-0 No 42, formerly GNR No 183 which was built in 1915. The crew seems to be Birdie Rankin and Paddy Ingram, both from Enniskillen. By now, the line had been closed for nearly three years and the weeds are very much in evidence. On the left is the neat crossing keeper's house with its occupants watching one of the last trains to pass this way.

A Donaldson, courtesy WT Scott

Left: SLNCR loco *Lough Gill* was sent to the GNR's Dundalk Works in April 1957 for a heavy repair but was still awaiting attention when the axe fell and there she remained until sold for scrap. Here GNR Apprentice Fitter Pearse McKeown (son of Driver Paddy, seen on page 118) is in *Lough Gill's* cab, in the midst of many GNR engines about to be scrapped and perhaps remembering his childhood days in Enniskillen and happier times all round.

Photographer unknown

rail ended in 1975. Even at that date Dublin-Holyhead was the only route still taking them.

Likewise the Bundoran branch could hardly have survived much beyond the early 1960s. Even in the 1950s it carried little passenger traffic in the winter and was dependent on summer holiday makers and Lough Derg pilgrims for revenue. However social changes were threatening this traffic also, with cheap continental holidays replacing the traditional week at the seaside. Today Bundoran would probably not attract enough day trippers to sustain a railway. Ballyshannon might have had some potential for replacing Sligo as a CIE freight railhead for south Donegal.

As to the other GNR lines, we can speculate that the healthy goods traffic from Enniskillen to Belfast and Derry would probably have declined in line with trends elsewhere. The UTA was to end all rail-borne freight in 1965, so that would have ended it in Fermanagh at that point, even if the Portadown-Derry line had remained open. If the UTA, and its successor NIR, had retained rail freight originating within Northern Ireland, it is possible that Enniskillen might still do some business in cement and timber traffic – perhaps three trains a week.

On the passenger side, the pattern elsewhere would suggest that the number of passengers travelling by rail (particularly local traffic) would have continued to fall until the early 1960s as car ownership spread. It would then have stabilised and, if the troubles in Northern Ireland had not taken place, the Fermanagh railways could well have benefited from

tourism. The emphasis would have been on a fast service to Belfast, with a connection for Derry at Omagh. Intermediate stations between Clones and Enniskillen would have been better placed for survival than those between Enniskillen and Omagh, where the stations at Trillick, Dromore Road and Fintona Junction were too remote from the villages they served. Even so, all of them would probably have become unstaffed halts.

South of the border a useful move would have been for CIE to change the track layout at Cavan, where there was an end-on connection with the old MGWR route from Inny Junction. This would have allowed through running between Dublin and the GNR branch from Clones. In this event a through service from Dublin serving Cavan, Clones and Monaghan might have been viable for both passengers and freight. The old GNR route from Clones to Dundalk could have been abandoned and, if the UTA/NIR had retained the Armagh line, there could have been joint operation of the Monaghan-Armagh section. Such a route should have been as viable as the Dublin-Westport line is today, and a connection at Clones would have fed traffic into and out of Fermanagh. If all this had happened we would probably today have two coach NIR trains from Belfast running to Omagh, changing direction and going to Enniskillen, to terminate at Clones, and connect into a Dublin-Clones-Armagh-Belfast service. Manned level crossings would have given way to automatic half barriers, and one signal box in Portadown or Omagh would control the entire route to Clones!

All speculation perhaps, but we are entitled to dream!

Left: As UTA No 26, *Lough Melvin* is seen far from home working a train of loco coal from 'The Low Docks' at Belfast's Queen's Quay to the former GNR engine shed at Adelaide, near Windsor Park football ground. Here *Lough Melvin* is climbing away from Ballymacarrett Junction at about where Bridge End halt is today.

IC Pryce

RECENT DEVELOPMENTS

It may now be more than fifty years since the scenes in this book were swept away by the forces of change and short-sightedness, but the memories have survived surprisingly well.

After a successful railway exhibition in 1997 to commemorate the 40th anniversary of the big closures, former GNR Fireman Kevin Love and local railway enthusiast Selwyn Johnston were inspired to find a permanent home for the material collected. Various options were considered but cost was always a problem. Selwyn's brothers Gordon and Nigel own Headhunters Barber shop in Darling Street, Enniskillen.

Happily, the refurbishment of the shop coincided with the 45th anniversary, so the three brothers decided to use the space available to display the many artefacts elated to railways in Fermanagh. Through their energy, the project has now become one of our most important, if not unusual, railway museums. They are working towards full accreditation.

Starting from small beginnings, but with the help of many former railwaymen and enthusiasts, the exhibits now cover every aspect of railway life in Fermanagh on the GNR, SLNCR and CVR.

All photos in this section are by CP Friel.

Lhis page: Our picture coverage of the last decade in Fermanagh begins at Belcoo with this general view looking towards Enniskillen. The present owner, Mairead O'Dolan along with her brother Charlie and sister Olive, has done much to restore the station house and recondition the signal cabin in fine style. The corrugated iron Post Office building (seen on page 149) has been removed.

Top: 11 August 1998 – a few months after the launch of the first edition of this book – saw the return of steam trains to Belcoo. As part of Belcoo Community Association's week of events for locals, holiday makers and returning emigrants, the committee organised the Belfast and County Down Miniature Railway to bring its portable 7¼ inch gauge line to the town and set up on the former up line at the station. The opening train is pictured with author Charles Friel at the controls. The loco is a Swiss 0-6-0T *Waldenberg* owned by Roger Lockwood, who has Fermanagh connections of his own. In the background, are several former railwaymen. Two Great Northern enginemen are facing us on the left; Jimmy Armstrong (left) and Douglas Armstrong. The man in the railway hat facing left is Jack Bell (once SLNCR relief stationmaster) while in the right background is former SLNCR Guard and author Michael Hamilton in his original uniform. Remarkably, both BBC and UTV sent their outside broadcast vans to Belcoo that evening, probably tempted by the poster that promised "The re-opening of the Belcoo railway".

Above: On 30 September 2001, Selwyn organised a bus trip for former railway employees along the route of the SLNCR from Enniskillen to Sligo using an ex-GNR Gardner bus. The event was videoed and here, at Florencecourt (now owned by Jim Stevenson), Fermanagh businessman and enthusiast Raymond McCartney is doing a piece to camera before interviewing Robin Gault (left), who had been Florencecourt's last Station Master, and his brother William, who was a Guard on the SLNCR.

Left: A little later, the GNR bus parked across the restored level crossing gates at Belcoo. You can see something of the work that Mairead had done to reinstate the gates and some of the signals. The GNR bus is No 389 (IY 7383) a dual-purpose seated Gardner which dates from 1951. It is now operated by the Cavan and Leitrim Preservation Society at Dromod and their Michael Kennedy manfully struggled with the crash gearbox and the non-power-assisted steering in some tight corners. The bus in the bottom right is not approaching from Glenfarne! It is Ulsterbus N Type Tiger No 384 (FXI 384) based at Enniskillen and parked here over the weekend before resuming work on route 064 to Enniskillen.

Right: Independently, a community group in Brookeborough had fully restored the former station house here, extended it skilfully at the Maguiresbridge end, and laid a length of track. Most of the work was done in 1998. Later, the group also organised the building of this replica bogie coach which is on static display. This photograph was taken in 2002 when the group was hoping to fund a suitable locomotive but they are now concentrating on a CVR cattle wagon.

Left: On 28 September 2002, Selwyn and his group organised another bus run for former railway employees, this time from Enniskillen to Bundoran. At Bundoran Junction we see Fireman Kevin Love, Signalman Charlie McLaughlin (formerly at Lisbellaw), Signalman Vincent Beattie (formerly Bundoran Junction South and Enniskillen South) holding a staff, Fireman Paddy Love and Cecil Irvine (SLNCR clerk in Enniskillen). It was on this trip that Arthur Darragh and Billy Hawthorne met up again for the first time since the night of the closures!

Right: During the stay at the Junction, BBC Radio Ulster's Breege McCusker, the Fermanagh correspondent for "Your Place and Mine", caught up with Selwyn.

Left: The present owner of Irvinestown station, Mrs Reihill, kindly allowed the party in to see this splendidly-preserved station. Always a well-maintained place, this photograph is deliberately reminiscent of the photo reproduced on page 89 though the road overbridge is long gone - but the tidiness has survived the long years of closure.

Below: This is only part of the Headhunters' display as seen a few years ago - it is a lot busier now! To the left is a recreation of the SLNCR's General Manager's office using material kindly donated by Caroline Guy and Olive Creighton, daughters of Harry Taylor, the line's last Traffic Manager.

Bottom: On 30 September 2006, the anniversary of the closure was marked by the naming three paths in Enniskillen - the Great Northern Way along the former trackbed alongside the Irvinestown Road, the Manager's Walk which once linked the Pound Brae bridge to near the goods store, and the Sligo Leitrim Way which begins near the former SLNCR bay platform and leads towards the site of Enniskillen South signal cabin and then along the GN trackbed towards the Tempo Road. Here, near the then only surviving railway building, we see the group who gathered to mark the occasion and perform the unveilings; they are standing roughly in the same place as the picture on page 129 . . .

. . . The names of those pictured are:

Back row: William Clingen, Kevin Love, Jim Flanagan, Patsy Rooney, Norman Browne, Cecil Carson, Walter Brown, Harold McIntyre, Robin Gault, William Gault and Kenneth Elliott.

Front row: Douglas Armstrong, May Johnston, Marie Woods, Kathleen Morris, Ernie Louden, Cecil Irvine, Arthur Darragh and Sammy Fiddis.

Left: On Monday 1 October 2007, I presented a slide show in Enniskillen's Ardhowen Theatre which, Iam delighted to say, was standing-room only. Before the show got under way, the opportunity was taken to present this specially-commissioned painting to the Theatre to commemorate its long association with the former railway employees. Here we see William Gault (SLNCR) with Jackie Owens of the Ardhowen, the artist Michael McCarthy and Alex Baird, Chairman of Fermanagh District Council. The painting is based on the picture seen on our page 142. To the left, above the picture, you can see the remaining piers of the bridge itself. It was on this balcony that the conversation, mentioned on page 21, between Rev John McKegney and Gerry Burns took place – truly the wheel had come full circle!

Right: After years out of use and subsequent preservation in Mallow, former SLNCR Railcar B is seen in the shadow of Down Cathedral at Downpatrick where it is now in the care of the Downpatrick and County Down Railway. They have launched an appeal for its restoration and have assured everyone that the vehicle is in better order than would first appear. Consider yourself heartily encouraged to give your support!

Left: Fermanagh County Museum organised a Fermanagh-oriented railway exhibition as part of the "All Change – the Social Impact of the Railways" touring exhibition. It ran between May and October 2004. At the opening ceremony, on 16 May 2004, Arthur Darragh and Billy Hawthorne were invited to cut the cake, ably assisted by Harold Andrews, the Chairman of Fermanagh District Council. In the left background is Helen Lanigan-Wood, the Museum's Curator, supervises proceedings.